Environmental Debates and the
Public in Ireland

DAMASCHKE.

Environmental Debates and the Public in Ireland

Mary Kelly

IPA
INSTITUTE OF PUBLIC
ADMINISTRATION
50 Years
CELEBRATING PUBLIC SERVICE
1957 - 2007

First published 2007
by the Institute of Public Administration
57–61 Lansdowne Road
Dublin 4
Ireland

ISBN: 978–1–904541–55–4

British Library Cataloguing in Publication Data
A catalogue record for this book is available from the British Library.

Cover design by Slick Fish Design, Dublin
Typeset by Carole Lynch, Sligo
Printed in Ireland on recycled paper containing a minimum of 75% post-consumer waste by ColourBooks Ltd, Dublin

Contents

Preface

Economic and environmental policymaking frequently highlights the extent to which the environment is a contested arena. Whether the issue is waste disposal, water pollution, infrastructural developments, conservation of the countryside or the many other issues that impact on the environment, different groups articulate varying perspectives. This book, *Environmental Debates and the Public in Ireland,* explores these perspectives. It examines the kinds of environmental discourses generated by different groups, the social, organisational and cultural contexts giving rise to these discourses, and the conflict between them. A companion volume written by Hilary Tovey (2007), *Environmentalism in Ireland: Movement and Activists* (Dublin: IPA), explores the pathways through which people become activists for the environment and the ways in which activist groups organise their activities.

Both books are the outcome of a larger research project entitled 'Research Programme on Environmental Attitudes, Values and Behaviour in Ireland', funded by the Environmental Protection Agency, under the National Development Plan (Environmental RDTI Programme 2000–2006. Grant number: 2001-MS/SE1-M1). This research programme included not only the research questions analysed and reported on in these two volumes, but the completion and analysis of a national survey. This research used a module on environmental attitudes, values and behaviour designed by the International Social Survey Project (ISSP). Thus the research had a comparative cross-national perspective. The module also repeated many of the questions asked in an earlier 1993 module on environmental attitudes in Ireland, enabling trends and changes over a decade to be examined. Three reports presenting an analysis of this data, *Trends in Irish Environmental Attitudes between 1993 and 2002; Cultural Sources of Support on which Environmental Attitudes and Behaviours Draw;* and *Environmental Attitudes and Behaviours: Ireland in Comparative European Perspective,* are available at http://www.ucd.ie/environ/home.htm.

The research team of Mary Kelly (School of Sociology, University College Dublin), Hilary Tovey (Department of Sociology, Trinity College

Dublin) and Pauline Faughnan (Social Science Research Centre, University College Dublin) would like to acknowledge the invaluable contribution of many excellent researchers to the successful completion of this extensive research programme. Undertaking and analysing the focus group research reported in this volume were Sharon Bryan, Fiona Gill, Carmel Grogan and Brian Motherway, while the qualitative interviews with activists were completed by Noelle Cotter and Adele McKenna. The interviews for the survey research were completed by the Survey Unit, Economic and Social Research Institute, while the quantitative survey data was analysed by Fiachra Kennedy and Brian Motherway. We would also like to thank Colette Dowling and Ellen Gallaher for their valuable contributions at different stages of the research process. The Social Science Research Centre, University College Dublin, provided administrative support ably orchestrated by Philippa Caithness along with the Office of Funded Research Support Services, while the Geary Institute, University College Dublin, as well as the School of Sociology, University College Dublin, and the Department of Sociology, Trinity College Dublin, provided research accommodation and highly supportive environments in which to complete social scientific research.

Institutional support was also readily offered by the Steering Committee of the Environmental Protection Agency, including Loraine Fegan (EPA), Kevin Woods (EPA), John Kiernan (DoEHLG) and Andreas Cebulla (National Centre for Social Research, London). Andreas' insightful and rigorous reading of each of our five reports was particularly appreciated. The Institute of Public Administration's enthusiastic response to the proposal to publish the two present volumes was very encouraging, and we would like to particularly thank Declan McDonagh in this regard, and Julie O'Shea for her excellent editorial advice.

This research programme could not have been completed without the active co-operation of the 1,257 survey interviewees, the 168 participants in 22 focus groups, and the 38 environmental activists who completed qualitative interviews. All of these respondents willingly gave of their time to enthusiastically respond to our questions. For this we sincerely thank them and hope that the experience was as enjoyable and as worthwhile for them as it has been for us.

Mary Kelly, Hilary Tovey and Pauline Faughnan, Dublin, July 2006

1

Environmental Discourses

Introduction

How do Irish people think and talk about the environment? What are the central themes and topics they raise? In these discussions, what kinds of perspectives or discourses do they draw on? Do groups in different social and class positions articulate or prioritise different perspectives? Are there differences between those living in rural and urban areas? Furthermore, how do these different ecological discourses impact on environmental policymaking, on discussions in civil society regarding economic and social as well as environmental change and, consequently, discussions regarding the kind of society we want to live in now and in the future?

These are important questions, not only in terms of seeking to identify the different ways in which Irish people define their relationship with nature, but in exploring the social, economic and cultural contexts within which these different definitions arise and are maintained over time. Understanding these different voices and their sources is imperative if democratically agreed ways of addressing current threats to the environment are to be found and ecological sustainability ensured. They are also particularly urgent at this time of rapid social change, growing environmental threats, and increasing environmental conflicts.

That the environment in Ireland is under considerable stress is well recognised (EPA, *Ireland's Environment 2004*). A rapidly changing and growing economy, growth in population and affluence, and an explosion in housing, car ownership and waste generation have all begun to raise questions regarding protection of the environment and the kind of society we want. This issue, however, does not concern Irish society alone. There are also the global environmental responsibilities of increasing CO_2 emissions and climate change, over-use and pollution of the world's natural resources, decreasing biodiversity, and the unequal global distribution of environmental degradation.

As new roads, houses and waste facilities are seen to invade the Irish countryside, and increasing economic development and car ownership contribute significantly to rising CO_2 levels, do Irish people raise these issues when talking about the environment? When talking about them, what kinds of discourses or perspectives do they draw on? The sociological literature, both international and Irish, reveals the possible presence of five types of environmental discourses:

1 Moral discourses, which articulate different ways of perceiving the relationship between humans and the natural environment, and consequent moral responsibilities
2 Radical political discourses regarding global environmental responsibilities, as well as perspectives on the activities of more radical environmental activists
3 Romantic and aesthetic discourses, which emphasise subjective, emotional and imaginative experiences and perceptions regarding the natural world, in particular the countryside. These experiences may be articulated in terms of, for example, a sense of place
4 Scientific discourses regarding the role of science, scientific 'expertise' and scientific 'facts' in protecting the environment. These concerns may be articulated in terms of a discussion of the use of science by the state, industry and the lay public, either to justify or to question major state, economic and environmental interests
5 Regulatory discourses regarding the relationship between economic growth and its environmental consequences, and the need for state environmental regulations.

In order to explore how these discourses were articulated by a wide range of groups in Ireland in 2003, two-hour discussions were held with twenty-two focus groups, generally consisting of eight participants. In total, 168 individuals participated in the discussions. Open-ended trigger questions regarding the groups' perceptions of the environment and environmental issues were discussed during the first hour, and more focused 'discourse statements' were explored during the second hour. (For discussion of focus groups as a research method and discourse statements used, see Appendix 1 and Table A1. The objective in selecting the groups was to get as broad a range of both groups and environmental discourses as possible.

Five types of groups were selected:

- environmental regulators and scientists (three groups)
- business representatives from industry (two groups)
- farmers (two groups)
- environmentally active groups (four groups)
- groups drawn from the general public (eleven groups drawn from a wide range of occupational and educational levels).

Roughly half of these groups were based in Dublin, and broadly equal numbers of men and women participated overall, although not necessarily within each separate group. The aim was to explore the kinds of environmental discourses different groups generate, and to explore the social and cultural contexts within which they are generated and argued for.

The Sociological Analysis of Environmental Discourses

Continuing conflict regarding the environment and its uses is prevalent in contemporary society. Differences persist regarding, for example, genetically modified (GM) crops, the use of fertilizers in intensive farming, the best use of the countryside given increased road and house building; how to limit waste generation and dispose of the waste mountain; and whether or not to place a tax on carbon-based fuels to discourage car usage and achieve lower CO_2 levels. All of these indicate the highly contested nature of definitions of the environment and its proper use and protection. Conflicts surround not only this definition but also responsibilities: who is responsible, what should be done, who should pay, and, ultimately, what kind of place do we want Ireland to be, not only in terms of the environment itself, but also in terms of the relationship between self, society and nature? These questions are central to democratic decision-making in relation to society and ecological sustainability.

One of the roles of sociology is to identify and make visible these environmental discourses; to describe how they operate by exploring how different groups elaborate, support or contest them; and to examine the cultural and institutional contexts within which they develop. Through this analysis sociology contributes to '… making visible the whole spectrum of different experiences, perceptions, frames and knowledges' that contribute to contemporary environmentalist thinking, as well as contributing to that 'self-reflexivity and self-transformative public discourse worthy of a democratic society' (Strydom 2002: 158, see also Fairclough 2003).

Discourse analysis is a way of identifying and examining discourses as meaningful elements or segments within a broader culture. Discourses can be defined as ways of representing aspects of the world from a particular perspective (see Fairclough et al. 2003). A discourse is a cultural lens or frame shared by groups of people, used in communication with others, influenced by social and cultural history and relatively stable over time. Discourses construct identities in particular ways. They define and construct a sense of self and of others, the latter often differentiated in terms of 'us' and 'them'; a sense of societal differentiations and power structures; and of the natural and physical world. Discourses not only represent the world as it is seen to be and has been, but also as it might, could or should be. They may construct moral as well as imaginary worlds and projects for change (see Fairclough 2003: 123–4).

Discourses are related to the different positions and relationships that people have within, and to, the social and natural world. Differently positioned social actors tend to 'see' and represent the world and social life in different ways. Those in positions of power are particularly influential in constructing discourses that ensure the maintenance of their power and in inculcating these discourses in the less powerful. Nonetheless, strong discourse traditions resistant to, and critical of, those of the powerful frequently exist among groups who feel dominated or marginalised in society.

The various themes or frames that characterise a discourse may not be totally coherent. They may be contradictory and ambivalent, and thus open to change. In relation to other discourses, they may complement, compete with or attempt to dominate each other. Hajer (1995) proposes an 'argumentative approach' to the analysis of the social and political process of struggle for 'discursive dominance'. Strydom (2002) adds the important roles of credibility, acceptability and trust in inculcating and maintaining discourses over time. In elaborating a new discourse, different elements from a range of previously different discourses frequently combine.

Analysis of environmental discourses articulated by focus groups facilitates the exploration of how the environment is seen, talked about and negotiated by group members; how these constructions are challenged within the group; and how open or resistant to change they may be. The analysis of discourses is thought to be especially pertinent at times of social change as it allows the exploration of this fluidity (Fairclough 2003: 208), as well as the linkages between particular discourses and power relations. The extent to which powerful groups are seen to be proposing and maintaining particular discourses in their own interest can be explored, as can the extent of 'reflexivity' or questioning of society and its future trajectory by all groups.

In analysing the five environmental discourses nominated in this research – moral, radical political, romantic, scientific and regulatory discourses – there was also a concern to explore overlapping themes between discourses, the extent to which there was coherence within and between discourses, or whether, on the contrary, it was apparent that a high level of fragmentation and incoherence existed. The extent to which there was agreement within and between groups on the discourse themes articulated, and the degree of resonance between the discourses of the five sets of groups – regulators, business groups, farmers, the environmentally mobilised and the general public – were thus explored.

Related questions concerned the role of science in environmental policymaking and in environmental disputes; the relationship between economic growth and sustainable development and the role of the state in promoting ecological modernisation; the responsibilities of the public as citizens and consumers; and the role of both citizens and the state in relation to global environmental threats.[1]

The Participants

The selected focus groups reflected a range of possible positions on environmental issues. Included were those with particular occupational interests in the environmental domain, those actively and voluntarily mobilised around environmental issues, as well as a considerable number of groups from the general public. The groups included were:

1 Environmental regulators and scientists (three groups, including a group from the Department of the Environment, Heritage and Local Government (DoE), a group of heritage officers who work at local authority level, and a group of environmental scientists)
2 Business representatives (two groups, including a group of environmental managers and a group of engineering consultants)
3 Farmers (two groups, including a group of large dairy farmers and a group of small, West of Ireland farmers; a decision was taken not to include organic farmers as considerable research on these farmers already exists, see Tovey 1997, 1999, 2002a).
4 Environmentally mobilised groups (four groups, including a group from the Cork Environmental Forum (CEF), a group of returned Catholic missionary priests and nuns taking an ecology course, an anti-incinerator group and a group of hillwalkers)
5 General public groups (eleven groups representing a broad educational, age, gender, locational and occupational spread. Differences in educational level were considered particularly important as education was found to be the most strongly related of all demographic factors to differences in environmental attitudes and practices in the quantitative survey research carried out as part of the 'Research Programme on Environmental Attitudes, Values and Behaviour in Ireland' of which this exploration of environmental discourses was part (see analysis of the quantitative survey data at http://www.ucd.ie/environ/home.htm). The eleven groups chosen included: commuters to white-collar work in

---

1 For discussion on focus groups as a research method, on its appropriateness in exploring participants' discourses, on best practice in selecting, recruiting and facilitating groups and how these were undertaken in this research project, on the discourse statements used and with what groups, and how the data generated was analysed, see Appendix 1.

Dublin, nurses, the retired, primary teachers, shop workers, a group of skilled building workers, two university student groups, a group of Traveller women, an unemployed group of men, and a group of young working-class mothers working in the home (see Table 1).

Table 1: Focus Group Participants

Groups	Gender		
	Male	**Female**	**Total**
1 Regulators			
Department of the Environment	6	–	6
Heritage officers	3	5	8
Environmental scientists	7	1	8
2 Business Groups			
Environmental managers	2	3	5
Consultant engineers	4	2	6
3 Farming Groups			
Dairy farmers	8	–	8
Small farmers	9	–	9
4 Activist Groups			
Cork Environmental Forum	7	4	11
Returned missionaries	6	2	8
Anti-incinerator group	–	8	8
Walkers	4	4	8
Sub-total	**56**	**29**	**85**
5 General Public			
Commuters	4	4	8
Nurses	–	6	6
The retired	4	3	7
Shop workers	–	7	7
Skilled building workers	8	–	8
Students 1	–	5	5
Students 2	1	5	6
Teachers	4	4	8
Travellers	–	9	9
Unemployed	9	–	9
Young mothers	–	10	10
Sub-total	**30**	**53**	**83**
Overall total	**86**	**82**	**168**

Information about the demographic characteristics of each of the participants, along with their levels of community involvement and public policy preferences was elicited through brief questionnaires to the farmers, the environmentally mobilised groups (apart from the CEF), and the general public groups. For the environmental regulators, scientists, environmental managers and the CEF a shortened exit questionnaire was used to elicit demographic information on each of the participants. This information is drawn on in the brief descriptions of each of the groups below.

Environmental Regulators and Environmental Scientists

1   Department of the Environment, Heritage and Local Government (DoE)
    The six male members of the DoE focus group were assistant Principal Officers and Higher Executive Officers working in relevant environmental areas. All but one had a higher educational qualification, generally in the humanities, and the age range was twenty-six to fifty-five. The group had an interesting debate on the real-life difficulties, challenges and constraints facing environmental policymakers in Ireland today.

2   Heritage officers
    Heritage officers work at the local authority level and are responsible for the development of local heritage plans (both of the natural and built environment) in consultation with local groups; they also get involved in public awareness campaigns and, on occasion, in local planning consultation with inputs into policy strategy documents, such as county development plans. The focus group consisted of five women and three men, five of whom were aged between twenty-six and thirty-five and three between thirty-six and forty-five. All had a third-level qualification in such disciplines as botany, geology, agricultural science, archaeology and geography; five had Masters degrees or higher. They appeared to enjoy good working relationships with one another and felt that they could draw on each other's expertise.

3   Environmental scientists
    The group of environmental scientists consisted of seven men and one woman. Six held doctorates and two Masters degrees in disciplines ranging from chemistry and biology to engineering. There was a wide spectrum of ages: three were aged between twenty-six and thirty-five, one between thirty-six and forty-five, two between forty-five and fifty-five, while the final two were aged between fifty-six and sixty-five. There was also a spread in levels of seniority. All recognised the need to be objective in their work, while some also recognised the need to be somewhat passionate, especially in the face of opposition from, for example, polluting groups and interests.

Business Groups

1 Environmental managers

This group of two men and three women was contacted through the Irish Pharmaceutical and Chemical Manufacturing Federation (IPCMF) of the Irish Business and Employers Confederation (IBEC). Three came from the chemical/pharmaceutical industry and two from the mining industry. In educational terms, most came from a scientific background, while in age terms two were between twenty-six and thirty-five and three between thirty-six and forty-five. As with many groups, the attraction of attending the focus group was to talk to, and share ideas with, others in a similar position to themselves. The members of this group also wanted to represent their industry, feeling strongly that, despite their efforts, they were an easy target for both government and the general public when environmental problems occurred.

2 Consultant engineers

This group of six consultant engineers, four men and two women, was contacted through the Institute of Engineers of Ireland (IEI). Group members were mostly in relatively senior positions in engineering consultancy firms that offered a consultancy service to private and public companies, especially those involved in building large infrastructural or other projects requiring environmental impact assessments. An exit questionnaire was not completed with this group.

Farmers

1 Dairy farmers

The eight men in this group were large dairy farmers from the midlands, recruited on the basis of having herds of at least 100 cows and a milk quota of at least 1,500 gallons. Their ages ranged from thirty to sixty-five, and their educational level also varied greatly – one had completed primary school; three had their Junior Certificate and two their Leaving Certificate; two had a tertiary education in agriculture, of whom one had a Master's degree. The differences in age and educational levels did not appear to make any difference within the focus group discussion of this lively and articulate group. All had been born and reared in the country, and six were married and living with their spouses and children, and occasionally parents. Four of their wives worked, two as teachers and two as nurses. Two of the farmers lived alone. The environment was preceded by health, the economy and education on their public policy priority list.

2 Small farmers

The nine men in this group were small farmers from the West of Ireland aged between thirty and fifty years of age. Of the nine, seven were part-time farmers, mainly in dry-stock cattle and sheep, who also worked at a number of other full-time jobs. These ranged from driver and postman to white-collar clerical, computer and teaching work. Their educational range also varied: two had left primary school at fourteen; three had completed their Junior Certificate and one his Leaving Certificate; two had a post-Leaving Certificate diploma; and one had a degree. All had grown up on farms in the area and all but one were married. Four of their wives were also working outside the home. Most had children, some of whom still lived at home, while others were third-level students. Thus, in family terms they were well integrated into their communities, in voluntary groups, particularly the GAA, and in political organisations. The environment as a public policy issue was not a priority for this group; health, crime, education and the economy were regarded as more important.

Mobilised Groups
1   Cork Environmental Forum
In order to hold a focus group with a number of representatives of voluntary environmental organisations or NGOs, the Cork Environmental Forum was contacted. This forum was established in 1995 by the local authority county manager in the aftermath of the Earth Summit in Rio de Janeiro and, in particular, in response to its Local Agenda 21 and sustainable development initiatives. Its purpose is to bring together four sets of environmental stakeholders: public representatives, including local authority representatives and those from the Cork City and County Development Boards; business and farming groups; community NGOs and environmental groups; as well as interested others, including environmental consultants. One of its main objectives is to provide a forum for all parties with an interest in the environment to engage in debate on current environmental issues and seek agreement on a way of resolving them, as well as to stimulate and sustain the level of active environmental awareness, concern and care among the people of Cork.

Eleven members joined the focus group, seven men and four women. They were representative of an impressive range of groups including, for example, community, housing and tidy-towns associations, anti-incinerator groups and alliances to promote the protection of the Irish landscape and marine environment. The participants had given long-term commitments to these voluntary organisations, typically being members of local as well as national groups. In educational terms, all but one had received third-level education, four in the humanities and four in the biological and applied sciences, while two combined both. Six were also involved in environmental issues as part of their main occupation, for example, as environmental consultants or as community or environmental organisation co-ordinators.

As might be expected, this was a vocal and committed group, and many of the participants built care of the environment into regular work practices and articulated and practised a holistic view of the world. Their ages ranged evenly from twenty-six to sixty-five.

2   Returned missionaries

The returned missionary group of six men and two women, between the ages of fifty and sixty-five, had all served as missionaries for a numbers of years, mostly in developing countries. They were one of the most environmentally mobilised of all the focus groups, with all of the participants reporting that they had signed petitions about environmental issues and had devoted time to environmental causes over the past five years. Health and the environment were at the top of their public policy priority list.

3   Anti-incinerator group

This group included five women who were centrally involved in mobilising an anti-incinerator campaign and three other women who had offered their support by signing petitions and giving money. As might be expected, this group was both committed and lively. They were aged between twenty-five and forty-five. Four had a third-level education, two being qualified teachers, one a nurse. Four worked full-time in the home, while, outside the home, two continued to work full-time and two part-time. They were strongly locally integrated into the rural community in which they lived. In terms of their public policy priorities, only health was prioritised over environmental issues.

4   Walkers

This Midlands-based group was particularly committed to the environmental protection of the hill and mountain areas in which they walked. They were a group of four men and four women aged between forty-five and sixty and predominantly middle-class. Three of the women were involved in education, a fourth had a science degree and worked in the home; all were married and three had children. The four men included a farmer and three others who worked, or had worked, in small businesses. Two lived with their spouses, two alone.

All but two stated that they had been involved in some pro-environmental mobilisation over the past five years. They were well integrated into their local communities through sport and hobby groups or residents' associations. Regarding public policy issues, they placed the environment along with health as their top priorities.

General Public Groups

The selection of these groups was influenced in particular by an attempt to ensure a broad educational range. The survey research carried out as part of this research programme indicated that there existed a strong correlation between education and differential attitudes to the environment. Selection by occupation not only ensured different educational levels but also sufficient similarity in experiences within groups to facilitate discussion.

1   Commuters

   This group of four men and four women, aged between eighteen and twenty-six, commuted to Dublin from Counties Louth, Meath and Kildare, spending several hours travelling to and from work each day, mainly using public transport. Five had spent their childhoods in these counties and continued living with parents while commuting to work in Dublin. Three had been reared in Dublin but moved to live in Drogheda because of Dublin house prices. All but one were single, and all worked in white-collar clerical and customer service jobs. Most had some tertiary level qualifications, either a degree (three) or a certificate or diploma (four).

   While interested in discussing environmental issues with their peers, they were not seriously animated by them, and most had not engaged in promoting environmental concerns in the past; neither were they deeply integrated into their local communities. In terms of policy priorities, health, crime, the economy and education were most important to them.

2   Nurses

   Of the six nurses – all women – who constituted this group, five were working either full-time or part-time in palliative care. Most were between forty and fifty-five, married and living with partners and children. Although Dublin-based, all but one had grown up outside Dublin. They were well integrated into local voluntary groups, whether sporting or hobby groups, further education classes or residence associations. They had also contributed at some level to environmental campaigns in the past. Not unexpectedly, health issues topped their public policy concerns, followed by education and the environment.

3   The retired

   This was a mixed group of four men and three women, aged between sixty-five and seventy-five, who had been born, reared and lived all their lives in Dublin. Most had finished school at primary level and entered skilled or semi-skilled work. All of them lived with other adults in the home. They were well integrated into their local communities, either through sporting, hobby or religious groups, further education classes or residence associations. Only a minority had been mobilised regarding an environmental issue in the recent past. Their main policy concerns were health, followed by crime.

4   Shop workers

The seven young women, aged between twenty and thirty-five, who made up the shop workers' group had all been born and were living in or near the Midland town in which they worked in large nationally based supermarkets. Five still lived in the parental home, while two had established their own homes with partners. All but one had their Leaving Certificate. Although they all knew one another, in their lifestyles, interests and contributions to the focus group, two sub-groups were apparent. One included three participants who were slightly older than the others and had worked together for a longer period in the same supermarket. This sub-group tended to participate more fully in the focus group discussions, and the environment was among their top public issue priorities. For the other sub-group, who were younger and regarded their supermarket work as temporary, health and education were prioritised over the environment in terms of public policy concerns.

5   Skilled building workers

The eight male members of this group were Dublin-reared and Dublin-based, and aged between twenty-two and thirty. Most had completed their Leaving Certificate before taking up an apprenticeship. The group included three carpenters, three painters, a bricklayer and a plasterer. Three still lived in the parental home, three had established their own homes with a partner, while two lived on their own. In terms of voluntary association membership, they were not a highly mobilised group, although three were members of sporting organisations. Nor were they mobilised on environmental issues – two had signed a petition about an environmental issue in the past five years. In terms of public policy issues, economic growth, followed by health, crime and education were placed before the environment.

6&7   Students 1 and 2

There was only one male participant in these two groups of university students. The majority were under twenty-two years of age. Their family backgrounds were generally managerial or professional, and seven of the eleven came from Dublin and lived at home. Their areas of study included the humanities, social sciences, and science. Although the environment was not among their public policy priorities – health and education being more important – most of them had been involved in some capacity in environmental campaigns, seven having signed petitions.

8   Teachers

This mixed gender group of eight primary school teachers (four men, four women) taught in village-based schools in the West of Ireland and had grown up in the country. Five were married with children, and their ages ranged from twenty-five to fifty. All were highly integrated into their local communities, involved in sporting groups, especially the GAA, in community and residence associations, religiously based groups and further education classes. They were interested in environmental issues and could almost have been classified as a mobilised group. Over the past five years, six had signed environmental petitions: four had given time to an environmental cause, while two had taken part in environmental protests or demonstrations. Their interest in environmental issues was also evident in the topics, practices and forms of teaching which some of them had introduced to their pupils. Teaching was a vocation for this group and they shared their enthusiasm within an open focus group discussion. Regarding public policy issues generally, health and education followed by the environment defined their major priorities.

9   Traveller women

The group of nine Traveller women between the ages of twenty-five and fifty were all married women, and had, on average, four children. Eight of the women lived with other members of the Travelling community, and one lived in a house among the settled community. They were all Dublin-based and most had also spent their childhood there. All but one had left school at the earliest possible opportunity and remained working in the home thereafter. Except for two women taking Fás or Youth Reach programmes, they were not involved in any other formal groups outside the home. None had ever been involved in any form of environmental protest or campaign, nor was the environment near the top of their priority list; instead, health and crime predominated. A discussion regarding environmental issues was not easily attained.

10   Unemployed

The nine male members of this group were aged between thirty and fifty and from a city in the West of Ireland, where the majority had also grown up. Their previous employment had been mainly in semi-skilled or unskilled work. In educational terms, two had completed their Leaving Certificate, three their Group Certificate, while four had left school before the age of fifteen. Two of the latter had trade certificates. Their living arrangements were more varied than any other group: four lived alone, two with parents or parents-in-law, one with a partner and child, and two with friends. Sporting groups provided a source of involvement with others, along with other groups such as an unmarried fathers' group and a pipe band group. In terms of mobilisation on environmental issues, four were quite active, signing petitions and giving time to environmental causes. Overall, however, health, crime and the economy had higher salience in the issue agenda of most of this group, with the environment and education following.

11   Young mothers

The ten participants in this group of single mothers lived on a working-class housing estate in Dublin and all were under thirty years of age. Over half of the group had left the educational system at sixteen or younger and entered mainly service-type occupations such as hairdressing, waitressing and shop work. The majority had one child. All but one were involved in some sporting or hobby group, while half were taking some further education classes. Most had not supported an environmental issue in the past, and crime, health and education were prioritised over the environment in terms of policy concerns.

As might be expected of the relatively complex interactional context of focus groups, some groups worked better than others. It is difficult to identify precisely the factors that contributed to this. Familiarity with this form of semi-formal and focused interaction and the linguistic skills required may have been a factor. However, in order to avoid the potential problem of a practiced focus group participant dominating the discussion, it was required that recruits to the general public and farmer groups had not participated in such a focus group before. It was, of course, difficult to control all aspects of the setting in which the group took place, and some settings facilitated easier discussions than others.

Organisation of the Chapters

Each of the following chapters addresses one of the five environmental discourses (moral, radical political, romantic, scientific, regulatory), starting with a review of the relevant Irish and international sociological literature related to the discourse, and identifying which groups most clearly articulated some of the central themes in the discourse. In general, the chapters first look at the extent to which these themes were articulated spontaneously during the first hour of discussion, and secondly, how they were articulated in response to the discourse statements. Each chapter then recaps by identifying how each discourse contributed to the definition of self, others and the environment.

While repetition and overlap between the themes within different discourses will be noted as the chapters proceed, these will be particularly addressed in the concluding chapter. Here three overlapping themes will be examined – empowerment and the importance of local identification and involvement; consultation regarding environmental decisions impacting on the local area; and trust, or more accurately distrust of those seen to be imposing decisions on the locality. These were the most prevalent recurring themes within which discussions on the environment were embedded. Evidence from the quantitative survey research undertaken as part of the broader 'Research Programme on Environmental Attitudes, Values and Behaviour in Ireland' will also be briefly drawn upon here. The importance for policymakers to take account of these themes is finally and briefly addressed.

2

Moral Discourse: An Ethic of Environmental Care

Introduction

Under the rubric of moral discourses is included a range of ideas, concepts and categories which address environmental issues in terms of a moral imperative regarding human–nature relationships. Moral or value discourses question and explore the relationship between the well-being of self, others and the ecosystem in which human beings live; establish principles regarding what is considered good, desirable and just; and prescribe appropriate behaviour. Individuals, social groups and societies as a whole may or may not accept or find it possible to fulfil these prescriptions.

Among environmentalists, one of the major discourses concerning environmental ethics is a debate about the most appropriate source of environmental values. Ought these values to be anthropocentric or biocentric? An anthropocentric discourse takes human beings and their welfare as the focus of environmental attitudes and behaviour. Nature is seen primarily as a resource for human use. These human-centred values tend to be predominantly utilitarian, and concerns regarding the environment tend to focus on those that affect the self, the family, the local community, or the state as a whole. They may also extend to a concern for global environmental damage, again to the extent that human welfare is threatened. This approach may draw on a range of motivations and values. It may be based on purely egocentric interests about one's own welfare or the welfare of one's business; on concern to protect one's family and future generations; on a concern by the state to limit environmental destruction through, for example, sustainable development policies; or on environmental justice discourses concerned with exploring and changing the social, political and economic factors underlying environmental destruction at the local, national or international level.

In contrast, radical biocentric or ecocentric perspectives give nature itself intrinsic value, independent of human interests. For some of these biocentric thinkers a rights-based approach is adopted; for example, the right of sentient animals to continue to exist. These rights may be seen as equal to those of human beings, and justice requires that these rights be protected and vindicated. For others, all living beings and the ecosystems on which they depend have a moral status, whether or not they matter to human beings.

Between the anthropocentric and radical biocentric poles lie further sets of values that may contribute to environmental protection. These discourses focus on the interconnectedness and interdependence of human and non-human nature and a feeling of oneness with all things. There may be an emphasis on nature as a holistic system, on the essential oneness of life and, hence, on a desire to protect it. Three sources for this identification with nature can be identified.

Firstly, it may be based on a strong sense of interdependence and interrelationship between human and non-human nature, leading to an ethic of mutual care and partnership. This approach, sometimes called a relational approach (see Plumwood 1993, 1996, and 2002), is not new (see, for example, Leopold's land ethic, 1949; new edition 2001) and has recently been further developed by ecofeminists. Secondly, it may be based on a romantic and emotional identification with nature and a sense of oneness with it (see Chapter 4). Thirdly, it may derive from a religious source, whereby God or some other spiritual element is perceived as the creative source of both human and non-human nature and of the interconnectedness of all things, and which implies an obligation to respect and care for the earth.

Some of the sociological and other literature on each of these five ethical perspectives – anthropocentrism, a relational approach, romantic, spiritual and radical biocentrism – will be reviewed briefly below. The extent to which, and how, these themes were articulated by the focus groups will then be explored. Further aspects of an anthropocentric perspective, as articulated in the focus group discussions in relation to scientific, regulatory and radical political discourses, will be addressed in later chapters, as will further aspects of the relationship between moral and romantic discourses.

Anthropocentrism

Anthropocentrism, which defines nature purely as a resource for human use and benefit, is acknowledged as the dominant moral ecological discourse of our time. The consequences for the environment are everywhere, from experiments on animals to road building that carves through the countryside. The former are justified in terms of human health, the latter in terms of economic growth and travel convenience. They may be justified in terms of the welfare of others and not just oneself. Kempton et al. (1995) in their study *Environmental Values in American Culture*, based on survey and in-depth interview data, found that in their attitudes to the environment Americans were most likely to emphasise not just the fulfilment of personal needs but those of the family and future generations. Concern for the future of children and descendants emerged as one of the strongest values related to an ethic of environmental protection. While this had a personal and emotional resonance when one had children, it was also stated by others (Kempton et al. 1995: 95–102). Other strong themes within an anthropocentric ethic include some scientific, regulatory and social justice discourse themes.

Some historians argue that anthropocentrism has its roots in Christianity, roots that have been further reinforced by Enlightenment rationality. The historian Lynn White (1996: 189) has argued that 'Especially in its Western form, Christianity is the most anthropocentric religion the world has seen.' Roderick Nash (1989: 88–9), in his history of environmental ethics, comments on White's article, noting:

> For evidence White needed to look no further than the first pages of the Old Testament where, after shaping man 'in his own image', God commands his favorite artefact to 'be fruitful and multiply, and fill the earth and subdue it; and have dominion over the fish of the sea and over the birds of the air and over every living thing that moves upon the earth.' Every creature was assumed to be created to serve a human need. Human beings were, quite literally, the kings of beasts; every other being was inferior in the Judeo-Christian hierarchy.

Nash draws particular attention to the Old Testament, which instructs humans to 'increase and multiply and dominate the earth' (Genesis 1: 27–28). He notes that the Genesis account was interpreted as God having created the world 'explicitly for man's benefit and rule; no item in the physical creation had any purpose save to serve man's purposes'. The Genesis command was reinforced by the Christian denunciation of pantheism and animism, leaving, Nash argues, nature exposed to human greed, indifference and exploitation. Analysis of US survey research also shows a correlation between Christian fundamentalism and a lack of environmental concern (see Greeley (1993); Eckberg and Blocker (1989 and 1996); and Guth et al. (1995)).

White (1996: 193) also argues for the possibility of a revolution in Christian values, a revolution that would draw on the example of Saint Francis of Assisi who radically challenged Christian anthropocentrism. Likewise, Nash (1989: 97) notes the example offered by the Benedictine monks who emphasised Christian stewardship of the land, but recognises the anthropocentric kernel of the stewardship ethic in which humans had the authority to use nature in their own interest but always 'with a feeling of reverence for what was ultimately not [their] possession but God's'.

The Irish Columban priest and ecologist, Fr Seán McDonagh (2001: 39 seq.) has revisited the anthropocentric nature of the Genesis account. Although he points out that contemporary scripture scholars find the interpretation of giving licence to dominate the earth and its animals and plants to be mistaken, he sees its continuing influence in recent Catholic Church teaching. He notes of Vatican II's central text, *Gaudium et Spes*, that the anthropocentric bias is particularly marked in its statement, 'according to the unanimous opinion of believers and unbelievers alike, all things on earth should be related to man as their centre and crown'. He rather caustically comments, 'The cultures of tribal people and Hinduism and Buddhism, the great religions of the East, can hardly be used to bolster this claim' (McDonagh 2001: 40). He believes that the Christian churches, both internationally and in Ireland, have arrived late to the challenges of environmental destruction and have provided little leadership in this area. Michael Viney (2003: 4), likewise, has pointed to the continuing legacy in Ireland of a Christian discourse of human mastery over nature and the duty to subdue and exploit other species, stating that 'its assumptions still run strongly through our culture'.

Reinforcing this anthropocentrism in the Western world are the rationalistic tendencies of the Enlightenment. This places humanity as endowed with reason above and superior to the non-human natural world, and produces an instrumentalist conception of nature. It emphasises the development of administrative, regulatory as well as scientific and technological tools to subdue non-human nature in the interest of humanity. It also tends to marginalise as inferior any emotional relationships of love and care both between humans themselves and between humans and non-human nature.

A Relational Approach

It is precisely for these rationalistic, instrumentalist and purely anthropocentric tendencies that Enlightenment thinking has been criticised by ecofeminists, among others (see for example, Merchant, 2003). Elaborating what some have called a relational or partnership approach, they argue that rather than non-human nature being seen as simply for humanity's use and benefit, it should be seen as having an autonomy, integrity and purpose in its own right. The appropriate ethical focus thus becomes the type of relationship that humans should establish with non-human nature. Given its autonomy and integrity, the appropriate ethical relationship, a relational approach argues, is one of respect, care and co-operation rather than domination and exploitation. This, it is argued, will break the 'instrumentalisation' of nature, defined by Plumwood (1993: 142) as 'a mode of use which does not respect the other's independence or fullness of being'.

Ecofeminists, in their elaboration of a relational ethic, draw in particular on Carol Gilligan's work, *In a Different Voice* (1982). In this she criticises a developmentalist approach to ethics which prioritised the development of 'objective', 'detached' and abstract rules and principles. This formal rationality is contrasted with an emphasis on the development of an ethical self in and through relationships of closeness and attachment to others, the making of ethical judgements relative to particular situations and contexts, and the recognition of a plurality of interests. The ecofeminist philosopher Val Plumwood (1993: 154) argues that 'a view of self as self-in-relationship can not only explain how instrumentalism can be avoided but also provides an appropriate foundation for an account of the ecological self, the self in non-instrumental relationship to nature'. She continues, 'The relational self delineates the general structure of a relationship of respect, friendship or care for the other as a variant on Aristotle's account of friendship: wishing for the other's good for their own sake' (Plumwood 1993: 155). This self, however, in respecting the other, does not merge with the other; it respects the difference between human needs and the great variety of the needs of non-humans: it is thus 'crucially important to maintain both empathy and the sense of the difference of our needs and desires from those of the other' (Plumwood 1993: 160). In this Plumwood differentiates the relational from the ecocentrism of, for example, Naess (see below).

The relational approach seeks to break down a series of dichotomies, which, it argues, lie at the ideological centre of modern society since the Enlightenment. These are the dichotomies between mind/body, reason/emotion, culture/nature and male/female, in which the mind, reason, culture and male are valued, while the body, emotion, nature and female are denigrated. It would replace these dichotomies with an emphasis on care, friendship and respect for nature. These ethically based relationships should draw on both reason and emotion to inform human–non-human interaction. Consequently, these relationships would be respectful, contextually sensitive and empathic. Val Plumwood is particularly associated with articulating a relational ethic of care. She consistently emphasises the need to break the reason/emotion dualism, and the related bias which prioritises reason and generalised, abstract principles over the emotional, the relational and the context-dependent, and which identifies the emotional with egoism and the private sphere. She argues (Plumwood 1996: 159) that:

care for particular others is essential to a more particular morality ... For as Blum ... stresses, special relationships form the basis for much of our moral concern, and it could hardly be otherwise. With nature, as with the human sphere, the capacity to care, to experience sympathy, understanding, and sensitivity to the situation and fate of particular others, and to take responsibility for others is an index of our moral being. Special relationship with, care for, or empathy with particular aspects of nature as experienced rather than with nature as abstraction are essential to provide a depth and type of concern that is not otherwise possible. Care and responsibility for particular animals, trees, and rivers that are known well, loved and appropriately connected to the self are an important basis for acquiring a wider, more generalized concern.

Plumwood (1996: 172) argues that this approach offers an alternative to anthropocentrism. It constitutes 'a relational account of self, which clearly recognises the distinctness of nature, but also our relation and continuity with it'.

The environmental historian Carolyn Merchant (1996: 216) calls this a partnership ethic that transcends some of the problems of both anthropocentric and biocentric perspectives: 'A partnership ethic sees the human community and the biotic community in a mutual relationship with each other. It states, "The greatest good for the human and nonhuman community is to be found in their mutual, living interdependence".' She reaffirms this approach in her later (Merchant 2003: 226) publication:

A partnership ethic is a synthesis between an ecological approach based on moral consideration of all living and nonliving things and a human centred (or homocentric) approach based on the social good and the fulfilment of basic human needs. All humans have needs for food, clothing, shelter and energy, but nature also has an equal need to survive. The new ethic questions the notion of the unregulated market, sharply criticizing egocentric ethics – what is good for the individual is good for society – and instead proposes a partnership between nonhuman nature and the human community.

She (Merchant 2003: 228) emphasises that in this ethic the capacity of humans to control nature is limited, and that it must be recognised that non-human nature is itself a dynamic actor, and not amenable to the type of total domination and control envisaged by Enlightenment thinkers and the scientific and industrial revolutions. However, humans can become a sensitive partner of nature by listening to its voice and working with it through new forms of design and planning.

This relational or partnership perspective had been articulated in the 1940s by Aldo Leopold and published in his collected writings, *A Sand County Almanac*. The land ethic he proposed argued that the abuse of land in Western industrial societies was due to the overwhelming emphasis on economics and 'progress', so that the land and the biotic community were seen as commodities belonging to humans, to be exploited without any obligation to conserve it. He (Leopold 2001: 171) proposed instead a holistic approach, a land ethic that 'enlarges the boundaries of community to include soils, plants and animals, or collectively the land', and the extension of moral concerns to it, as is done to persons in community. Thus, humans should become 'biotic citizens' and change 'from conqueror of the land community to plain member and citizen of it. It implies respect for his fellow members.' This ethical relation could not exist 'without love, respect and admiration for the land'. Economic questions also had their place, but economic and ecological questions should be examined in terms of 'what is ethically and aesthetically right, as well as what is economically expedient. A thing is right when it tends to preserve the integrity, stability and beauty of the biotic community. It is wrong when it tends otherwise' (Leopold 2001: 189). Merchant (2003: 162) notes that the land ethic might be considered as 'one foundation for an ethic of partnership among humans and between human and nonhuman communities ...'

The Romantic and the Moral

A romantic perspective privileges the experiential as well as the imaginative, the intuitive and the holistic. This emphasis on the experiential and the emotional may contribute to an ethic of care and to a relational approach, to prudence and humility in the face of non-human nature. It can contribute both to insight into human interdependence with non-human nature as well as to the motivation not to destroy either that on which humans are dependent, or the source of that perception of beauty and joy which can give meaning to human life.

In his argument for the preservation of biodiversity, the biologist Edward O. Wilson (1993: 348–51) notes the important role of biophilia (love or affection for life) in this regard. He points to its importance as a motive underpinning the 'ethical imperative' of prudence in relation to non-human nature, and the importance for human well-being of the opportunity to experience and wonder at the diversity and beauty of nature and to acknowledge that '... humanity is a part of nature, a species that evolved among other species'.

The philosopher Ronald Hepburn (1984: 134–5) also acknowledges the links between the sense of wonder at human and non-human nature and the consequent moral imperative to care for all of nature. In his essay

'Wonder', he argues that a close affinity exists between a sense of wonder, which is in itself non-exploitative and non-utilitarian, and moral attitudes which seek to respect all other beings as well as the virtue of humility.

A romantic approach to nature may thus be characterised by a sense of awe and wonder at the existence and beauty of living and non-living nature and of the cosmos as a whole. Such a romantic approach, when it emphasises a self-merging and close identification with nature, has contributed to the development of 'deep ecology', which sees itself as fundamentally opposed to the instrumentalist and anthropocentric view which gives humans the right to dominate and control nature.

As already noted regarding Plumwood's relational perspective, she recognises the important role that care for particular animals, trees and rivers plays in acquiring a more generalised concern for non-human nature. However, she has also offered a critique of an overly romantic, deep-green perspective. While placing the caring relationship between human and non-human nature at the centre of her ecological ethic, she is critical of a lack of adequate acknowledgement of the differences between human and non-human nature and of an identification with non-human nature which leads to the submerging of the self. She has critically identified three aspects to this form of self-identification with nature – indistinguishability, expansion of self, and transcendence of self – and notes that deep ecologists appear to feel free to move among them at will.

Indistinguishability rejects boundaries between self and nature. It emphasises mystical and holistic intuition, and a merging of the self and other. This mystical connection to nature will heal, it is argued, Western dualisms. Plumwood (1996: 165) argues, however, that this approach allows no space for recognising that the needs of non-human nature are distinct from, and different to, human needs, an essential aspect of a relational approach to environmental ethics. The expanded self of deep ecology sees identification with nature as leading to an enlarged sense of self. Plumwood notes that this can just lead to expanded egoism rather than recognition of the independence of non-human nature. The transcendence of self is based on a detachment from the particular concerns of self and a deep identification with particular parts of the natural world, often seen as sacred places, and with the cosmos as a whole. This approach does not allow for what Plumwood (1996: 167) sees as 'the deep and highly particularistic attachment to place, to the land and to the natural world which are central to a relational ethic of care'. This latter ethic thus draws strongly on romantic sentiments in terms of a 'highly particularistic attachment to place', sentiments which will be a major focus in the chapter on romantic discourses.

Religion as a Source of an Environmental Ethic

A Christianity based on a literal reading of the Genesis account of creation has been criticised as legitimating an anthropocentric and utilitarian definition of nature. Furthermore, when reinforced by the rationalist, instrumentalist and science-based Enlightenment and subsequent industrial revolution, it has led, some would argue, to today's wholesale destruction and exploitation of nature. However, some ecologically oriented Christians have argued that there are other traditions and practices within the Christian tradition which are more ecologically friendly. One is the biocentric tradition of Saint Francis of Assisi, for whom all God's creatures, human and non-human, equally praise the Lord and are worthy of ethical consideration (see Nash 1989: 93–4; White 1996: 193). Seán McDonagh (2001: 45) has written of this perspective, looking in particular at the biblical affirmation of the creation as good and as loved by God. Drawing on the Psalms and the Book of Job, the purpose of the creation is seen as lying not 'primarily in its ability to meet human needs. It has its own dignity, its own rights and reasons for being, quite apart from its role in sustaining humans … Creation has intrinsic value because it is created by God and sustained by God's Spirit.'

Creation spirituality is also the focus of the work of Thomas Berry, among others, in the US. The desire to consider the natural world, and the cosmos as a whole, as sacred is a major focus in their writing. There is strong criticism of the estrangement of humans from the natural world evident in contemporary society, which overly emphasises an exploitative and 'extractive economy' on the one hand and consumption on the other. Berry (1999: 136–7) sees this as a movement away from early Christianity when:

> The natural world was considered as a manifestation of the divine and the locus for the meeting of the divine and the human. Yet the sense of the Earth as a single community, with every being having inherent value and corresponding rights according to its mode of being, and with the human as one of the component members of this great community, was in the course of centuries diminished by excess emphasis on the human as a spiritual being aloof from the physical universe.

God's love of creation and the recognition that the beauty of creation gives glory to God should be mirrored in human respect, love and protection of nature. McDonagh (2001: 50), in seeking to promote a Christian-based ecology, states:

> I believe authentic creation spirituality would help regenerate Irish Christianity, and, especially Irish Catholicism. Celtic spirituality

celebrated the goodness of God that was manifested in the beauty of the world around us. Many Celtic monasteries were sited in remote and beautiful places like Skellig and Iona. It is no wonder that the monks came to love the cry of the curlew, the flight of the gannet, the bark of seals, the beauty of trees and wild flowers and the buzzing of bees and insects.

Another Christian tradition argues that humans are the stewards of God's creation, and as such are required to respect and care for it, and to acknowledge it as sacred (see Nash 1989: 96 seq.). Some theologians go further, emphasising the goodness of all creation, its holistic qualities and the joyous human response to it. Greedy and thoughtless exploitation of God's creation is seen as immoral and as bringing destruction to human and non-human nature alike. McDonagh (2001: 45) has also examined this perspective:

A theology of creation will also have to deal with the fact that human well-being, both for individuals and communities, depends on other creatures and a fertile environment. Here again the Bible has much to teach us in regard to how we relate to the rest of creation. In Chapter two and three of the Book of Genesis humans are challenged to be stewards of God's creation and to live in companionship with the rest of creation. The command of God to Adam and Eve is 'to till and to keep' (Gen. 2:15).

This tradition of stewardship thus criticises an emphasis on 'domination' and 'mastery' over non-human nature. Rather, as Merchant (2003: 25) notes,

In Genesis 2, the earth is a garden – a local plot of land rather than a vast area for spatial conquest – and the man is commanded to 'dress', 'keep', 'tend', 'guard', and 'watch over' it. According to ecologist René Dubos, God 'placed man in the Garden of Eden not as a master but rather in a spirit of stewardship'. For many religious sects wishing to embrace an ecological ethic, stewardship is the most persuasive ethic that is also consistent with biblical traditions. Stewardship is a caretaker ethic, but it is still anthropocentric inasmuch as nature is created for human use. Moreover [in this perspective], nature is not an actor, but is rendered passive.

Radical Biocentric Values

An ecocentric or biocentric perspective argues that nature has moral standing in itself; it is of intrinsic value or inherent worth and, some would argue, has moral rights. The Norwegian philosopher and deep ecologist Arne Naess (1989: 29) has argued that the 'richness and diversity of life forms are values in themselves and contribute to the flourishing of human and non-human life on Earth', and that, 'Humans have no right to reduce this richness and diversity except to satisfy vital needs.' Emphasising the vastness of nature and, in comparison, the puny nature of human beings, Naess (1989: 187) is critical of the tradition of Christian stewardship, arguing that it reinforces the arrogant idea of human superiority over nature, 'The wisdom of God is ridiculed if he is said to have engaged so ignorant and so ignoble a creature as *Homo sapiens* to administer or guard the vastness of nature, of which we understand so little. Nature is not a vegetable patch.'

In *Respect for Nature* (1986), the philosopher Paul Taylor has also articulated an ecocentric perspective, arguing for the equal rights of all living beings, whether human or non-human, sentient or non-sentient.

> When one conceives of oneself, one's relation to other living things, and the whole set of natural ecosystems on our planet in terms of this outlook, one identifies oneself as a member of the Earth's Community of Life. This does not entail a denial of one's personhood. Rather, it is a way of understanding one's true self to include one's biological nature as well as one's personhood. From the perspective of the biocentric outlook, one sees one's membership on the Earth's Community of Life as providing a common bond with all the different species of all animals and plants that have evolved over the ages. One becomes aware that, like all other living things on our planet, one's very existence depends on the fundamental soundness and integrity of the biological system of nature. (Taylor 1986: 44)

For Taylor (1986: 67), all living organisms have 'inherent worth' and a 'good of their own' which entails the full development of their biological goal. Humans have a duty to every living being, 'to give consideration to its good and to see to it that it does not suffer harm as the result of our own conduct. None of these ways of thinking and acting with regard to it presupposes that the organism values anything subjectively or even has an interest in what we may do for it.' These duties require that humans protect the very complex ecosystems on which living beings depend.

The biocentric tradition thus places human beings on an equal footing with other life forms. For Tom Regan (1984) the concept of rights is extended to include not only humans but both domestic and wild animals.

And if animals have rights, justice requires that humans secure and vindicate these rights. In arguing its point the rights-based approach tends to draw on the Enlightenment emphasis on reason rather than on care and concern as the source of values – although these emotions may be the consequence of certain 'rationally' argued rights.

Val Plumwood (1996) notes of a rights-based approach such as Regan's that it appears to give humans almost limitless obligations to intervene massively in all sorts of far-reaching and conflicting ways in natural cycles to secure the rights of a bewildering variety of beings. She is particularly concerned about the possibility and appropriateness of doing this in relation to wild animals. She is also concerned that the rights-based argument frequently opposes its own 'rationally based argument' to an ethic based on a responsiveness to, and feelings of care for, the natural world. She notes that it is precisely this overly rationalistic approach which has given rise to the anthropocentric and utilitarian destruction of nature in modern society. She argues (1996: 160) that:

A more promising approach for an ethics of nature ... would be to remove rights from the center of the moral stage and pay more attention to some other less dualistic, moral concepts such as respect, sympathy, care, concern, compassion, gratitude, friendship and responsibility.

These virtue-based concepts are 'resistant to analysis along lines of a dualistic reason/emotion dichotomy ... [Rather t]hey *are* moral "feelings" but they involve reason, behaviour and emotion in ways that do not seem separable.' She concludes (1996: 161):

The ethic of care and responsibility ... seems to extend much less problematically to the nonhuman world than do the impersonal concepts which are currently seen as central, and it also seems capable of providing an excellent basis for the noninstrumental treatment of nature many environmental philosophers have now called for.

The question asked in the remainder of this chapter is: to what extent were these five moral perspectives evident in our focus group data? The first section looks at one focus group in particular, the returned missionary group, as this group most clearly articulated some of the moral themes reviewed above. It ends with a brief analysis of how the discourses of other groups compared with the discourse articulated by the returned missionaries. The second section looks in some detail at the discourses of these other groups, especially their discussions on the themes of care and greed, as articulated spontaneously by them in the first hour of the discussion. The third section examines their responses to the moral discourse statement introduced for discussion in the second hour; while the fourth and concluding section identifies how these moral themes contributed to the constitution or definition of a sense of self, of 'we' and 'they', and of the environment.

Elaboration of Moral Discourse Themes by Returned Missionaries

There was an identifiable moral discourse about the environment in the focus group data. The question is to what extent this discourse articulated anthropocentric, relational, romantic, religious or radical biocentric themes. These themes often overlap; thus, a sense of the spiritual interconnectedness of all things may draw on religious themes as well as anthropocentric and/or romantic themes. It is argued that a set of values that could be considered an ethic of environmental care was evident in our data, although often in fragmentary forms.

Moral Themes Expressed by the Returned Missionary Group

A strong and elaborate environmental ethic of care was evident in the spontaneous discussion of the religious group but was rather more attenuated in other groups. For the returned missionary group this ethic had become part of their whole way of life. While it was clearly integrated into their God-centred worldview, it was also clearly anthropocentric in nature. One participant noted that, while an environmental consciousness had not formed part of his education in the seminary, it was now '*very much part of my religious consciousness*' (1).[3] Another added that the environment had become '*a moral issue rather than just an environmental one*' (8). Their awakening to an environmental consciousness, however, had developed not in Ireland, nor through their institutional membership of the Catholic Church, but while working in developing countries:

> 8   *Well, personally I got interested, I came from Ireland, I saw the forest being destroyed, I saw the topsoil just gushing into the rivers. I mean*

---

3 Transcription conventions used in the report: quotations from focus group transcripts are italicised, and when longer than three lines, indented. When the quote is indented the number before each intervention is the number of the relevant speaker, while 'F' indicates that the facilitator is speaking. '…' indicates that some phrase, sentence or brief intervention by another speaker has been omitted, or, when at the end of the speaker's quotation, that the speaker continued further. When the quote is not indented it is also italicised and where appropriate, the speaker number is given in brackets after the quote. When a particular characterisation of a participant might lead to his/her identification, it is omitted or left ambivalent.

you didn't have to be a genius to say '... there has to be something wrong with this ... This cannot be right and it cannot be right as a Christian missionary here and not saying anything about it' ... And you build on it from there. You get into other campaigns and you learn something about it and you try to connect it to your faith and there's no end to it actually, unfortunately.

Returned missionaries

Recognising the difficulties of bringing about the radical political and economic changes needed to protect the environment, another participant noted the potential role of religious groups generally:

6　*Religious groups – I mean I am talking about Buddhists, Muslims, everybody – I mean if you look at the population of the world religious whatever ... or a huge percentage of people believe in God anyway, and I think you have to have strong motivation for change and I think religious motivation or God or whatever is a strong motivation and this would include all people. I am not talking about people going to Church, because I think that change has to come from the bottom not the top ...*

Returned missionaries

However, as the last sentence begins to indicate, their God-centred environmental ethic was not inspired by the institutional Catholic Church. Indeed its lack of pro-environmental awareness and action was a major source of critical disappointment to them.

This discourse, while religiously based, was also strongly anthropocentric. Describing her ministry in a refugee camp, a participant noted:

7　*When I first went there I noticed there was no animal life, no birdsong. But that's because people have very little food to eat so they kill off even the tiny baby birds, the new-born birds ... because they are so poor they cannot buy anything. They cut down the forests to build homes but they are not supposed to. They are put in jail if they are caught cutting down the forests. But they need to burn wood to cook.*

Returned missionaries

Furthermore, there was no clean water. The participant tried to help:

7　*Well we do try to find them some other way to get clean water. Give them some money but that only lasts ... there are 20,000 people there.*

F   *And are you doing that to help them survive or are you doing that to protect the environment …?*

7   *It is mainly to help them survive.*

Returned missionaries

On the other hand, aspects of a biocentric perspective were also aired, if not agreed upon. The issue raised was that of animal welfare and the protection of animals when this was against the economic interest of humans. One participant noted that, when he was young, the attitude to killing animals assumed that humans were superior and the killing justified in terms of '*it's only a rabbit*', '*it's only a hare*', '*it's only an animal*'. Now he felt more open to seeing:

1   *that the environment is part of a whole … it is our Mother in a way, it produces so much, all these things for life and if Jesus said 'I have come that they may have life' then this is all part of this life, you know – this broader community. And it is kind of my vision has just broadened out to include those things.*

Returned missionaries

Another participant queried a species-equality perspective, taking the example of the Compassion in World Farming protest at the export of calves. She noted that in England it appeared that:

6   *Animals are more important than humans … I mean the calves they were supporting and I mean I agree they were being treated badly, but they honestly don't seem to get as upset about children in the streets begging as they do about foxes in the back garden – you see them feeding the foxes now. If my brother saw that he would have a heart attack because he would just shoot them all because they are killing the lambs. … He is a farmer so that makes it different. But you can overdo the animal bit as well, that's what I'm saying, living in England. In Ireland I think we are a bit more balanced.*

2   *Free the mink and the swan dies.*

Returned missionaries

This discussion regarding animal rights was not taken further however, as another participant moved the discussion on by highlighting his recent fascination on viewing the interdependent 'life system' evidenced in some '*stone, mud and dirt and weeds*' dug up from the local river when viewed under the microscope: '*It was just fascinating here to see that when you looked at it through a microscope there … so each little thing, I would never have been conscious of that before, and that they all have a role. They looked stupendous ...'* (4). Thus a romantic perspective was drawn upon to move away from a potentially contentious area.

A religious and anthropocentric ethic was underpinned for some by an aesthetic appreciation of the beauty of God's creation and by an appreciation that non-human nature was worthy of respect and protection in its own right. One member noted:

4   *... I was incensed on Sunday morning. I was going to say Mass in .... and as you go beyond ... there's a ... lovely spread of daffodils on the left-hand side ... to see that people probably who had gone home from the disco the night before, had cropped the heads off daffodils and they were lying strewn on the footpath. ... It's an attitude that you cut off the head of something ... it made me incensed I would say on Sunday.*

Returned missionaries

He continued by describing how he had incorporated this into his homily:

4   *You know the beautiful day and you know everything is fresh with life. It was new summertime, the newness of life, the daffodils, the primroses, the new mown grass. So it's a sign of new life and just to help people to express their appreciation for the beauty of God's creation, tying it in with another part of the Gospel, you know? And maybe just to bring out that dimension – that it is a new beginning and how we can ... maybe not meaning it, but just destroy them – and they are not there for destruction, you know.*

Returned missionaries

Religious, anthropocentric and romantic themes were interwoven into the discourse of this group, all contributing to respect and care for non-human nature. A sense of the interdependence of all things was also articulated: '*And you realise you are dependent on nature and the whole structure for your own survival*' (5). They were also acutely aware of forces operating against an environmental ethic of care, particularly economic forces. One noted that environmental regulations would not be necessary:

5   *If we are in harmony, if we are integrated people and if we are in harmony with creation, it should be all part of us.*
F   *Yes, but that's not the case?*
5   *No.*
1   *Economic pressures.*
8   *Economic pressures, yeah.*

Returned missionaries

Responses of Other Groups

While no other group spontaneously articulated a God-centred or religious perspective as narrated by the returned missionaries, different aspects of an environmental ethic of care were evident across all groups. This was evident both in response to the moral discourse statement and in moral comments made spontaneously during the first half of the discussion, during which two themes predominated. One was the frequent, if sometimes brief, articulation of a discourse of 'care' for the environment and its opposite, 'careless' and 'greedy' behaviour. The emphasis on environmental care was often linked to a concern for others or to protecting the environment in the interest of children and future generations. It was thus anthropocentric, but social rather than individualistic in nature. In contrast, the theme of greed as fuelling environmental destruction was seen as linked to economic self-interest. A further theme, although much less frequently articulated, was cruelty to animals. Here there was an occasional opening up of a biocentric discourse, but this was either ignored or closed down by others.

The moral statement offered to the focus groups was biocentric in focus. It was offered in two formats. The first stated, 'Trees are not commodities. Trees are nature. They are nature's gift to us and we should protect them.' It was an adaptation of a statement made on RTÉ news by a woman protesting against the cutting down of trees in Ayer Square, Galway city, at the time the research project was being designed. This statement was presented to twelve groups (see Table A1 in Appendix 1 for a list of statements and groups to which they were presented) and elicited an interesting discussion regarding the relationship between human and non-human nature. Some groups and participants strongly contradicted the statement, emphasising the anthropocentric perspective that nature was a commodity for human use and benefit; others raised romantic and occasional relational perspectives. A radical biocentric approach tended to be rejected, or if raised, sidelined. Many of the groups associated the statement with the sentiments articulated by 'tree huggers', 'eco-warriors' or radical ecocentric groups, with which most groups were not at all enamoured.

An alternative statement format was offered to seven groups in which a God-centred rather than nature-centred perspective was offered. It read, 'Trees are not commodities. Trees are nature. They are God's gift to us and we should protect them.' Two of the mobilised groups, the CEF and the anti-incinerator group, were offered this version of the statement. Some gave its God-centred perspective a brief acknowledgement, others gave a more negotiated and distancing response, apparently because of the style of the statement, which a CEF member stated was 'dictatorial'. While one member of the anti-incinerator group stated, '*They are all gifts from God*' (4), another wondered who might have made this statement, speculating that '*Nobody in power would have said that*' and, drawing on *The Lord of the Rings*, suggesting, to much laughter, that it might have come from '*a voice living in a tree … A hobbit*' (7).

Of the five groups from the general public who were shown the God-centred statement, only one, the retired group, agreed unreservedly with it, but did not discuss its religious sentiments or its mode of address. The group of Traveller women also nodded assent, but took this discussion no further. In the three remaining groups, the predominant response was, as with the mobilised groups, to the style of address rather than the substance of the statement. While an individual participant might acknowledge the statement as true or at least true for some, the more general discussion focused on their sense that the statement was dictatorial and patronising, like something that would be said to children in kindergarten. These groups occupied less powerful social positions, including the unemployed, students 2, and shop workers. The students, for example, complained that they felt they were being '*preached at*' by it, that it was like something out of a '*first year religion book*' (2) and '*a very attacking statement which makes me feel defensive as if they are accusing me of cutting down all the trees*' (5). Looking more at the substance of the statement, a shop worker stated that '*Some people don't believe in God. We should protect* [trees], *but I believe in God like, but some people don't*' (6), while another in this group reinterpreted God's gifts as '*mother earth's gifts*' (3). There was little evidence among most groups of a strong and articulate underpinning of an environmental ethic by God-centred Christian sentiments or beliefs.

Moral Themes Articulated Spontaneously by Other Groups

Although a God-centred ethic of environmental concern was infrequent, focus groups spontaneously elaborated a moral discourse regarding what they defined as careful or, alternatively, careless attitudes and behaviour in relation to the environment, as well as a moral disapproval of the greediness of contemporary society which, they argued, supported carelessness.

Care and Carelessness
Fifteen of the twenty-two focus groups spontaneously used the terms 'care' or 'carelessness' in talking about people's environmental attitudes and behaviour, while nine used the term 'greed'. The usage of the term 'care' was more frequently articulated by the general public and mobilised groups than by scientists, consultant engineers or the farming groups. Mobilised groups and the general public used the term in two ways: one

was to complain about others – 'they don't care', 'people don't care', 'nobody cares', 'the powers that be don't care'; the second was to embed the discussion about environmental care in discussions regarding familial relationships, the home, women, children, future generations and, outside the home, respect for other people. Thus, care for other humans was closely associated with care for the environment. This was the case for the four mobilised groups as well as for the teachers, nurses, skilled workers, shop workers, the retired, and young mothers. It was an anthropocentric discourse, but one that stressed social relationships rather then egoistic interests. In contrast, the moral discourse on greed as fuelling environmental destruction, while also strongly anthropocentric, emphasised the egoistic demands of producers for profits and consumers for material goods.

Regarding a lack of concern for other people contributing to careless environmental behaviour, the retired group noted that the reason dog owners did not clean up after their dog, causing other people to walk in it, was due to:

2   *Carelessness, I'd say.*
–   *Exactly.*
6   *People just don't care about the other person.*
–   *No, no.*
4   *No respect for other people.*
7   *People don't care about the environment.*
F   *Do you think not?*
7   *Yeah, a lot of people don't.*

Retired

The familial context and an emphasis on children and occasionally women were particularly evident in discussions on environmental care. An environmental activist in the CEF, reporting on her experiences in attempting to mobilise support, stated:

7   *... when* [people] *are informed, almost to a man they do care, especially women. I've stood in the street many afternoons just stopping people and talking about this* [environmental issues] *to them and a lot of them don't want to know, they want their machines and that's it ... but women and children actually are amazingly caring and I think that's partly perhaps because women are the nurturers, they do care about the environment a lot and I've found that's a very interesting thing.*

CEF

This member of the CEF also reported how in her NGO:

7 *... we have three highly qualified chemists who are giving up their time for no money purely on a voluntary basis because they care about the environment in this area and the future of children in ... And they want to get it right and they have researched other methods, for example, of dealing with toxic waste ...*

CEF

Also frequently noted was the role of the family in inducting children into caring for the environment. Regarding littering, the unemployed group noted that '*... as regards throwing papers on the ground, some people won't do it because that is the way they were brought up, but other people do it because the don't give a ****, they just don't care at all*' (2). The young mothers also noted the disrespect shown to the environment, especially by adolescents:

— *But you see kids, say you were walking to the shops, and you see kids not with their parents, old schoolchildren, you see them probably kicking trees and all, they haven't got the ... knowledge or the understanding like, they are important, you are not supposed to do that, have respect like.*

Young mothers

Teachers spoke of the role of education: '*I suppose being teachers and I mean, I was thinking of kids and, you know, how we teach them care and respect for the environment in which they find themselves*' (7). They noted the responsiveness of their rural primary school students to environmental issues. Describing the response to a retired local environmental expert who visits the school:

4 *He could have our whole school say from first class to sixth class in a hall for two, two and a half hours, and there's no discipline problem ... You can actually leave him in the hall with the children and he holds them in the palm of his hand.*
F *Why is that?*
4 *Because it's animals, it's creatures, it's living.*
8 *It's living, moving, it's interesting, it's alive, it's real.*

Teachers

However, they recognised that what they taught their students did not always tally with their own practices at home. One expressed concern about:

3   *... my own poor performance in terms of care of the environment and recycling – personally as an adult and as a parent and as a householder – and the contradiction that places me in and that places me off-side with what I'm expected to espouse in the classroom.*

Teachers

Skilled building workers spoke critically and extensively of wasteful building practices, placing them in the context of a lack of care by builders both for the environment and for workers on site. They particularly noted builders' emphasis on getting the job finished irrespective of the cost to workers (in terms of lack of safety) and to the environment. One worker described the supposed sorting of building waste:

2   *Yeah, a system, there's no system. You get like a wheelie bin on the site for metal, you get one for old paint cans but you don't, you should have one for timber, you get one for ****** plasterboard or whatever, right, but the thing would be half full of metal, know what I mean, next of all the sticker is gone off it, wood is on this, gets thrown on top, no one cares ...*

Skilled workers

And because of work pressures from the builder to get the job done, and from the worker not to lose his job, the environment was given very short shift. They contrasted this with their experiences at home:

2   *... you're more aware* [of the environment] *at home, you know what I mean, you're more relaxed and ...*
6   *It's yours.*
–   *It's yours.*
8   *You're more protective of your own area.*
7   *With the work, that's at work, there is none ...*
–   *There's none.*
7   *When you're finished with your cans you **** them ...*
1   *There's nobody to take them and recycle them ... get out the cheap way.*
F   *And there is no systems possible in work?*
–   *It's getting the job done.*

Skilled workers

Greed and the Environment

The home is also a major site for consumption, and there was recognition among the groups that the drive for economic growth, the desire to make a profit, as well as their own demands as consumers, were causing environmental damage. Greed was often the simple term used to describe all of these motivations, and it was used across all five focus group subsets – regulators (DoE), the environmental managers, the dairy farmers, the mobilised groups, and, among the general public, the commuters, the skilled workers, the young workers and the unemployed. Thus, for example, the DoE felt that there was *'only care for the environment when you appeal to people's self-interest'* (4); dairy farmers noted that illegal dumping by private interests was *'down to economics and greed'*; while the walkers claimed that the fencing off of the mountains by farmers to qualify for government grants was due to their *'selfishness and greed'* (6). This greed was seen as a characteristic of contemporary society and as having increased with Ireland's recent economic boom. Greed was the reason people showed a lack of care. Commenting on the recent rapid economic changes experienced in Ireland and their consequences for the environment, the commuter group noted:

7   *And I think we are a greedy enough race of people actually ...*
4   *We want our mobile phones.*
7   *We want everything and I don't think we put the environment really into perspective at all ...*
–   *No.*
7   *... we have gone from like having* [little economic development] *... and then just grab, grab, grab, because the 90s just went boom and nobody really cared about the environment. It was just grab, grab, grab.*

Commuters

Young mothers agreed. They pointed out how the food industry and supermarkets, catering for consumer demand, supplied strawberries in January and daffodils in December. They also thought that *'everything is being force-grown'*, which was not good for the environment and *'not good for any of us'*, but despite this *'we are still willing to pay for it'* (7). They continued:

–   *We are looking for them, that is why they are doing it. The more we want it, the more they will do it.*
–   *We are just looking for it.*
F   *Where will it all end though?*

10 *It won't end coz people are too greedy.*
– *Yeah, they are, they are all greedy.*
10 *You are right, they want things like this* [snaps fingers a few times], *you know.*
– *That is why they are cloning all these sheep.*
1 *They have already cloned the babies.*

Young mothers

Environmental managers agreed and, furthermore, legitimated greed as 'human nature':

1 *It's greed, it's what we want, we want more and we want it cheaper and we want it quicker and we have to pay that price* [of environmental destruction]. *I think greed definitely sums up a lot of it, like economics runs the world, you can't avoid economics, it's how you deal with economics possibly but like you say greed is driving* [it]. *It's human nature. And people want more and the more they have, the more they want, and that's driving the economic system we have.*

Environmental managers

The DoE focus groups concurred, one participant noting that it was '*people's selfishness that motivates everybody*'. It was only after '*they have their two cars, they have their holiday home, they have all the comforts, then maybe they'll do their bit for the environment*'. And particularly so if it simply meant a smaller box of detergent, or recycling the wine bottles, then people will be '*happy enough, it's not going to make a big impact on their lifestyle*'. On the other hand, it was also recognised that such minimal practices were not going to solve environmental problems in the long term – '*it's in many ways just rearranging the furniture on the Titanic, rearranging the deck chairs*' (2).

The difficulty with this egocentric ethic, in which greed is linked to individual self-interest and the harvesting of economic and social capital as well as being underpinned by a sense of economic inevitability, is in finding a way out of the deterministic nature of this discourse. Were alternative modes of arguing for an environmental ethic, whether relational, romantic, religious or radically biocentric, raised by the focus groups, and, if raised, how did others respond to them? These questions will be examined in the next section.

Cruelty to Animals: A Biocentric Ethic?

Three groups, apart from the religious group, spontaneously brought up the issue of possible cruelty to animals. One of the most interesting was the discussion by large dairy farmers. They brought up the issue of the live export of calves and the protests by Compassion in World Farming:

3   *Remember them crew of hairy lads that were jumping on the trucks when they were taking the calves over to ...*

4   *Compassion in World Farming.*

–   *Yeah, they are sucklers.*

3   *Ah the poor calves.* [Ironic]

4   *They were being exported but the regulations saw them board.*

–   *Everything was above board only ...*

F   *Why do you think they* [protesters] *did ...?*

–   *You get extremists.*

F   *What was motivating them?*

2   *Obviously cruelty.*

5   *But they look at the calves as having a soul and having ...*

F   *Do you look at the calf having a soul?*

–   *No, you can't.*

–   *In fairness you can't be cruel either.*

4   *You have to be removed; if we looked at them like that we would never sell any of them.*

5   *You have to be cruel to be kind.*

–   *Being transported* [they] *were getting nothing to eat.*

–   *They have to be looked after.*

5   *But you have to be cruel to be kind like ... That even goes for human beings as well.*

Dairy farmers

Thus, while some were opening up the subject, others were successfully closing it down with the non sequitur, '*you have to be cruel to be kind like*'.

The hillwalkers (among them a farmer (5)) also brought up the issue of cruelty to farm animals. On their walks in the mountains they had come across sheep which they felt had not been looked after properly:

6   *... they don't really look after them.*

5   *I don't think they are that bad now.*

6   *Well, look at the ... fence after we went back from the foot-and-mouth, there was three sheep caught in wire and obviously no farmer had checked them for months, they just died ... that's pure neglect.*

–   *Yeah.*

4   *I reported sheep to the guards up at ... that were eaten alive with maggots, their backbone exposed let me tell you, about five years ago.*

3   *They were still alive you were saying.*

4   *Walking and their backbone exposed, I come from a farming background.*

–   *That's true, it's terrible.*

–   *Yeah.*

4   *There was a farmer up there that was neglecting sheep.*

–   *Yeah.*

5   *They're a minority.*

4   *They are a minority, yeah.*

5   *They are, yeah.*

6   *But then again that goes back to what I was saying, there's no policing of it like, there's laws there to say all these sheep should be dipped and the farmers even get paid to dip them ...*

Walkers

A further extensive discussion of the treatment of farm animals was taken up by the teachers (in response to the discourse statement), in which they noted, in very unfavourable terms, recent changes that had occurred. The teachers' group, many themselves spouses and children of farmers, discussed changes in farming practices consequent on Irish membership of the EU:

4   *I think farming is a scandal. It totally, absolutely infuriates me. It has destroyed our environment and our farmers are being funded to continue to destroy the water, destroy the environment, just change the whole pattern ...*

1   *... I was born on a farm, was raised on a farm and I can watch the difference.* [My father] *had a huge respect and love and care for the animals – every damn one of them, and would hate to see an animal mistreated. What the new type of farming has done and what the headage, the whole headage business has done, is made the animals again commodities, numbers. And like, if you put sheep into a pen, if a few of them die – so what, like. Whereas, if one animal died for his generation, they would really feel it.*

4   *Because it was probably 10 percent of their overall ten cows.*

–   *It wasn't so much that though. I think they had a huge ...*

8   *Well there was a one-to-oneness there.*

–   *There was ...*

–   *They had a great love for them.*

8 *Because they were forking them stuff personally almost, but now it's run up and down the feeder or whatever and churning out ... you know.*

– *I'm not casting aspersions on modern-day farmers because they ...*

8 *They are paid to do it; they are encouraged to do it. But they need to do it as well to survive. Your thirty-acre man might as well pack his bag, you know – they have to work the system to make a living, you know.*

Teachers

The possibility and superiority of a caring and relational approach (a 'one-to-oneness') to farm animals were acknowledged here, even if present-day economic constraints in the agri-food business did nothing to encourage this approach.

The young working-class mothers spontaneously took up another issue – the testing of cosmetics on animals and the use of leather belts and fur jackets. While one stated that she did not agree with such testing at all, the word of another appeared to carry more weight: '*Like, I'm a beautician and I believe in testing on animals, because I don't want to break out ...* [laughing] *you know what I mean. The* [name of brand] *makeup right is not tested and you do be in bits after it*' (3). Most agreed that when buying make-up they did not check for animal testing. Others gave examples of their bad reactions to hair dyes, but the query by one participant, '*why put the animal through that?*' elicited no concerned response from the others.

Thus it would appear that in this domain of caring for domestic animals and the use of animals for testing cosmetics, alternative moral discourses were available and articulated. However, for those whose own personal interests (e.g. dairy farmers and users of cosmetics) were seen to be most affected by the cruel treatment of animals, there was a tendency to close down the discussion fairly rapidly and little evidence of a willingness to change. For teachers and walkers, perceived ill-treatment of animals was observed in areas emotionally close to them: the home farms of teachers and the mountains for walkers. Teachers, looking to the past, sought a more relational approach, but also noted the economic impediments to this. The walkers noted that it was only a minority who neglected their sheep and sought the enforcement of state regulations. There was no evidence of a rights-based approach, but the area was a contentious one, raised spontaneously by members of these groups and often discussed with feeling and high modality.

Community, Care and the Environment

Another research question concerned the occurrence, or not, of a discussion regarding local communities of residence and a sense of obligation to care for others and the environment in that community. An idealised sense of community was seldom articulated, but a number of groups used the term 'community' as a moral category, articulating a sense of responsibility to other community members and to protecting and maintaining the community's physical environment. Some participants gave examples of their own efforts with others to do this. For many, however, this sense of community was seen as something in the past. With increasing wealth and changing lifestyles, nobody had time, so community-based traditions were seen to be declining rapidly, with rural communities in the West facing the further problem of depopulation. Thus, care for the local environment had also become more problematic, and resources to mobilise protest had been weakened. This was the view of the urban-based retired as well as small-town and rural-based teachers and commuters, large and small farmers, and walkers.

A second issue was the relationship between industry, especially what was perceived as a potentially dirty industry, and its local community. Here the environmental managers emphasised the desirability of gaining the goodwill of the local community. One described the industry's open community days and environmental schools' competitions organised by the firm, also noting:

1   *We do try and make an additional effort because community relations obviously are very important to us and having a good corporate image is very important to us and I suppose having good employee awareness ... If we started polluting or started getting prosecutions or started getting a bad reputation as an environment polluter, it affects our employees, affects everybody. If you've got a good reputation you generally like to keep it.*

Environmental managers

From the opposite perspective, the anti-incinerator group, when describing an industry not seen as environmentally conscientious, noted the double bind of community members. When family and neighbours were also employees, especially at times of high unemployment, differential power relationships meant that the mobilisation of local complaint was not seen as an option.

A third community-related perspective was raised by the DoE. Here the lack of environmental care for one's local neighbourhood, especially evidenced in littering, was explained as follows:

1   *The Irish live in Ireland as though they* [are] *living in rented accommodation. There's this kind of post-colonial mentality: 'Well, I'm in the landlord's house, sod it, I won't bother'. Whereas if you live in the UK, or Scandinavian countries, people obey, they don't seek the chance, take the opportunity to slip one by the authorities. There's that kind of post-colonial mentality.*

DoE

This lack of a sense of ownership was reiterated by another participant:

4   *I pick up litter in my local park because I figure it's my park. I own it just as much as anyone else. But the kids who throw the litter there, they obviously don't feel a sense of ownership and a sense of community. And this is the big cultural change that needs to be made ...*

DoE

Later, the same participant noted the work of local authorities in funding and encouraging local initiatives, a point also made by the heritage officers and responded to positively by the CEF.

To recap, moral themes were frequently, if rather briefly, articulated spontaneously by almost all of the focus groups. In particular, the theme of the obligation to take care of the environment was prevalent, and this was linked to the anthropocentric but also altruistic theme of respect and care for others. However, the latter sense of community was seen as rapidly declining. Environmental carelessness was often associated with self-interest, greed and the workings of the economy. The moral issue of cruelty to animals, when raised within a minority of groups, was contentious, and related more often to emotional feelings and identifications than a rights-based approach.

Responses to the Moral Discourse Statement: Range of Moral Discourse Themes

How did the focus groups respond to the ecocentric statements: 'Trees are not commodities. Trees are nature. They are nature's / God's gift to us and we should protect them'? The responding discourse was predominantly anthropocentric. However, occasional romantic, religious and relational perspectives were briefly articulated. Each of these will be outlined and exemplified below.

Anthropocentric Responses: Managing Nature
For many of those proposing a mainstream anthropocentric perspective, the statement was seen as somewhat contradictory and, for some,

ridiculous, as trees for them were defined both as part of nature and as commodities for human use. Moreover, the statement was seen as over-generalised. Rather than the generalised category of trees, it was thought more relevant to offer a classification of different types of trees and the appropriate human behaviour relative to each class, in particular how to appropriately 'manage' each. This emphasis on classification and/or management was the predominant sustainable development or ecological modernisation discourse among the regulators, the environmental scientists and the heritage officers; the business groups; both large and small farmers; the anti-incinerator group and walkers among the mobilised groups; and the teachers, students, skilled building workers and young mothers.

As most clearly delineated by the environmental scientists, trees as commodities represented the first category. Within this category, several of the groups placed evergreen and coniferous trees, which had been planted as a cash crop and which humans could use as they saw fit. The second and third categories were, respectively, broadleaf native woodlands and trees in urban or residential areas. These were seen to have a different value to those in the first category and should be treated with greater sensitivity. The environmental scientists articulated these differences most precisely:

7   *I have a particular view on certain types of trees, coniferous, and where they're planted. They can have a nuisance value if they're not planted in the correct areas. Broadleaf trees, oaks and things like that, yeah great, everybody likes to see those …*

–   *…*

6   *Yeah, again I was thinking of the difference between commercial forestry and more native forestry, the commercial forest is planted as a commodity and sometimes it spills over into a social, has a social role in the picnic areas and that sort of thing but essentially it's planted for harvest, it's just a crop.*

–   *…*

5   *Yeah, I suppose I'm thinking of trees in an urban area where there are trees planted in various parts of the city and so on, but at the same time, you know, it's not an absolute thing. If a tree is blocking out all the light from my house I'd have objections to it, so it depends where it is.*

–   *…*

3   *Yeah, I think it's all in the context of where they are. A tree in a forest that's all the same height and on the side of a mountain in a nice big square, that's a commodity and there's no value to that. But, you know, in terms of urban areas, you know, there is a significant value*

in having, you know, mature trees in, say, estates and all that and I
think in that sense they should be protected.

Environmental scientists

For these three categories of trees, the appropriate term for humans'
relationship to them was 'management'. A central aspect of this
anthropocentric management discourse was that, given that trees were a
renewable resource, they should be planted (in appropriate areas) and used
in the interests of humans. There was an emphasis on achieving a managed
balance between different interests in doing this, and a belief that if trees
were felled, they should be replanted. As the environmental managers
noted:

3   *... trees are commodities.*
–   *Yeah.*
3   *And can be treated as such. They're a renewable source of energy, it's*
     easy to plant, so long as you ensure that they are replanted, I've no
     difficulty with trees.

–   *...*
4   *They're a resource like, to be managed properly.*
–   *Yeah.*
2   *It can actually be shown that trees properly managed are more*
     beneficial to the environment than just letting them grow. If we look
     at all the issues, carbon dioxide for instance now, it's a proven fact
     that trees in their first ten to fifteen years of growth in a managed
     forest will tie up more carbon than mature trees.

Environmental managers

Later, the environmental managers noted the need to maintain a 'balance'
between big native trees and evergreens in order to 'try to encourage some
of the wildlife back'. The engineering group, articulating a managerial
discourse, attempted to be specific regarding ideal replacement targets:

3   *Trees can take up to 100s of years to grow fully, an example – an oak*
     tree and you can cut it down in a minute.
F   *And how does that make you feel ...?*
3   *So I'm saying if we have to cut down trees we should replace them.*
     Maybe 1.5 of a factor. They've been there 100s of years. A factor of
     two or something.

Consultant engineers

Romantic Responses: The Mystery of Trees

It was thought that trees in urban or residential areas should be protected in particular. A number of groups, having accepted that forest trees were a commodity and a business, gave examples of their concerns regarding their unwarranted destruction by housing and road developers. Groups drew on an aesthetic appreciation of trees and, occasionally, as in the quote below, a recognition of their uniqueness, which might indicate a relational approach:

1   *I know you can get a chainsaw and run it through. I lived in ... for ten years and there was a lovely tree ... absolutely fantastic, beautiful and they just did eight of them on the trot to widen a footpath ... Huge trees, now you can preserve or you can even go and replant your oaks and get a couple of saplings but nobody is going to see those trees again.*
–   *Yeah.*
–   *Yeah.*
–   *You see that's past.*
–   *It's gone.*
–   *You can't go back.*
–   *130 years to grow and it's gone in a minute.*
–   *...*
F   *And what do you like about trees from a personal point of view?*
3   *I think their age and how attractive ... They're there so long, I think trees have always been part of ...*
1   *They're unique, you don't get the same ...*
3   *As a child you always learned how to count the rings like, you know, like ...* (Laughter) *That sense of mystery about a tree, that it has seen so much or ... just something about it.*

Environmental managers

However, despite the first environmental manager's concerns regarding particular trees and a recognition of their uniqueness, he/she was also concerned not to attract the taint of being an environmentalist activist. During the discussion on trees this participant pointed out: '*I'm not a very environmental sort of, I haven't got the woolly jumper with me in the car*' (1).

An aesthetic appreciation of trees was not felt to contradict an anthropocentric perspective. Thus, a recognition of trees as a commodity was often held alongside an appreciation of the beauty of particular trees and a desire to protect them. One of the dairy farmers spoke of his appreciation of such a tree, to the agreement of the group:

8   *I had the same problem four years ago, the ESB were running their wires ... across my farm and what we called the walnut tree – a horse*

chestnut tree, and the kids from all over the area were coming to get the conkers every year, and they wanted to knock that tree. I said you can move the line but you can't move that tree.

F   *Why did you not want that tree* [to be knocked] ...?

8   *It was a beautiful tree for starters, plus the entertainment the kids got from it, they come on their bicycles there and taking the conkers and they would look and see would I be in the yard ...* (laughing)

Dairy farmers

He concluded, '*I think a tree that is there for generations and has a bit of character to it, it is wrong to cut it down*'; but if it was a danger to the public, '*that is a different matter altogether*'.

One of the small, part-time farmers described his own changing attitude to trees on his land. In reply to the facilitator's question, 'Would there be many cutting down their trees?' he replied, 'I used to cut them down practically every winter' (2). He went on to say that he didn't any more as '*the family would rear up*' if he did, as '*they think it isn't right*'. He now regretted having cut down so many. In general though, the small farmers' attitude to trees and tree plantations was almost entirely pragmatic. While recognising that '*they are visually attractive*' (6), they emphasised their utilitarian value: they '*have their place, do their job*' (3). They provide '*shelter for livestock*', '*they are good wind breakers*'. One had got into forestry as '*a way of utilising land that wasn't great for agriculture. There was an income in it*' (5).

The Absence of a Religious Perspective

As noted above, only two of the mobilised groups, the anti-incinerator group and the CEF, and one of the general public groups, the retired, having been given the 'God's gift' statement, articulated a religiously based discourse, but very briefly. The anti-incinerator group discussed the dilemma of trees as a commodity, on the one hand, and as a part of nature, on the other:

4   *Each feature has its purpose in life as well.*
–   *They are there for a reason.*
–   *They are all gifts from God like.*
2   *Definitely.*

Anti-incinerator group

The CEF tended to place humans and trees within the one interdependent sphere of nature. However, they also noted, somewhat heatedly, some of the difficulties associated with a radical biocentric approach in assuming the rights of all species to exist:

2   *The human perception of, you know, trees are commodities for us to use, we're nature, they're nature, you know. Nature needs each other and suits each other.*

10 *We are a part of nature too.*

9   *And they are put there so that we can make things out of them and use them.*

2   *That's why I get angry at that statement. It's so limited.*

7   *If you said that to an elephant, you know, you can't eat that, it's not your commodity.*

10 *Yeah, say that to the mountain gorilla that you can't break that branch off and eat it.*

7   *It's a contradiction in terms to say it's not a commodity because everything in nature is a commodity for another part of nature.*

    …

3   *You only protect nature because of the God entity … If you like* [the] *old Christian Victorian kind of view on it that humans are kind of stewards of the world …*

CEF

Yet even this statement did not go unchallenged: one participant noted that a Christian ideology was used to legitimate colonialism and the extermination of indigenous peoples. However, others in the group neither pursued this line of reasoning nor a God-centred perspective on nature.

A Relational Approach

Some hints of a relational approach came through in the discussions of the anti-incinerator group and the CEF, as well as among environmental managers and the teachers' group, all quoted above. This was also the case with nurses and the unemployed. This approach acknowledges the autonomy and uniqueness of non-human nature, the interdependence of human and non-human nature and thus the appropriate ethical response of care and co-operation with it. As an approach it does not preclude using nature as a commodity to meet human needs, but strongly emphasises respect for non-human nature and its needs, and care regarding over-exploitation and ecological destruction. It draws on human rational, emotional, aesthetic and relational resources to forge a relationship of mutuality and empathy with non-human nature.

The nurses agreed strongly with the 'nature's gift' statement. Referring to the eco-warriors protesting about the destruction of trees at the Glen of the Downs, while one participant stated that many people thought they were '*eccentric and over the top*' (2), others said that they respected and admired them. They noted the destruction of the rainforests and the time and difficulty involved in replacing trees: '*It's the years it takes for them to grow ... And once they go then it's going to take so many years before they can be replaced again, if they are ever replaced*' (1). They also emphasised the interdependence of human and non-human nature:

4   *Well, you need that environment for our grandchildren, you want the earth preserved, a love of the earth, you know, and nature, everything. Why should we destroy it? We need it. We go hand in hand, humans and the land, so we need to look after our environment.*

Nurses

A participant in the unemployed group also emphasised the age of trees and that an individual tree could never be replaced, unlike a manufactured commodity. As he noted: '*You can plant another tree but you can't reinvent it*' (9). However, this potentially biocentric view could be cut off mid-stream in the name of 'realism':

6   *I think trees and plants and all that, they are all a gift, they all grew long before man was about. So it wasn't man that ...*
7   *It's an ideal sentiment to have, but once again if there is money involved they are all gone out the window. There is a profit to be made out of trees, and somebody wants to cut them down, they will be cut down and make money.*

Unemployed

Conclusion: Anthropocentrism and a Fragmentary Moral Discourse

This chapter explored the extent to which anthropocentric, relational, religious, romantic and radical biocentric themes were articulated in the focus group discussions. The range of possible themes was thus broad. The research was particularly interested in exploring the extent to which, if at all, utopian or critical moral perspectives were raised. In this context the comment by Smith (2001: 164) regarding the ethical space opened up by environmentalist discourses is appropriate. He notes that such discourses can give rise to '... a new reality ... creating the cracks and fissures through which we can glimpse the existence of an/other possible way of life'.

Overall, it might be argued that while such perspectives might be glimpsed in places, they were fragmentary and weak. While all five ethical themes were articulated at some point, giving evidence of their relatively wide availability in Ireland, an anthropocentric perspective was by far the most dominant. It was not, however, an exclusive perspective but was often held alongside others, especially romantic sentiments. The main anthropocentric perspective articulated an ethic of environmental care while at the same time recognising how greed fuelled environmental destruction. Mediating between care and greed, an administrative and scientific concern to classify and manage the ecological system was articulated. Greed was seen as a characteristic of the economic system, both in terms of production and consumption, and was believed to have increased exponentially over the past decade, and to have become a pronounced characteristic of 'we, Irish people'. There was little articulated sense of the possibility or willingness to change. This toleration of what was readily and spontaneously identified as greed was rationalised partially by a sense of disempowerment given the dominance of global capitalism. It was considered 'unrealistic' to propose change because of how deeply embedded 'we, Irish people' were in this economic system and because of a desire to hold on to the lifestyle that had been achieved in the last decade.

However, alongside this perspective of a greedy and destructive (but highly pleasurable, in lifestyle and consumption terms) economy was an ethic of environmental care. If the major forces supporting greed were seen as located in the economy, the forces supporting care were located by many groups in the home. Thus, there was a radical distinction made between public and private: in the public sphere, greedy economic interests were destroying the environment, while care and concern for the environment were identified with the private sphere of home, children and future generations. Young children, in particular, were seen as open to learning to care for the environment. Narratives of romantic responses to nature were told of the participants' own childhood or of the behaviour of children they knew. The home was also seen by some as a sphere protected from the harsh economic and environmental realities outside. This was certainly the case for the skilled workers who very clearly contrasted the environmental destructiveness of the building site with the care concerns evident in their homes. For farmers, however, it was less easy to make this distinction. Their work place was also their home. Thus, family members put pressure on one small farmer not to cut down trees. Teachers who were farmers' wives were particularly distressed by the forms of animal husbandry they saw practiced around them. The incursion of the greedy economic system had entered into the very life world of their home, contributing perhaps to their anger in discussing this.

Yet the home was also the centre of greedy consumption practices and lifestyles that were recognised as environmentally destructive. Teachers, as well as some other groups, recognised their own contradictory and less than morally pure behaviour: teaching their young pupils an ethic of environmental care while enjoying in their home a lifestyle which they acknowledged was environmentally exploitative. 'Managing' the environment may operate in this context as an ideological mantra, appearing to resolve or hide these contradictions.

A central aspect of an anthropocentric ethic is a focus on 'managing' the environment, in particular trees, due to the discourse statement offered to the focus groups. Here the classification of different types of trees in different types of locations gave rise to what were seen as 'appropriate' practices, drawing on scientific and administrative knowledge with an emphasis on protecting human interests whether in terms of utility or aesthetics. It is a perspective that allows and tends to encourage further economic development and legitimate this in terms of 'progress'. This discourse of modernity, emphasising order and classification, science and management, will be raised again in the science and regulatory chapters.

Religious support for an environmental ethic was noticeable by its absence – although given the general disinterest of the Catholic Church in the ecological sphere, this is perhaps not so surprising. Some groups expressed a certain hostility to the form of the discourse statement in terms of nature being 'God's gift'. Only the retired group openly endorsed this statement, with the CEF and the anti-incinerator group briefly acknowledging a God-based justification for environmental protection. The returned missionary group was the only group to spontaneously articulate a religious ethic, integrating into this both romantic and justice perspectives.

A romantic perspective was an important resource drawn upon by some to support an environmental ethic of care. A number of focus groups articulated an emotional identification with, and an aesthetic appreciation for, particular trees, especially broadleaf trees and those sited in residential areas. There was also recognition of nature and its processes as existing apart from humans – leading to a sense of its mystery, for example, in the uniqueness and longevity of trees.

This shaded into a relational approach that recognised both the otherness of nature but also human interdependence with it. If both human interdependence with non-human nature is recognised, as well as the latter's uniqueness, the elements of a partnership ethic or a relational approach are in place, or as one teacher noted, 'a one-to-oneness' can be established through a close and caring relationship with non-human nature. This approach was not, however, elaborated on in any detail within the groups, but its potential could be glimpsed on occasion, opening up a utopian space and a space in which to criticise current practices, for example, the treatment of animals.

This relational approach offers a language with which perhaps few are sufficiently acquainted to articulate with confidence. On the other hand, it may be a discourse with which all may not wish to become acquainted or to support. If it comes to be seen as the language of those defined as extreme environmental protest groups – *'them crew of hairy lads'* – it may tend to alienate. If it too fundamentally questions one's economic, lifestyle or other interests it may tend to be marginalised or rejected – as with the dairy farmers and young mothers. However, the evidence from all the focus groups was that these ethical questions are being raised, and there is a search for a language in which to express them. When command of an ethical perspective or critique had been gained, personal identification with it and the modality in which it was expressed was high. The examples among our focus groups were the four mobilised groups – returned missionaries, CEF, walkers and anti-incinerator groups, as well as some of the teachers and nurses. It was hinted at on occasion by some of the environmental managers and the unemployed. Regarding the groups that expressed a high level of moral concern, there was also a high level of frustration and, for some, guilt, at an inability to deliver on high environmental ethical ideals, both at societal and individual levels.

For the remainder of the groups, the scientists, the consultant engineers, as well as the rest of the general public groups, a discourse of care and greed, strongly underpinned by an anthropocentric and regulatory perspective predominated. Here there were references to the moral feelings of 'we, Irish people', but little strongly articulated sense that 'I' ought to be morally committed to getting up and doing something about the environment. Some may hope that a regulatory discourse of the state, mediating to 'manage' the environment, will absolve the 'I' from responsibilities in this regard. For farmers, the theme of care was not articulated. The extent to which all groups were mobilised by a romantic rather than, or perhaps along with, a moral discourse will be further examined in Chapter 4. However, prior to this, a further aspect of moral discourses will be examined by looking at the themes articulated around radical political discourses, including the issue of the fair treatment of developing countries and perceptions regarding radical environmental groups.

3

Radical Political Discourse: The Possibility of Change

Introduction

Radical political discourses on the environment argue that current levels of environmental destruction must be curtailed in the interests of both the environment and humanity. The solution, it is argued, lies not just with the sustainable development policies of further economic development complemented by strict environmental regulation and green consumerism (a set of policies frequently entitled ecomodernisation); nor with individual commitment to biocentric values or local environmentally friendly initiatives. What is needed is global change, in particular a change in the relationship between the economically dominant North and the dependent and impoverished South. This requires an examination of global patterns of capitalist development, which, it is argued, are based on the 'power and greed' (Khor 1999: 73) of transnational corporations (TNCs), the support they receive from multilateral international institutions and the major Western and G7 nations, and the free-trade ideology which promotes and maintains their power. Mobilisation and protest at international, national and local levels are also required to bring about this economic and social change. Such protest is expressed in the so-called anti-capitalist, anti-globalisation movements, or, to use the title preferred by some of the participants, the 'global justice movement'.

Among the many aims of different segments of this movement is to protest at what are seen as the existing exploitative relationships between the wealthy North and the impoverished South and the exploitative and destructive relationship with nature which this economic system upholds, and to explore alternative ways of improving the quality of life for all, in both the developed and the developing worlds. The distribution of goods in both of these worlds, it is argued, should be more closely related to 'needs' rather than 'wants'. Goods should be less standardised and commodified according to the interests of globalised markets. There should be respect for difference, both that between human beings and that between all things in nature. Relationships should not be characterised by the increasing levels of inequality and exploitation, of both people and nature, which global capitalist development has brought. (For discussion of some of these issues, see Gadgil and Guha 1995, International Forum on Globalisation 2002, Agyeman et al. 2003, Peet and Watts 2004, Sklair 2002)

One of the most important radical environmental discourses at the present time, both in Ireland and at the international level, is a criticism of capitalist globalisation. McMichael (2000), in his analysis of capitalist development, has argued that since the Second World War, what was initially a 'development project' has evolved into a 'globalisation project'. The 'development project' emphasised national economic growth. In economically dependent countries this growth relied on assistance from sets of alliances established within the competitive and militarised terms of the Cold War. Although the proposed national economic development was under the supervision of individual states, the subsequent economic growth, when it occurred, led to dependent economic development. In the drive for development, national governments gave environmental issues low priority, as did assisting states, multinational institutions, and TNCs (Bryant and Baily 1997).

The globalisation of capitalist industrial development, some would argue, has led to an intensification of patterns of dependency, poverty and environmental exploitation. New forms of global authority and discipline according to the laws of the market are insisted upon by the developed world (especially G7 states) and enacted through such multilateral institutions as the World Bank, the International Monetary Fund (IMF) and the World Trade Organisation (WTO). These institutions can impose market-based policies on developing countries, while 'market power is in the hands of transnational corporations and financial power in the hands of transnational banks' (McMichael 2000: 187). The consequence is the further intensification of environmental destruction. As noted in a World Bank (2001) report:

Long-term poverty reduction and sustainable economic growth are now being undermined by the continuing degradation of soils, the increasing scarcity of freshwater, the overexploitation of coastal ecosystems and fisheries, the loss of forest cover, long-term changes in the earth's climate, and loss of biological diversity at the genetic, species, and ecosystem level. What is clear is that the roughly 2.8 billion poor and near poor people in the world ... are disproportionately affected by these bad environmental conditions. They are particularly vulnerable to shocks from environmental change and natural catastrophes. Every year around 5 million people in developing countries die from waterborne diseases and polluted air. The livelihoods of around 1 billion rural people are at risk because of desertification and land degradation. And up to two-thirds of the world's people are likely to be affected by water scarcity.

The change from 'development' to 'globalised' economic regimes has been analysed in some detail by sociologists in terms of a movement from Fordism to post-Fordism or neo-liberalism. (For succinct reviews of Fordism and post-Fordism, see Bonanno and Constance 1996, and of neo-liberalism, see Portes 1997). Fordism, dominant during the development period up to the early 1970s, was characterised in the industrialised developed world by national economic growth based on mass production and mass consumption; highly centralised mass production according to Fordist methods; centralised and concentrated ownership and control of capital; and stable labour markets which offered unionised employment. Political stability was maintained by the nation-state offering a 'class compromise' based on redistribution through the welfare state and protection of workers through labour legislation; and using protectionist policies to ensure that national industries had access to markets. In post-Fordism, the national economy is dependent on the growth of TNCs and constant expansion of the world market, particularly that of the First World. In this economic regime, ownership and control are increasingly concentrated and centralised. However, production is decentralised and fragmented through global sourcing, and labour markets are deregulated and non-unionised to ensure greater 'flexibility'. Thus the 'class compromise' of the Fordist era has been weakened, there is less redistribution and protective labour legislation, and free trade and the market are promoted in all production sectors.

This regime change has major consequences for agriculture and for the environment. In the Fordist era the emphasis was on state support, through subsidies and protectionism of national productivist agriculture (regarding Ireland, see Tovey 1990). This included increased use of industrially produced inputs of pesticides, fertilisers and farm machinery. It also contributed to the over-production of food and to the decline in food prices in the First World. The state showed little concern for environmental destruction, while environmental groups and environmental awareness began to develop. In post-Fordism, agriculture was restructured: agri-business became globalised and grew in size and power, and agri-food complexes developed based on the global sourcing of food ingredients, 'flexible' industrial food production, vertical integration of farmers, and the targeting of fragmented global markets. Markets began to be deregulated and there was a regulatory shift from the nation-state to the WTO. In the developing majority world, mono-cropping and the intensification of production for export increased to pay off debts to the developed world, contributing to increased poverty and environmental destruction.

The late 1990s saw the mobilisation of protest by environmental, peace, Third World, labour and other groups, against what was seen as the exploitative and destructive nature of this globalised, capitalist neo-liberal regime. Tony Juniper, Director of Friends of the Earth, UK, described this evolution in environmentalist thinking, (quoted in Mike Bygrave, 'Where did all the Protesters go?', *The Observer,* 14 July 2002):

> For the past 10 years we've been locating ourselves more in the bigger economic debate and less in the 'save the whales' type debate. Talking about rainforests led us into talking about third world debt. Talking about climate change led us to talk about transnational corporations. The more you talk about these things, the more you realise the subject isn't the environment any more, it's the economy and the pressures on countries to do things that undercut any efforts they make to deal with environmental issues. By the time we got to Seattle, we were all campaigning on the same basic trend that was undermining everybody's efforts to achieve any progressive goals. That trend is the free market and privileges for big corporations and rich people at the expense of everything else.

The placing of environmental issues in a much broader economic context and, in particular, the analysis of the consequences of free trade and globalisation for both the developing majority world as well as the developed world, marked a change of consciousness which is expressed in the mobilisation of the global justice movement. It also had roots in everyday experiences at the local level, whether of dependent development as TNCs opened (and closed) factories and farmers produced to the specifications of giant supermarkets and Brussels, or of customers attempting to detect GM ingredients on labels. The slogan was 'The World is not for Sale'. Protests were held, for example, in Florence in November 2002, which included Irish people among its 400,000 participants. While not widely covered in the media, an editorial in the *Irish Times* (12 November 2002) noted the 'extraordinary amalgam' of groups involved and the seriousness of purpose and the range of topics discussed, including globalisation and militarism, development in Africa, migrant rights, and vegetarianism. Their mobilisation was interpreted as 'an alienated cry of rage from decent young people at real global injustice and the inability of a system of plenty to share either wealth or power that must be heard and engaged with'.

In the 1970s and 1980s in Ireland, there was local mobilisation against dependent development and its environmental consequences, often drawing on a nationalist rhetoric, and organised as anti-toxic, anti-mining and anti-nuclear energy movements (Baker 1990). These were not always successful. Indeed research by Curtin and Shields (1988) regarding Tynagh Mines and by Eipper (1989) regarding the Gulf Oil Terminal on Whiddy Island, confirm the weakness of local communities in a situation of dependent development.

Globalised, post-Fordist agri-business practices became evident in Ireland from the mid-1980s. Tovey (1990) has argued that the globalised nature of the contemporary food industry has had major consequences for Irish agriculture and agri-business. There has been a concentration of ownership in food-processing industries, internationalisation by expansion overseas, diversification in production and vertical integration into international agri-food chains to globally source ingredients for convenience food production for a global market. The consequence for agriculture, she argues, has been the creation of a dual food system. One food system feeds into and supplies internationalised agri-food complexes and requires intensified production of highly standardised products for sale to TNCs or major supermarket chains. In fragile environments this can lead to environmental degradation. The consequence of transnational control over food production is loss of local and national control over the food system. The second food system, concentrated on small farms, is what Tovey calls 'artisanal food production' for the local market. Here there are both traditional small farmers and a small number of organic farmers. Both may be subsidised by the Rural Environmental Protection Scheme (REPS), encouraging extensive land use, conservation and tourism. (Regarding organic farming in Ireland, see Tovey 1997, 1999, 2002a).

Also occurring at the local level are small-scale alternatives to involvement in the money-based, globalised economy, which is seen as faceless and exploitative. These include such initiatives as LETS (Local Exchange Trading Schemes), food co-operatives, and local or farmers' markets (see Woods and Davie 1999). These groups frequently network with each other and with other larger and more nationally based organisations such as Sustainable Ireland and Earth Fairs. Sustainable Ireland, Feasta, Greenpeace and Voice also network with global groups offering a radical critique of the globalised power of TNCs. They are a conduit of radical political discourses. Thus, Martin Khor, Director of the Third World Network, Malaysia, writes in *Sustainable Ireland Sourcebook 2000* (Woods and Davie 1999: 73–4; see also Korten 2001) that:

Countries in the developing world are no longer able to have control over their currencies and financial systems. The destabilisation that this causes is undermining their trade, investment and development prospects. These latest events are only part of a series of developments that have combined to make the developing countries poor, dependent and helpless. Much of Africa and Latin America have had two 'lost decades' in which declining commodity prices and the external debt trap had bled their countries of resources and reduced them to the status of beggars.

He continues by describing the 'apartheid-like situation' in the ever-widening gap between rich and poor countries, the 'globalisation-cum-liberalisation' policies of international monetary institutions and TNCs, and the links between large corporations and rich Northern governments. However, he notes the number of groups in the North who are working with groups in the South to put pressure on the World Bank and the IMF to introduce more transparency and socially responsible policies; and the mobilisation of citizen groups against Third World debt, the patenting of life forms and genetic engineering, and their promotion of environmentally sound and socially just ways of production, consumption and living. He concludes (Khor 1999: 77):

These efforts by ordinary people, their communities and organisations, are the building blocks of a different world where markets and technology are to be used to serve humanity, and not the other way around. And where the interests of community and the satisfaction of human needs instead of materialistic greed and the drive for individual or corporate power are the driving forces and the sources of fulfilment.

In Ireland, returned development workers, both religious and lay, have added their knowledge and mobilisation skills to this campaign, as have such economists as Richard Douthwaite in *The Growth Illusion* and *Short Circuit,* not only criticising contemporary patterns of capitalist economic growth as unsustainable, but seeking alternatives based on local rather than global imperatives. Feasta, the Foundation for the Economics of Sustainability in Ireland, has likewise provided a forum for critical thinking (see, for example, *Feasta Review*, No. 1, 2001 and other subsequent publications).

There is also a less radical discourse regarding global and neo-liberal forms of economic development and its ecological consequences. This is the dominant discourse articulated by international agencies, particularly within the UN and in the World Bank, as well as some Irish and international non-governmental organisations (NGOs) concerned with development issues. This discourse, while not specifying or criticising global neo-liberal economic policies, recognises the increasing levels of poverty in the developing majority world and the severe and increasing levels of environmental destruction. Furthermore, it recognises that these problems are likely to grow and become more severe. To counter these problems this reformist discourse argues for policy-based manageralist and technocratic solutions. Although there are no quick fixes, change can be managed within the current economic system, as argued in the UN-sponsored *Millennium Ecosystem Assessment Synthesis Report* (2005: 17–18):

> An effective set of responses to ensure the sustainable management of ecosystems requires substantial changes in institutions and governance, in economic policies and incentives, social and behaviour factors, technology, and knowledge. Actions such as the integration of ecosystem management goals in various sectors (such as agriculture, forestry, finance, trade, and health), increased transparency and accountability of government and private-sector performance in ecosystem management, elimination of perverse subsidies, greater use of economic instruments and market-based approaches, empowerment of groups dependent on ecosystem services or affected by their degradation, promotion of technologies enabling increased crop yields without harmful environmental impacts, ecosystem restoration, and the incorporation of nonmarket values of ecosystems in management decisions all could substantially lessen the severity of these problems in the next several decades.

There has only been limited focus group research on perceptions of global issues. In Britain, research by Myers et al. (1999: 10), entitled *Global Citizenship and the Environment,* found that while focus group participants manifested a 'cosmopolitan' sense based on an awareness of 'distant' and 'different' lands, peoples and ways of life, developed through tourism, the media, and, for some, work, associational and leisure-based relationships, few claimed an identity as a 'citizen of the world'. They were much more deeply embedded in local and national identities. They were aware of global flows of images, money, commodities and pollution, yet uncomfortable and ambivalent regarding more abstract questions of global responsibility. They preferred to talk of particular exemplary figures such as Nelson Mandela or Mother Teresa, or the giving of particular charitable gifts to a particular family or child in a developing country, rather than discussing abstract concepts of being a global citizen. Furthermore, the behaviour of these exemplars was not thought to suggest that they themselves should behave in a similar fashion. For respondents it was sufficient to respond in what was considered a morally appropriate way, while giving priority to care of their own family and the local community, and acknowledging their rights and duties as citizens of the nation rather than the world.

Comparative research in a number of European countries, which draws on the responses of group participants who had been exposed over a number of weeks to the input of 'experts' regarding such global environmental issues as climate change and global warming, observed the tendency within groups to shift the conversation from narrowly defined climate issues to a broader social perspective 'including more local concerns, personal experiences and moral/ethical issues' regarding what was considered fair both at home and internationally (Darier et al. 1999: 367). It is also important to note the linkages participants made between experiences at the local and national levels on the one hand, and a sense of global responsibilities and actions on the other. Thus, negative sentiments regarding the national or local were translated to the international level, and mistrust of the national government was projected onto international bodies (Darier et al. 1999: 364–5). Furthermore, when individuals felt powerless to effect change at local and national levels, they also tended to feel powerless in relation to effecting change at the international level. Thus interconnections were readily made between local, national and global experiences and a sense of moral responsibility.

The literature reviewed above indicates three major themes within a radical political discourse:

1   recognition and analysis of the economic power imbalances between the developed North and the developing South, and the consequent exploitative relationship and its negative effects on both the people and the environment in the majority world; added to this knowledge may be serious moral concerns regarding what is fair and equitable, and a sense that something should be done

2   discussion of the dependency of Ireland on the globalised economic system, and its consequences in terms of production, consumption and the environment

3   how a sense of empowerment or disempowerment at local and/or national levels may be translated to the international sphere.

How the focus groups articulated these themes will be discussed below, as will the participants' views on radical environmental protests and protesters.

Spontaneous Articulation of a Radical Political Discourse

Three focus groups spontaneously articulated a radical political discourse: the returned missionaries, the CEF and one of the student groups. The returned missionaries, who had worked in the majority world, spontaneously articulated a radical political discourse in most detail. They emphasised the unequal balance of power between the North and South, the North's exploitation of the South for its own benefit and gain, the role of TNCs and multilateral organisations, the dominance of the US, and the immorality of the consequent poverty and environmental destruction of developing countries. They pointed to the patenting of the genes of staple foods as one example, drawing the judgement:

6   *It is unbelievable ...*
8   *The staple crops of the world.*
6   *Yes, the staple crops of the world – unbelievable, immoral ...*
    ...
8   *The corn ...*
1   *It is unbelievable.*
4   *And I think it is a huge issue.*
    ...
8   *They* [TNCs] *took out a patent on Basmati rice. I think they were beaten on that.*
6   *Yes, they were beaten on that one.*
8   *But that's only one. I mean, there are something like 100,000 patents have been taken out in the last six years and again it got no coverage in the paper in Ireland when it went through the European Parliament. The multinationals – they launched the biggest PR job on the Parliament for it ... Now actually it means not just the ... like the old colonial thing, you went and you took the gold, silver, precious stones. Then you took their labour, and now you take everything. And the irony is that the Third World is rich in life. Like, there are more species in a single hectare of tropical forest where I live than in all of these islands, more different species of wood ... In a single hectare ... so now they are going to take that too. And there is very little discussion about it. In other words, the Monsantos of the world or the Cargills will own the staple crops of the world.*

                                                           Returned missionaries

They continued by noting the role of international economic organisations, including the WTO, in ensuring the continued economic dependence of developing countries, concluding: *'It's worse than colonialism. It is totally robbery, rape ... '* (6).

They recognised the pressure that increased poverty and debt placed on the environment and the concerns of local people: *'We worked in Third World countries,* [and we have seen] *how people who are poor care for the environment and how their poverty inhibits their ability* [to do this]*'* (7). Likewise they noted the destruction of species and water privatisation, and the role of Third World elites in this dependent development: *'No multinational can work unless they get counterparts inside'* (2).

Dependent development and its consequences in terms of poverty, debt and environmental destruction was not just a problem for developing countries, it was an international problem – as was climate change. They criticised the US position on Kyoto:

8   *Mr Bush has no problem spending probably 500 billion running a war and he wouldn't sign up to Kyoto, you know, which will do enormous damage to people. So I think that … the environment would need to be much higher on the list of concerns of people. Because it is not at the moment, it is generally at the end of* [their concerns].

Returned missionaries

They were entirely in agreement with the radical political discourse statement: 'It is the worldwide economic system today that is not only destroying the environment but destroying many Third World countries. We need to do something about that', although they felt it did not adequately recognise *'the contribution of our own greed'* (2). They discussed the statement further in terms of the support given to the contemporary economic system by governments and multilateral agencies: *'You can look at the politicians, all … the multilateral agencies in the world – the WTO, IMF, World Bank – these are the big hitters all over the world and they are all locked into it big time.'* And while these agencies recognised the problem and their own contribution to it, they did nothing. For example, at the World Conference on Sustainable Development in Johannesburg in 2001, it was noted that *'none of the politicians or the multilateral agencies took it seriously. In actual fact what they said was, "OK, we are the ones who have destroyed the world, but what you need is more of us if you are going to care for it"'* (8).

When their focus moved to Ireland, they pointed out its own dependent position within the globalised economic system, the 'consumerist', 'disposable' and 'greedy' lifestyle on which it was predicated, and the dominance of economics as the driving force. They noted in particular the pressure of the globalised system on farmers (some of the contributors were members of a religious order which managed a farm in Ireland):

8   *I would also say though, to be fair to farmers, particularly modern farmers – they are under enormous pressures. They were told to do things like 'increase your yield', but now with increasing costs their income is falling, a lot of them feel, 'I'm the last generation, my kids are not going to be able to farm', so they are angry, they are frustrated. They don't know who to blame so they'll blame anyone. And there's no one actually helping them to understand that it isn't the hen harrier[4] that's the enemy, it is actually the policies that have supported cheap food and industrially produced food ... We should have taken here twenty years ago a clear decision in Ireland that the only kind of food that would make any sense for us here and abroad would be organic food.*

Returned missionaries

The Irish government, they felt, had not supported environmental policies due to the priority given to economic interests. However, politicians were following the electorate on this: people would *'prefer to have a job than clean water'*. Furthermore, there was a tendency to *'just keep quiet'* (6), rather than question major economic interests. As might be expected this group supported the anti-globalisation movement.

One of the student groups (Students 1) spontaneously reproduced this discourse but did so only briefly. They focused on the economic power imbalances between North and South, and the role of *'multinational corporations moving in and taking over, destroying the natural environment and destroying their* [indigenous people's] *livelihood'* (5). They noted the attraction of developing countries for TNCs in terms of their provision of cheap labour and lack of environmental regulations, and that it was 'we' in the developed world who benefited through cheaper goods and TNC profits. They also noted weak internal leadership and the destruction of indigenous communal ways of life in developing countries, while the perceived attractions of the global economy were increased employment and the need to repay debts. While this global economic system was seen as unfair by the students, their discussion was more abstract than that of the returned missionaries and not characterised by the same level of moral outrage.

The CEF focused on the impact of globalisation on Irish people. Here, ambivalence, recognition of conflicts of interest and of difficulties in bringing about change, were evident:

6   *... the people of Ireland perceive themselves as net beneficiaries of what I would describe as globalisation, they perceive themselves as*

---

4   Hen harriers are birds of prey and a protected species.

> *net beneficiaries of the boom and they perceive themselves as net beneficiaries of the lifestyle we have.*
>
> 2   *That's right.*
>
> 6   *Which are destroying our coast.*
>
> 2   *There's an implied threat there all the time that if you don't join you'll be left out.*
>
> 6   *Yeah, and we're living in a country that has been used to having a very prominent mindset ... and it's shifted from a Judaeo-Christian mindset to an American consumer mindset, you know, as the dominant theology or ideology of the country. And concepts like sustainability will always be entertained as intellectual pursuits but it's never going to be ...* [unclear] *with the current mindset and that's a cultural problem we have now ...* [However] *I've got a bit of optimism about that because we've got the anti-globalisation movement and young people and the Seattle and the Genoa and no logo generations, there's an awful lot of energy and idealism and activity in those generations that will bear fruit in twenty years' time.*
>
> 2   *Oh yeah.*
>
> CEF

However, another member of the group argued that once protesting young people moved into the sphere of work and mortgages '*... you're back to square one, it's a cycle'*.

The CEF also articulated the third theme, linking local empowerment and international concerns, but also acknowledged that little had been done as yet by the forum on the issue of unequal development. They noted the relationship between global justice issues and environmental destruction, pointing out that *'those issues are linked in with trade issues* [and] *consumer issues ... Stories around indigenous people from Africa or America tie in very much with lifestyle issues in Ireland and the impact on the environment, locally as well as globally ...* ' (6) The group was reminded that a few years previously a three-week run across Ireland was undertaken by a group of American Indians, hosted by an environmental group. A relay run between ancient sites was completed to:

> 6   *... raise awareness of the simple message which was that all life was sacred ... Bringing an environmental message, bringing a social justice, human rights message and rekindling an empathy with ... landscape, visiting the ancient places ... places you might have access issues* [with], *so their stories ... tie all those issues in a very tangible way – and there would be a bit of craic involved!*
>
> CEF

Responses to the Radical Political Discourse Statement

Apart from the three groups discussed above, a further ten groups were presented with the radical political statement (quoted above). Responses ranged from agreement, through negotiation to disagreement. Two groups unreservedly agreed with it – the walkers and the nurses. This appeared to be strongly related to the fact that both groups contained at least some individuals who linked personal action (whether in the private domestic arena or in the local public sphere) with perceived global environmental consequences. The DoE group also agreed with the statement but acknowledged serious difficulties in bringing about change. The two farming groups gave negotiated, nuanced responses, drawing on their own experiences of productivist agricultural policies and strong international competition in the food sector, while also acknowledging that many in the developing majority world were starving. Young skilled building workers were divided in their responses, some agreeing and some disagreeing with the statement.

Four groups, the environmental scientists, the heritage officers, the environmental managers, and the consultant engineers, all of whom held relatively high and influential positions in social-class and status terms, elaborated responses that were toward the negotiated–rejecting end of the scale. This appeared partly due to a rejection of the emphatic style of the statement which they characterised as 'extreme' (environmental scientist), 'simplistic' (environmental managers), or too 'confrontational' (heritage officers). Some also saw it as 'too negative', and as not recognising our own responsibilities (environmental scientists and heritage officers). They also drew on substantive arguments regarding (1) the contribution that Third World countries themselves made to their own lack of development, and (2) the positive effects of globalisation, including Ireland's economic success, which offered a lifestyle that Irish people would be loath to give up, despite recognising its negative environmental consequences (articulated especially by the environmental scientists and managers).

The responses of the latter four groups and the young skilled building workers will be examined below, followed by those of the farmers and the DoE, ending with the responses of the two groups who perceived themselves to be more empowered – the nurses and walkers.

Power Differentials between North and South

The storyline of the industrialised and rich North exploiting the majority world in its own interest was strongly challenged by the consultant engineers, some of whom had also worked abroad. For some members of this group the developing countries themselves were: *'the worst offenders'*

(1), *'because the population is rising and ... they haven't the ability to civilise and get the infrastructure in place to contain the development and try to use all the land to the best ability and it's actually making the land worse'* (1). Thus *'... it's not the economic systems that are making them worse, it's the people themselves ...'* (4). This was challenged by another member of the group:

6   *... that can be a bit harsh on them, even when they really do damage ... there's a stone wall of, like, the European agricultural policy .... Even if they organise properly, they might find it impossible to sell into markets and there's all sorts of cartels, and lots of other things are worse, blockades, economic blockades.*

Consultant engineers

However, this challenge was ignored by the next speaker who reaffirmed the first's perspective, although softening it somewhat:

2   *Sometimes you find that a lot of Third World countries don't know how to manage resources. And the second thing is corruption and it's very disheartening to see both these things and that's quite apart from the developments good or bad. These things are big problems.*

Consultant engineers

Likewise with regard to environmental destruction, a participant in the environmental scientists' group noted, *'David Bellamy reckons over-population is the major environmental* [problem].*'*

A further contributory factor to the rejection of the statement was that it was read as blaming all environmental destruction on the economic system and thus appeared to discount individual responsibility. The heritage officers noted:

1   *I only partially agree because you can't blame everything on the worldwide economic system. I mean local factors like ignorance and in some cases maybe just bad minds, just creating damage or disruption, they have to be factored in as well, sometimes it's very easy to blame any kind of environmental damage on forces that, on the face of it, are outside our control, but really I think we have a lot of, we can take responsibility for a lot of our own actions ourselves.*

2   *To say that means that it takes the responsibility away from people.*

–   *Yeah.*

–   *Yeah.*

2   *Because you're saying, it's implying that there's nothing really we can do. What can we do? What can we do about the world economic system?*

1   *Yeah, exactly, exactly.*
2   *So that's grand, you carry on destroying what you want to destroy and take no responsibility for your own environment.*

Heritage officers

The heritage officers also felt it was the kind of statement made by anti-globalisation campaigners, of whom they were quite dismissive:

2   *And, you know, it's sort of been said by some of those people who don't really know what they're talking about.*
4   *Yeah.*
2   *Those people in Genoa and places that are going ...*
3   *Yeah.*
–   *Yeah.*
2   *... and anarchists, as they call themselves* [laughs], *they don't really know what they are saying.*
–   *Yeah.*
7   *It's far too broad-sweeping and catch-all and blame-all and 'nothing to do with me'.*
5   *Yeah.*
2   *With no real understanding behind it.*
4   *Yeah.*
5   *... This is the message that* [people] *are getting from the media and a lot of it, that it's all a big scale and we don't have to bother.*
7   *And it means that my friends who don't bother to use the bottle bank ... it doesn't matter.*
5   *Exactly, exactly.*
7   *That's exactly the problem ... and what* [name of member of group] *was saying ... that it depersonalises, so there's no point in me going to the bottle bank on Saturday morning, it's not going to make any difference anyway ...*
2   *Because you can't affect the worldwide economic system.*

Heritage officers

There were two interrelated elements in this rejection. One was that all could not be blamed on the economic system and that countries in the majority world themselves had to take some of the responsibility. The second was that even if it was impossible to change the economic system, this did not absolve the individual from environmental responsibilities. This individualisation of everyday environmental responsibilities rather than a sense of moral outrage at injustice and consequent environmental exploitation characterised this rejection of a global justice discourse, although it was not exclusive to these groups.

The group of young, skilled and Dublin-based building workers were divided in their response to the statement. Some agreed, articulating a global justice discourse, while others rejected it. Those who agreed with the statement observed that the fault lay with the *'superpowers* [who] *are making decisions for everybody in the world'* (2) and *'the big companies, the big, huge multi-conglomerates'* (5) exploiting the Third World. Others, however, noted that government corruption, dictatorships and wars in developing countries contributed significantly to their weakness. As one respondent noted: *'Sure have you ever noted in any of these countries, Somalia and Ethiopia and all that, every little kid seems to have an AK47, yet they're all starving, you know what I mean?'* (8) He concluded that he had *'no pity for Third World countries, none whatsoever.'* Whether sympathetic or not to the difficulties faced by developing countries, none articulated a sense that it was possible to successfully challenge and change existing economic power structures. Bob Geldof and others mobilising against Third World debt were *'just wasting their time'* (5).

Ireland and Globalisation

A number of groups (the environmental scientists and managers most strongly) argued that, economically, Ireland was a major beneficiary of a globalised system and that this was a gain they themselves, or indeed Irish people generally, would not wish to give up, despite its destructive effects on both the environment and people of the majority world:

7   *Yeah, this anti-globalisation thing is something that's catching on and I mean people are beginning to see that globalisation ... is coming at a price. Whether it's going to destroy the world or not is another matter. There would be people that would argue that, say, Central America is being destroyed by globalisation, Africa has been definitely destroyed by globalisation.*

8   *But the whole Celtic Tiger phenomenon depended on globalisation here.*

7   *That's what I was getting to; my wallet says good luck to it.*

Environmental scientists

Likewise, the environmental managers noted of the statement, *'Is it* [the globalised economic system] *destroying the environment? Yeah it probably is. Is it destroying Third World countries? Yes it is'* (1). But they went on to say that this was not simply the consequence of the economic system *per se*, but, of an economic system that was based primarily on greed, which was part of 'human nature'. Furthermore, the possibility of making any change was severely limited:

1   *Well, you see, this is it, how do you take such a broad global issue and tackle it, you're kind of going, oh my God, I can't even look at it because what do you do? Like, if you really wanted to do something, ok, you'd stop buying products from a particular country because they're not treating the people right and then what do you do to their system, you destroy more people ... Ok, it's not the way you want it done like ... We can't not live the way everyone else is living. I mean society drives how we live and you're part of that society, you can't just step out of it. I mean you wouldn't survive outside of it and you have to be involved in it, you've no real choice about that, but it's very difficult to tackle something as big as that.*

Environmental managers

Greedy individualism was thus justified as human nature, and an inability to act any differently was seen as due to economic and societal processes beyond people's control. It was recognised that Ireland's Celtic Tiger had been the beneficiary, while the developing majority world paid the cost. Guilt or moral outrage did not appear to enter into it.

Globalisation and the increased possibility of manufacturing firms moving their production to regions where labour and environmental laws were weaker were also noted by a participant in the environmental managers group. In particular, he commented negatively on the role of EU labour and environmental legislation which *'added to the cost of production in Ireland'* and *'tie manufacturing companies' hands with environmental stuff when they can go off to Ghana or go off somewhere else'*. While companies in such developing countries still *'have to be environmentally reasonable'*, they *'don't have this regulatory stuff'* (1).

The dairy farmers concurred with many of the sentiments described above. They recognised the negativities of the present economic and agricultural policies for the environment, *'the more intensive farming that we go into, the more pollution we manufacture'* (6), and the severe consequences of globalisation for the Third World:

4   *Well, they are still starving in the Third World ... and like that statement is very applicable even to the whole focus of Trócaire, even in the Lenten campaign this year. Even the people that are in Guatemala, like there is a native tribe out there that are being displaced by so-called economic progress, cutting down the trees and kind of invading their territory and they are literally pushed aside.*

There is ... a whole history of a generation of people and they are just being disposed with for so-called economic progress.

Dairy farmers

Yet in order for Irish farmers themselves to remain viable, they felt they had to produce more. They noted that:

4   *But the whole economic policy, and even go back to farming, and the whole future of farming, like we are being told, like, that we will all have to double or triple output just to generate the income ... and to do that possibly would create an environmental disaster to a certain extent ...*

    ...

3   *Our national advisers, Teagasc ... had their own conference down in Killarney in November and the bottom line out of it, you will have to have seventy or eighty thousand gallons of milk quota.*

–   *You will double up ...*

4   *To maintain your same standard of living.*

5   *Then you have more people out there looking for jobs.*

Dairy farmers

They commented that since milk quotas were introduced in 1983, the number of dairy farmers had declined by two-thirds, and that in five years' time there would be a further decrease by three-quarters: *'They intend that there will be only 8,000 dairy farmers in five years' time.'* They felt trapped by the multinational and Irish retail sector, by agricultural policies and *'the ****** politicians'* (3), but could only ask the question, not offer solutions, *'What can we do about it?'* (3).

The small, mostly part-time beef farmers living in the West of Ireland likewise could offer few solutions: *'You can't really change anything'* (6), *'The superpowers call the shots'* (6), *'We are only one small cog on the wheel'* (8). Within the world food regime they recognised the disadvantages faced by developing countries, which *'have to compete with all those subsidies paid to the bigger countries'*. Yet they also recognised their own need of subsidies in order to survive, and the difficulties they faced in competing with cheap beef imports from the developing world. They felt disempowered by the continuing imbalance as *'the Third World are starving and we are over-producing and there's no way of sending the surplus there'* (5). These contradictions, in which they felt trapped, appeared to sap their energies. One possible solution they offered was for Irish consumers to become more loyal to buying Irish produce, even if offered at a higher price.

The response of the DoE to the radical political statement exemplified the contradictions and difficulties many groups experienced in relation to it. All members of this group agreed with the discourse statement, but their discussion concentrated on the difficulties associated with bringing about any change. They began by discussing the attractions of a consumer lifestyle to 'people', despite its unsustainability, but ended with questions regarding what 'we' can do:

2   *It* [the statement] *is basically true. I mean it's what drives* economic *development and consumer lifestyle that the West have enjoyed and the rest of the world is clamouring to. A party that they're clamouring to join and it's not a statement that people want to listen to. When you switch on your telly tonight you'll get the glamorous ads telling you to get a car, it's sexy and it will give you a lot of freedom and status. You'll not get ads coming on* [with] *a spokesman from the Department of the Environment saying 'the party is over', so it's true and it's what drives it ...* [The statement] *could be addressed to everyone but I think most people wouldn't listen to it. People don't want to know that the party that everyone is enjoying, the lifestyle that they enjoy isn't sustainable and that their children and grandchildren are going to inherit a very much poorer environment ... The party will have to end sometime but nobody wants to listen ...*

    DoE

The discussion continued, *'hard decisions on what we're actually going to do'* would have to be taken, but there was no indication of who would have the power to do this or how it could be done.

Local, National and Global Mobilisation
Two groups, walkers and nurses, articulated a positive and empowered response to the radical political statement, showing similarities to the CEF in this regard. Both criticised the 'greed' and 'selfishness' on which contemporary society was based, while the walkers also discussed the power invested in the US. Both groups also sought to take up the challenge of the statement, 'We need to do something about that.'

Participants in the walkers' group, particularly those who were teachers, noted the alliance between big business, their political champions such as George Bush and aligned Third World elites (often due to debt burdens), and the consequences for the environment, including the threat to rainforests, to environmentally sensitive areas such as Alaska, and the non-signing by the US of the Kyoto agreement. In light of this, one participant noted that the statement made her feel powerless (1). Others stated, however, that what was needed was *'to put pressure on our own government'* (3) and that while *'individually we might not be able to do anything, but if we organised as a group ... '* (3). Another noted how consumers could help by buying Fairtrade goods – as encouraged by this participant's son (4). Nonetheless, they also suggested that among the population generally there was apathy, complacency and the desire for someone else to act. They argued that this was a relatively recent shift in attitudes:

4   *I think it's a whole change in lifestyles, we were much more, well we spoke out a little more I think in years gone by but now people are so busy working, doing this, that and the other.*

8   *We're a more affluent society today.*

4   *They've lost, well, I don't know, there's something being lost as well, people have got too complacent about things.*

–   *Yeah.*

5   *They don't care.*

Walkers

Nurses also agreed with the statement, with some expressing a particularly high level of empowerment: *'Well, you see, we are the power, so every voice is important, not just the government, we change the government, we vote them in'* (4) and that it was necessary to *'keep on at the government'* (1) to act. This could be done by *'raising our voices, keeping aware'* (2), noting that Bono's campaign against debt repayments was *'making people aware and people will listen'* (2), and was influencing young people. It was proposed that even the smallest pro-environmental action such as recycling could make a difference:

4   *But I feel we do do something about it, we plug at our politicians, like saving the rainforests, people come over from different organisations here and speak about the rainforests, you know what I mean, different ethnic groups and they want protection, so the world is being informed constantly. And you know maybe people like Bono or maybe people like, it doesn't matter who they are, Joe Soap will pick up on it and do something. You think of* [inaudible] *who went out to East Timor, there are lots of people who work in Africa that do a lot of this work. So I don't feel one bit ... I think actually it's very positive. You know what I mean, we are making a, you know, it depends on how strong you feel about it.*

–   *That is true.*

Nurses

It should be noted that the nurses, as well as the walkers, were two of the most mobilised groups in terms of participation in local community voluntary groups.

Environmental Protesters and Eco-warriors

Another set of discourse themes that arose in the focus groups was a discussion regarding radical environmental protesters and their actions. This discussion often occurred, not in response to the statement regarding the global economic system and its environmental consequences, but in response to the moral statement about the protection of trees discussed in Chapter 2. This statement frequently elicited a discussion regarding 'eco-warriors', 'tree-huggers' and anti-roads protesters. The latter included a focus on both tree-cutting at the Glen of the Downs and protests about the protection of archaeological sites, such as that at Carrickmines. Regarding the extent and type of comments made by different groups, none of the mobilised groups made very negative comments, while at the other end of the spectrum were the consultant engineers and a number of participants in the general public groups.

During the discussion on the moral discourse statement on trees, the facilitator asked the heritage officers whether they recognised who made the statement or where it was said. In response they noted:

1   *I can visualise them* [laughter]

     ...

–   *Bunny huggers.*
–   *Tree huggers.*
–   *Yeah.*
–   *Glen of the Downs people.*
1   *Is it a quotation from a real person?*
F   *It's actually somebody in Galway when they were going to cut down the trees in Ayer Square.*

     ...

2   *Tell her she'll never win with it.*

Heritage officers

The growing antipathy between the consultant engineers, given their commitment to 'development', and radical activists was evident in their discussion:

1   *Well the tree libbers and so on, the Glen of the Downs situation and so on, again it's a question of overall responsibility and we have to have some development and some people seem to be against*

    everything, whereas I would like to think that what we do, that we bring a balance, we do address their concerns and we mitigate and so on and so forth, and we develop with due care.

F   *Ok, is there a role for these people do you think, environmentalists, environmental activists?*

3   *They can highlight the problems maybe, make more people aware.*

   ...

2   *I always had this view that environmental activists are a very positive thing and I've had occasion lately to deal with these people and their facts sometimes can be wrong.*

–   *Yeah.*

–   *Absolutely.*

2   *... I suppose we're not as engineers equipped to deal necessarily with people who are ... we deal with the facts and we kind of assume people are professional and that they're not going to be misrepresenting and they do misrepresent things, environmental activists do. And for a person who would have thought they were a good thing, I don't necessarily think that now. And they know too much about too many things as well. You know what I mean? You can't be an expert on everything. You find the same people coming up everywhere.*

–   *Yeah.*

–   *Yeah.*

5   *I've heard a good description that an activist only has to have one statement right in 1,000 and they're hailed as a genius, and if an engineer gets one statement wrong in 1,000, they're damned forever.*

–   *Yeah.*

Consultant engineers

The environmental scientists also noted the 'dishonest' campaigning of some environmental groups, and their tendency to shift the grounds of their complaint when it suited them. However, their importance in placing environmental issues on the public agenda was also noted.

The mobilised activist groups generally did not raise the issue of radical environmental protest. The anti-incinerator group raised it briefly. This relatively recently mobilised group considered the idea of being identified as environmentalists or as a radical environmental group. Ambivalence was notable. If they continued to be mobilised, they argued:

–   *You would be going around following one good cause to the next, you know, the tree huggers.*

8   *There is a stereotype I find difficult to take.*

2 *A lot of them, like, would have lots of money and Daddy just keeps giving them money and they are living in the trees.*
8 *The knitted jumpers and ...*
– *The lunatic fringe.*

Anti-incinerator group

One noted that she was more likely to remain active '*if it threatened your own, like*'.

Among the general public, some among the nurses and students articulated a very positive response to radical protest. The nurses stated that the protesters at the Glen of the Downs '*will be heroes in the next century*' (4) and that even though, or indeed because, they were '*eccentric and over the top, yeah, I think an awful lot of people like that*' (2).

Students declared themselves sympathetic to the cause of protesters in the Glen of the Downs and Carrickmines but did not join in the protest themselves because of lack of time and because of a fear of being labelled: '*It seems to me that if you sign up with any of the issues you are categorised and you are put into the "tree lover", "dreadlocked"* [category] *... You seem to be pigeon-holed immediately as soon as you join any of these groups*' (Students 2: Participant 3). Some also expressed a fear of being totally sucked into a protest movement which would demand so much, but perhaps achieve very little:

5 *... you either have to take all or nothing it seems to end up ... Anyone I know who's gotten involved with green awareness or anything in that area, they get sucked in and have to do it all. ... You have to save the world. I know I can't save the world. It is a defeatist attitude ... You think of hard work and no reward, sort of thing ... It's like fighting a losing battle.*

   ...

3 *You are so small and it is such a big problem, it does seem very hard to imagine yourself making a difference.*

Students 2

However, the most frequent response among the general public and farmers was a negotiated discussion – some for and others against, with feelings generally veering toward the latter. In these responses a number of storylines tended to be articulated: an unease and ambivalence toward radical protesters as they questioned middle-class or comfortable lifestyles; a 'realist' rejection of their lifestyles in terms of the demands of everyday living and what were seen as the demands of 'development' and 'progress'; a noting of the democratic political contribution of protesters;

a perception that the protesters were often not locals and indeed sometimes foreigners; and a rejection and negative critique of their self-presentation and actions – *'them hairy lads with plaits'* (Dairy farmers).

Teachers articulated a number of these storylines:

3   *... For example, the ... issue and how suspicious we are of people who are pro-environment and their lifestyle and we're afraid of them – particularly if they have an English accent and a purple jumper and long hair.*

    ...

1   *Or if they are living in Dublin.*

    ...

3   *... I kind of start to smell a rat and wonder what are these people doing over here telling us about ... so I'm a bit uneasy around that dimension of ... you know, the eco-warrior. I'm suspicious and then I'd like to be more proactive and support them.*

F   *Why are you suspicious of ...?*

3   *Because they challenge me directly and my lifestyle. And by dropping their requirements of so-called middle-class life ...* [they] *show me what mistakes I'm making. I think that is an issue for teachers ... I'm uneasy with it.*

                                                    Teachers

This was followed by another teacher expressing a 'realist' storyline, *'Like we have to have the two cars to ferry the kids around the place, you know ...'* (6). Following some further discussion on the same themes – scepticism regarding outsiders, the contradictory behaviour of the protesters – another participant took up their positive political role:

6   *Yeah, but to go back to what you were saying about these people, you know, the eco-warriors, I love to see them challenging authority ...* [Drawing on the example of the Rainbow Warrior] *but the solving of a lot of the problems does come from below. And, like, I would be a little suspicious as well of some of these people and their motives, you know, it's those kind of people who actually ... bring issues to the fore, whether you like their methods or not.*

1   *I think it is very healthy for society to have groups challenging the accepted norms. I mean that's actually crucial for a healthy democratic society. I would agree with you totally.*

                                                    Teachers

Although protesting was not seen to work effectively to bring about change in the face of an intransigent government, one of the participants in the young mothers' group also reiterated her support for the approach. Regarding the prolonged save-the-trees protest in the Glen of the Downs, she said: *'I said fair play to them, they stuck it out for months and months'*, *'I have a lot of respect for them'*, and *'They really care'* (8). Others, however, highlighted a negative image of their self-presentation: *'Dreadlocks'*, *'unwashed'*, *'hippie'*, like *'Spider off Coronation Street'*. A realist perspective regarding their own world and the possibility of they themselves undertaking such a protest was reiterated: *'They don't have to look after a child or get a child to school or changed'* (7).

Radical environmental protesters also elicited suspicion among the unemployed who felt that protesters were possibly just middle-class hypocrites, mobilised because: *'It's just trendy. They will do it for two years and then they will drop out for a couple and then they will be walking around in a big suit'* (5). One member of the unemployed group had spent a brief period of time with the protesters in the Glen of the Downs, having been mobilised by some friends. He did not, however, report favourably on the experience: *'I think they are spoilt kids with nothing else to do ... I just remember them all smoking dope. I was up there'* (7).

The retired working-class group, in particular, criticised the protesters, frequently regarding them as foreigners, as *'living off the state'*, and as standing in the way of *'progress'*. One noted, to the general agreement of the group:

4   *When you think about progress of the country and you go up there to Carrickmines to see where they're trying to finish the M50 and you've a group of people up there at the present moment who, to me personally, are just a crowd of, for want of a better word, nig-nogs, they're just up there causing problems basically.*

Retired

The retired group regarded *'genuine'* protesters as local people who organised to protect their neighbourhoods and who used *'proper channels'* to bring about change *'rather than going out and causing problems'* (5). However, they also noted that while in the past governments did listen, *'they don't listen now, they've gone up there'* (6) – indicating the government's superior attitude, a strong theme which is taken up again in the regulatory chapter.

Conclusion: Causes of Global Inequalities and the Possibilities for Change

In terms of the first radical political theme raised at the end of the literature review, the analysis of the focus group data showed that there was wide recognition of the economic and power imbalances between the developed North and developing South, and of the negative consequences of this, both for the people and the environment in the South. Regarding the second theme, there was also a broadly based and clear recognition that Ireland's economy was highly dependent on the global economic system which produced such North–South inequalities. Where differences occurred between groups was in identifying the causes of these inequalities and in aspirations for change. A number of groups (returned missionaries, some students, some in the CEF, some walkers and nurses) identified the globalised free-market economic system, in which TNCs and multilateral organisations play a dominant role, as the main cause. These groups also felt something should and could be done. Others (especially some among environmental scientists, managers and engineering consultants) pointed to internal problems within the dependent states themselves as the culprit, and were also less likely to articulate a sense of obligation to mobilise for change. Other groups (for example, the DoE and farmers) gave negotiated responses – recognising the unfair and unequal realities of the present global economic system but feeling little could be done about it, especially given Ireland's own dependence on it and attachment to the pleasurable lifestyle it offered.

The third theme was also confirmed. A sense of empowerment at an international level was positively related to involvement in activities at a local level. The fourth theme regarding negative perceptions of radical protesters was spontaneously articulated by many group participants. Here there existed generally critical and conservative attitudes but also a recognition among some of their important democratic role. The more environmentally mobilised tended either not to raise this issue or to praise the protesters.

The strongest criticism of North–South power imbalances was made by the returned missionaries' group. Their discourse was characterised by a strong sense of self, drawing on their own personal experiences of working in developing countries among the poor, of involvement with groups promoting justice and the environment in Ireland, and particularly a sense of moral outrage. Thus, a powerful 'I' and 'we' was articulated: *'I think it is a huge issue'*, *'we worked in Third World countries'*, *'where I live ... '*. While recognising the role of Third World elites in reproducing inequalities, their representation of the Third World poor among whom they worked was of a caring people, impoverished by global economic forces and consequent environmental destruction. Change was being inhibited by the moral corruption of *'them'*, exemplified by the *'robbery* [and] *rape'* of the patenting of genes, by the activities of TNCs such as Monsanto and Cargill, and by US economic, political and military dominance.

The CEF, walkers and nurses likewise drew on personal experiences of local mobilisation, educational events, or individual actions such as buying Fairtrade goods, to underpin their discussion of the linkages between the contemporary globalised economy, environmental destruction and the possibility of contributing to change. Here again there was a sense of what 'I' or 'we' had done or should do – while also acknowledging the difficulties involved in the face of a culture of greedy individualism. In the students' more abstract articulation of this discourse there was no such strong 'I' or 'we'. The drawing on positive local experiences of mobilisation and empowerment and the projection of these to the global level in terms of the possibility of bringing about change, confirms some focus group research findings from other European countries (Darier et al. 1999). It is also worth noting that the same groups who reacted positively to the discourse statement, or spontaneously articulated concern and support for developing countries, were also the groups who articulated support for radical protest movements.

It was noteworthy that the occupational groups of nurses and teachers appeared to be particularly active at a local community level and were also among those who most frequently raised significant environmental concerns. Nurses and teachers featured not only in their respective occupationally based focus groups, but also among the mobilised activists in the anti-incinerator and hillwalkers' groups. The question may be raised as to whether involvement in the caring professions (and related educational experiences) may tend to encourage stronger moral concerns regarding others and the environment, as well as a sense of empowerment, leading to greater community-based activism. One is reminded of Szerszynski's (1997: 152) argument that:

> The possibility of achieving sustainability might depend as much on what sort of people we are as what sort of things we do, and thus that we have to pay attention to how our moral characters are shaped by the kind of institutions, both formal and informal, that our lives are caught up in.

He further (1997: 154) notes regarding voluntary community activities:

> Associational activity, even where it is not actually directed toward environment goals, helps to create the cultural preconditions for

sustainability by generating and sustaining dense horizontal bonds of trust and co-operation. It thus creates a generalized climate of trust where people are less likely to think simply of their own, narrowly conceived interests.

At the opposite end of the radical spectrum were the environmental scientists and managers and the consulting engineers. This was the case with regard to both the issue of developing countries and that of radical protesters at home. While recognising the poverty and environmental destruction occurring in developing countries, some of the participants in these groups felt that the people living in these countries were materially contributing to this destruction through overpopulation, incompetence and political corruption. They felt considerable distaste for what they saw as a simplistic blaming of the 'economic system' for global ills, and spoke of the fact that little could be done to change it: *'You can't affect the worldwide economic system'*. Some also articulated considerable scepticism regarding environmental protesters in Ireland, whom they regarded as 'they', the other.

Between these two extremes of mobilised groups on the one hand and environmental managers, scientists and consultants on the other, lay the farmers. Within this group the difficulties faced by developing countries were acknowledged as were the contradictions and frustrations involved in working with an EU agricultural policy that had encouraged overproduction without any way of sending the surplus to those starving in developing countries. There was also a strong sense of disempowerment: *'What can we do about it?'* (Dairy farmers), *'We are only one small cog on a wheel'* (Small farmers).

In their discussion the skilled building workers reproduced both sides of the argument regarding the role of the global economic system in the production of global inequalities and environmental destruction. For some the major fault lay with the excessive power vested in the few in the First World, for others it lay with the political and military elites in developing countries. For all, there was little sense in trying to effect change.

The globalised economic system was seen by all groups as based on greed. Irish people were seen as so attracted, indeed addicted, to the affluent lifestyle made available by the Celtic Tiger that they could not get off the gravy train. For most of the groups drawn from the general public, as well as the farmers, the environmental scientists and business personnel, this did not produce any major sense of guilt and certainly not moral outrage, or a desire for radical change. Teachers, nurses and students gave some of the most sympathetic accounts, debating difficulties, noting possibilities and stating moral concerns. Some groups, for example, heritage officers, emphasised that, although fundamental changes could not be made and collective efforts to attempt to bring such change were criticised, this did not absolve the public from individual responsibilities regarding protecting one's own environment. Thus was the individualising project which some (see Beck and Beck-Gernsheim 2002) would see as central to contemporary advanced capitalism articulated in the Irish context.

4

Romantic Discourse: A Sense of Place

Introduction

The nineteenth century romantic tradition in Europe developed in critical response to what was seen as destructive industrialisation and its rationalising tendencies. It is a perspective that privileges the intuitive and imaginative as well as the experiential and holistic. It allows a limited role for experimental science but does not prioritise it. The romantics, as David Pepper (1996: 191) explains, maintained that science was inadequate to explain all the phenomena with which humans are confronted. They regarded these phenomena – understandable through intuition, instinct and emotionally based knowledge – as the noblest aspect of being human. It is a discourse that frequently offers an idealisation of the rural, of harmony between the species, whether in the supposed domestic harmony of the small-scale and rural community or in the wilderness. Internationally, the romantic tradition has informed preservation and national parks' movements, the heritage industry, and popular travel, tourist and nature literature.

The research literature indicated three interrelated romantic discourse themes of potential relevance to the analysis of the focus groups' discussions. The first is a theme which draws on romantic nationalist sentiment elaborated in particular at the turn of the twentieth century in Ireland. The second is the articulation of a sense of locality and place, while the third is a theme which may disrupt or change this sense of place through a contemporary sense of the 'translocal', due to globalised economic forces moving capital, people and ideas translocally and transnationally.

Romantic Nationalism

To understand romantic environmental discourses in Ireland it is necessary to explore their interrelationship with the economic, political and cultural structures and traditions prevalent in society. As Jamison (2001: 100) notes regarding what he calls 'national shades of green': 'contemporary environmental politics have been shaped in significant ways by institutions and cultural patterns, or modes of social capital which manifest themselves in particular ways in particular national settings.'

Ireland's nineteenth century political history of union with Britain, supported by an Anglo-Irish, Protestant, land-owning class, and by a mainly Protestant, but increasingly Catholic, professional, bureaucratic and urban-based middle-class, was overturned by a successful nationalist mobilisation, both political and cultural, at the beginning of the twentieth century, leading to the establishment of an independent Irish state in 1922. This political history, with its attendant religious and class divisions, was the context within which cultural – literary, artistic and scientific – movements were formed and changed. One of the most important cultural movements in Ireland was the cultural revival of the 1890s, which included not only rapidly increasing interest in the Irish language and in the literature, archaeology, folklore and history of Ireland, but also interest in the natural history of Ireland, including botany, geology and ornithology. Like other aspects of the cultural revival in the Republic, the increasing interest in natural history contributed to a romantic construction of the West of Ireland and its islands. As Lysaght (1998: 40) comments, 'it was in the remote western regions particularly with their enduring Gaelic speaking culture and their uncatalogued biological heritage, that the romantic yearnings of [natural science] field club members, folklorists and antiquarians found scope for gratification.'

This interest in natural history and involvement in naturalists' field clubs was most frequently expressed by a Dublin-based Anglo-Irish and Protestant 'professocracy' along with some large landowners (Lysaght 1998). While sharing the same cultural and educational background among themselves, this was quite different from that of the majority of the population. Lysaght postulates that this group's interest in natural history at a time of political and social stress reflected a desire for self-transcendence in the face of the considerable insecurity they felt (Lysaght 1998; Foster 1997). Their interest lay in remote, 'wilderness' areas and in species in their particular natural habitat.

The natural historians and their field clubs that travelled to the West and to the islands, collecting and cataloguing species and publishing their findings, expressed a patriotic nativism. However, unlike many others in the cultural revival movement, this did not translate into nationalism and a desire to break with Britain. When nationalism triumphed, they were to fall victim (Lysaght 1998: 43).

The renowned Irish naturalist, Robert Lloyd Praeger (1865–1953), epitomised this group. An Ulster Presbyterian, from an upper middle-class industrial background who studied at Queen's University Belfast, Praeger came to work in the National Library in Dublin in 1883. Here he joined and became a highly influential member of the Dublin Naturalists' Field Club, along with others from a similar bourgeois and ascendancy background. Highly energetic and a leading figure in natural history, he organised field trips, often to the West, collecting species, determining their classification, cataloguing them and publishing his findings in the *Irish Naturalist*. He published, *inter alia*, *Irish Topographical Botany* (1901), and, along with others, carried out major scientific surveys of Lambay and Clare Islands. However, the economic and political position of this class was to be eroded in the new Irish state, and Praeger took early retirement from his National Library position in 1923. Natural history was of marginal interest in the new Ireland, in which national identity was to be promoted through the Irish language and an idealisation of the traditional small rural farm. In contrast, the natural history tradition on which Praeger drew was seen to be associated with the Victorian ethos of progress, power and empire, as expressed in the great exhibitions (Lysaght 1998: 112–3).

Praeger, however, forever energetic, published a typographical account of the thirty-two counties of Ireland – *The Way that I Went* (1937). It was a highly popular book, unlike his more scientific publications. Along with accurate scientifically based descriptions, Praeger expressed wonder and awe at the beauty of the landscape, especially that of the West of Ireland, exalting in solitary places and exhilarating walks, and the inspiration afforded by 'the mystery and majesty of nature' (Lysaght 1998: 154), in contrast to the rush and bustle of urban life. His Ireland was not one of historical conquests, but:

> It is rather the Ireland of the man who goes with reverend feet through the hills and valleys, accompanied by neither noise nor dust to scare away wild creatures; stopping often, watching closely, listening carefully. Only thus can he, if he is fortunate, make friends by degree with the birds and flowers and rocks, learn all the signs and sounds of the country-side, and at length feel at one with what is, after all, his natural environment. (Quoted in Lysaght 1998: 155)

The romanticisation of the West of Ireland was also strongly articulated by Yeats and Synge in the Irish literary revival, which identified its nature and its native Irish speakers as quintessentially Irish, the carriers of the traditions and aspirations of the nation. The nation was the primary romantic object, and what were seen as the wild and desolate areas of the West and its people represented the nation in its purist form. In fact the West of Ireland was densely populated, but the construction of it as an almost empty space lingered on strongly in pictorial- and tourist-oriented representations (see Torode 1984).

Some of the themes explored in the focus group data were the extent to which particular groups expressed an appreciation of the Irish landscape and associated this with pride in being Irish, and the implications of this outlook, if any, for a concern to protect the environment. Also of interest was any perceived identification between Ireland and rurality.

A Sense of Place

A focus on, and frequent idealisation of, a local sense of place also has a long tradition, especially in Irish poetry. Sean O' Tuama (1985: 25) notes that '[t]here is scarcely one of the many hundreds of poets writing in Irish in the seventeenth, eighteenth or nineteenth centuries whose poems do not focus in some way on his feeling for home or ancestral land.' Furthermore, this tradition survived the linguistic changeover from Irish to English and remains in the poetry of, for example, Montague, Kinsella and Heaney.

Geographers emphasise the importance of a sense of place. Regarding Ireland, Smyth (1985: 4) describes this sentiment as 'the rounded sense of place as experienced by the insider. This experience involves all the senses – of seeing, feeling, of sound, of touch and taste.' It is bound up with a sense of being at home, in a community, and strongly associated with identity and caring.

Torgenson (1999: 189), drawing on Bachalard's (1969) *Poetics of Space*, identifies his aesthetics of place as not alone a lived-in, highly valued and imagined space, but one that will be strongly defended. As Torgenson continues, 'What is primarily involved in defence of place is an effort to protect the culturally achieved meaningfulness of a particular way of life.'

Geographers also note the importance of the idea of place in the mobilisation of environmental concerns. Indeed for David Harvey (1996: 303):

> Place is the preferred terrain of much environmental politics. Some of the fiercest movements of opposition to the political-economy of capitalistic place construction are waged over the issue of the preservation or upsetting of valued environmental qualities in particular places.

Harvey further argues that in contemporary societies characterised by global flows of people, power and capital, the 'aestheticisation' of particular places 'becomes a means to explore an alternative aesthetic to that offered through the restless spatial flows of commodities and money'. Place comes to be seen as 'a locus of some potentially unalienating direct sensuous interaction with environs', thus becoming 'the focus for the imaginary, of beliefs, longings and desires' (Harvey 1996: 304, 316).

Place can thus be central to the construction of a sense of self, of others, of a particular way of life and of the environment. In the cultural politics of place 'individuals invest in places and thereby empower themselves collectively by virtue of that investment' (Harvey 1996: 323). However, places are also the product of institutionalised economic and political power and the local construction of place and strong defence of it may run counter to the more centralising project of the state. As Appadurai (2003: 338) notes, 'the production of locality challenges the order and the orderliness of the nation state'.

Regarding environmental mobilisation in Ireland, Tovey (1993) has also noted the importance of identification with the local for some of these mobilised groups. Her research on environmental discourses in the 1980s and early 1990s notes the conflict between the environmental discourses of mainly Dublin-based, environmental groups and those of environmental protesters with strong, local commitments. Each articulated a different discourse regarding Irish cultural and economic development and consequently different perspectives on the environment and its protection. The mainly Dublin-based and state-aligned group, which she sees as representing 'official environmentalism', mobilised around conservation organisations and a developing environmental 'knowledge' and 'civilising elite'. This elite saw Ireland as lagging behind other developed European countries and in need of modernisation and centralised, state-based regulation and public education in environmental matters. The second grouping of environmental activists was based within local populist movements for rural community development. These communities were experiencing peripheral underdevelopment with its attendant rural decline and unemployment. While favouring the development of local employment opportunities, they were suspicious of TNCs, which had not delivered in the past, and of the state, which did not consult them about the possible development of their own area, and they mobilised against perceived pollution threats and threats to their environment (see also Peace 1993, 1997). Her research on small organic farmers also notes the importance to this group of localism and communal relations in food production and consumption and their strong criticism of globalised food regimes (Tovey 1997).

This pattern of local environmental protest against what are seen to be the decisions of urban and state-based environmentalists can continue to be observed in contemporary protests against the refusal of planning permission for one-off housing in the countryside, and against the local siting of incinerators and waste dumps, and other infrastructural projects. (For detailed analysis of local environmental activists, see Hilary Tovey's *Environmentalism in Ireland: Movement and Activists*

Being born in the country and taking holidays there, as well as taking part in numerous outdoor pursuits, such as walking, camping and gardening, can also be major sources of emotional identification with non-human nature and a concern to care for and protect it. Research by Palmer (1998) in the UK on sources of continuing commitment to ecological interests among environmental educators noted the importance of such early socialisation and leisure-time activities. These were also reported by this group as contributing to a sense of wonder regarding the transcendental mystery of the natural world. It is not only the rural, of course, which can give rise to a strong sense of place and mobilisation to protect its environment. It can, and often does, occur in urban and suburban contexts (see Franklin 2002).

Translocality
With the increasing mobility of capital and labour, goods and services, and travel and ideas, sociologists and geographers have noted the possibility of a change in the sense of place (Castells 1997; Giddens 1990; Appadurai 2003; Rodman 2003). It is argued that post-Fordist economic restructuring is giving rise to a 'space of flows', which supersedes the local meaning of places. There is a growing tendency towards multilocality and hybrid cultural identities. Rodman (2003) suggests that multilocality has three dimensions: the first occurs when individuals or groups look at places through the eyes of others, for example, seeing one's own place through the eyes of tourists; this she calls 'decentred analysis'; the second is dislocation, which occurs when a contrast is made between a known and an unfamiliar place, as when a place changes or when comparisons are made between one's home place and elsewhere experienced as a traveller; the third is concerned with the many different meanings which one place may have – the multivocal dimension of place.

However, translocalisation is no new phenomenon in Ireland. Cultural theorists have noted that the nineteenth and early twentieth century romantic construction of the Irish landscape as a pastoral idyll, whether in literature, landscape painting (see Gibbons 1987), or travel writing (see Slater 1993), was frequently that of the outsider – particularly that of the Anglo-Irish landowning, and related professional, elite. It is a romantic image, effortlessly assimilated into the contemporary promotion of Irish tourism and heritage industries by urban, often state-sponsored, managerial elites (O'Connor 1993). This image may be accepted, negotiated, rejected or ignored by locals as their landscape and past is displaced and displayed for the consumption of others in advertisements, posters and postcards, and in interpretative and heritage centres. They may draw on a local oral discourse rather than an urban literate and pictorial one (see Slater 1993).

Alternatively, the outsider's image may be internalised, as Casey (2000: 263) argues. Noting the dependence on tourism, especially ecotourism, of a small village in the West of Ireland, she comments on how 'the locality is given its value mainly through the positive assessment that visitors make of it'. She quotes a local, 'They [tourists] say it's beautiful and somehow you feel responsible for how beautiful it is.' Locals who have returned from abroad, or outsiders who have settled in the area, have energetically promoted the construction of this landscape and area as an ecotourist market.

The extent to which the focus group participants accepted or rejected a romantic image of Ireland was explored through their spontaneous open discussion during the first hour as well as through the presentation of a romantic discourse statement during the second hour. The statement drew on the Bord Fáilte website advertisement which states: 'The central plain of Ireland is surrounded by a ring of mountains. Hues vary from the deep purple of heather to the black of the turf bogs and vistas range from the gentle Slieve Bloom mountains to the steep wooded valleys and the awe-inspiring Cliffs of Moher'. The romantic discourse statement was discussed with fourteen of the twenty-two focus groups. The aim was to explore whether or not the focus group participants adopted this romantic lens in 'seeing' the Irish landscape and emotionally responding to it, or, alternatively, if they distanced themselves from it, offering an ironic critique, as suggested by some contemporary artists and cultural studies theorists (see Graham 2001).

Elaboration of Romantic Discourse Themes

A romantic perspective was not predominant or spontaneously prevalent among most of the focus groups. Only seven of the groups spontaneously discussed, usually briefly, environmental or nature themes in romantic terms – the responses of the two farmer groups will be discussed separately below. Those general public groups who spontaneously elaborated on romantic themes included a number of the younger groups – the shop workers' group (women, and all under thirty-five), the two student groups (mainly women), and the commuters' group (a mixed gender group and all under thirty) – along with three older groups – the teachers, and two of the mobilised groups, the walkers and the returned missionary group (all mixed gender groups). None of the regulator, scientist, or business groups articulated this perspective spontaneously. There was of course further discussion in the context of the proposed romantic discourse statement, which will be analysed separately below.

Three romantic themes can be identified in the spontaneous discussions. These included the discussion of participants' emotional and pleasurable response to a particular natural phenomenon, typically locating and describing it in a specific place; a criticism of destructive 'progress' harming nature, again identifying and discussing this in relation to particular experiences and places; and an idealisation of the past, particularly drawing on rural childhood experiences.

An interesting set of participants who articulated a romantic discourse on each of these themes was three supermarket shop workers. These three workers had lived all their lives in the small town or its environs in which they worked. They each had their Leaving Certificate, had been employed for nine years in the same supermarket, and were deeply embedded in their local world of home, family and work. They differed from the other four participants in the group in being older, in the extent to which they were embedded in the locality, and in the priority they gave to environmental issues. They, unlike the other shop workers, perceived the supermarket as not only worker-friendly but also environmentally friendly.

These shop workers recalled a number of experiences regarding nature that they described in romantic terms. In particular, they described experiences of walking locally in wooded areas. One described trees in autumn:

4   *They are beautiful to look at, in autumn you have like, my daughter brought it to my attention one morning going to school, she said there is orange and yellow and red and green, Mammy, and white, she was amazed by it. Autumn and the leaves are on the ground; it's absolutely stunning. I live in the country but I live at the foot of ... Mountain, it's stunning, absolutely.*

F   *Now, she brought that to your attention, would you have noticed it otherwise?*

4   *I always do, it was just that morning, trying to get her to school and getting to work, but I was raised in the country and I have always noticed it. It's paramount to everything I think, nature.*

                                                              Shop workers

Another participant in this group described how she, as an alternative medicine practitioner, worked with energy fields, noting in particular that all living beings have an aura, and that humans are not superior to nature: 'I mean you should never think that anything is greater or lesser than yourself and that includes the land and the animals and everything like' (3). They decried some elements of 'progress', particularly using a negative image of concrete to contrast with what they perceived as natural. Regarding walking in the woods and the pleasures it invoked, they noted:

7   *It's the energy of the trees like, the sounds of them. You notice a child in a buggy, the first thing they see is the shape of the trees like. The leaves and the shadow.*

4   *And none of it is man-made, there is no concrete border. Or advertisements staring you in the face, it's just the trees, that is it.*

3   *A lot of meditation tapes and things like that are of wind, trees, leaves. Yeah, the whole lot.*

4   *The cracking of trees. All meditation tapes are of sounds of the environment, whales, dolphins like.*

Shop workers

They were very concerned about the protection of the environment. Discussing her strong motivation to recycle, one noted that this had been reinforced when her daughter was born:

7   *… when I had my daughter, you know what I mean, you would be thinking of her world. You know what I mean; will there be one for her?*

F   *How do you think her world will compare to our world?*

7   *It will be crap I would say. It's a hard world now, you know what I mean.*

F   *Environmentally, how will the world change?*

4   *Seasons seem to be different … in the summertime … we don't seem to have it anymore. We get the silage done in two days depending on how much land you have but we used to spend like a week and a half to two weeks treating the hay, turning, baling and whatever, that was the summertime and that was how you spent the summer in your shorts, and it just doesn't happen anymore.*

Shop workers

The two student groups also articulated certain aspects of a romantic discourse. In one of these groups, very early in the discussion, a participant raised the issue of light and smog pollution blotting out the stars:

5   [You] *can't see the stars in Dublin. It is really bad. …* [When] *I stay at home and I live in the middle of nowhere and you could go out in the middle of the night and just look at the stars and my Mam and I would go out and look at the stars, and you can see every single star. You can pick out the constellations and all and you can't hear a thing bar the sheep in the field beside you. You come up here* [Dublin] *and if you can pick out one star you are lucky. There's an alarm down the road from my Granny's* [where she stays when in Dublin] *that never stops going off – it's nerve-wracking.*

3   *I got a telescope for Christmas and I haven't been able to use it yet.*
5   *No, it is pointless.*
3   *Even when there is good weather it is useless pointing a telescope at the stars because ...*
5   *I think I saw the stars last week because it was just that cold.*
F   *So is that caused by smog, do you think, or is it caused by light or by both?*
5   *Both.*
F   *How do you feel about that? Does it worry or affect you?*
4   *I like the stars. Bring back the stars.*

Students 2

Both the student and commuter groups criticized 'progress', in particular road building. One student noted of the encroaching M50:

1   *Again it's related to the road. When you are out walking* [you see] *all the trees, and the lands, the fields. The M50 was built on my friend's back garden. We used to walk up there, used to be beehives and all that. Now it's just gone because of the road. You take the dog up for a walk on the extra section that is being built and I remember seeing a family of deer up there. And quite often they would get trapped because of the works. It's really sad when you see that. You are thinking the M50 and how far are they going to go into the mountains?*

Students 1

The returned missionary group, the teachers and the walkers also raised romantic themes, often integrating the emotional, the aesthetic and the moral. Some examples of this have already been examined in Chapter 2 under moral discourses. A further example is from the teachers' group:

4   *As a child now, maybe I'm an old romantic, I don't know, but I remember as a child going out into fields and you could walk among the animals and you could smell the animals and we used to grind turnips or put them into the pulper ... It was real hands-on and it was real healthy and the animals were happy. When I go down into our farmyard now – we're a REPS[5] farm – and I see animals just there pushed into sheds. The stink is deplorable.*

Teachers

Walkers expressed their love of walking in the mountains and their efforts to protect them. Speaking of a recent walk, one noted: *'You get up there*

---

5 Rural Environment Protection Scheme

*and you sit down and there's nothing but wind, clean air, like I was in ...
the other day ... it was beautiful like ... you really love it'* (6). They gave
many examples of recent attempts to protect the local mountains: from the
destructive erosion caused by scrambling bikes, from sheep farmers, from
'nouveau-riche' outsiders who had bought adjacent land and who would
deny access to walkers, and from the building of a wind farm. Regarding
the latter they noted that the walking club:

8   *... has been active in objecting to development on the mountain, in
fact I think the club has very successfully managed to prevent a wind
farm going up in an area that was very sensitive environmentally.*

6   *Yeah, we objected to it, there was strong feeling in the club about
wind farms, I suppose feelings were a bit mixed on it because
personally I think long term wind farms are going to come and I
don't have a problem with wind farms in the proper place. The
objection that I had personally to the one that we objected to strongly
was it was going to be in a scenic area and one of my main problems
was not so much the windmills themselves, it was the way they were
going to bring the power to the national grid which was over ground
and they were bringing it out over the* [name of local beauty spot],
one of the most scenic views [in this area].

Walkers

He also pointed out the importance of this beautiful area in attracting
tourists.

The walkers did not, however, romanticise the local community's
response to the proposed development, noting divisions within it in terms
of who might gain and who might lose, and who could be bought off by the
businessmen who proposed the development or their agents:

6   *... that's where the big bucks come from like and he* [the agent]
*actually threw neighbour against neighbour there because he was
promising some of the people who had small bits of grazing that he
would give them money for their rights to have windmills in their
place and then the guy down the road, typical Irish attitude like ...*
[there was] *the jealousy aspect of it ... 'Ah that fella, he's getting
€2,000 and I'm getting nothing' kind of a thing, and it threw kind of
neighbour against neighbour which was not nice really like, but that
actually happened back along that side* [of the mountain].

Walkers

Furthermore, the agent wrote to the walking club, *'... telling us we no longer had rights to walk on his mountain and that he was withdrawing all walking rights and we weren't going to be allowed on there in the future so. Nobody has taken any notice of it of course.'*

Romantic Discourses and the Rural: the Responses of Farmers

Because of the emphasis on the rural in spontaneous romantic discussions it was interesting to see if the farmers articulated such a perspective. Of the two groups, large dairy farmers were more likely than the small farmers to articulate a romantic perspective, albeit in a relatively weak form. For example, the dairy farmers identified closeness to nature as a motivating factor in their commitment to farming. When asked by the facilitator what they would miss most about farming if they were to leave it, they noted its healthy lifestyle, its tranquillity and its nearness to nature:

5   *That is a funny thing when you bring a live calf or a live lamb ...*
4   *See nature come to life.*
5   *You have to work at it, to bring the thing alive and get the thing right; it's serious satisfaction.*

Dairy farmers

A downside was potential isolation, *'the only thing about farming is that you are on your own, you could be found dead ... The loneliness can be fierce if you are on your own'* (3). Visiting neighbours was a thing of the past, and *'it's all rush, rush'; 'it comes back to not having time for each other'*.

The large farmers also articulated a deep sense of embeddedness in their farms and farm work in terms of both space and time, and indeed used this perspective to assess and, when appropriate, criticise 'expert' scientific advice (see Chapters 5, 6). They noted that they worked the land for 365 days of the year, that to farm successfully they needed to be highly sensitive to *'the balance of nature'* and the highly variable conditions of land, vegetation and weather. They appreciated the trees on their land and stated that they would miss particular trees as, *'you are looking at it every day of the week like'* (3). *'It's a landmark ... It adds something to your line of vision'* (4). Furthermore, trees could be *'there for generations'*, so *'there is linkage there'* (6).

Small farmers gave a different response to the question of why they continued farming, identifying pride in land ownership as a major motivating factor in continuing to farm:

5   *I think the pride in the land; it's not so long ago since they won it. Two generations or three generations, you know. People take pride in the place. It's what they've won. The right to own it.*

2   *... like it's their own.*
5   *Pride in working it.*

Small farmers

They had inherited their land, it was *'just a way of life for us, we were brought up to it'* (9). There was the added pragmatic *'satisfaction at the end of the day when you see your animals doing well, you get a good price for them'.*

There was also a strong recognition among these farmers that small farming was dying:

9   *... the younger generation aren't interested in farming, the lads of eighteen and twenty years of age, unless they have at least a couple of hundred acres, but I mean there is no lad going to take on farming forty or fifty acres of land now.*
2   *The present generation don't have the same interest as we had. They just drive the tractor and put on the radio. That's what they're like.*

Small farmers

They further noted that the destruction of this way of life was due to the fact that *'the costs are increasing and the price of the product is going down'.* Furthermore, *'the biggest problem, people aren't willing to put in the sixteen-hour day to be a farmer'* (6). Most wanted a nine-to-five job and to *'get on and have a quality of life after that'* (6). They were not a group to get carried away with romantic sentiment:

9   *You get satisfaction out of doing things right, if it goes wrong ...* [laughing]
2   *You get dead animals.*
9   *It has its ups and downs.*

Small farmers

Nor were they too upset by the thought that the next generation might not stay on the land. When asked by the facilitator, *'How would you feel if your own children don't stay on in your home, and what if they up and leave and there is nobody there?'* they variously replied that they would accept it, that they recognised that they were a different generation, and indeed that they would encourage them.

They were, however, concerned about what was happening and would happen to the small farm-based rural countryside as a whole if depopulation continued: *'Rural Ireland is in decline for a long time. Schools are closing. And if people can't live in the countryside ... Do we want rural Ireland to be a park or do we want people living in it?'* (1). They feared that depopulation would lead to the countryside becoming a wilderness:

7 *... You see it everywhere you go, places that haven't been farmed or lived in for ten or fifteen years. It's standing there in rack and ruin. And the land is just turning to pure wilderness. I don't think that anybody thinks that is attractive-looking. They would want to start thinking about it seriously because that is what the whole countryside will turn into if they keep doing what they are doing.*

Small farmers

The sentiments of small farmers regarding depopulation, and a recognition of parental acquiescence in the departure of their children from the land, were repeated by the teachers who lived and worked in similar small-farm areas.

Responses to the Romantic Discourse Statement

As noted above, the majority of groups did not spontaneously articulate a romantic discourse. However, a range of responses was elicited to the romantic representation of Ireland as presented in the statement: 'The central plain of Ireland is surrounded by a ring of mountains. Hues vary from the deep purple of heather to the black of the turf bogs and vistas range from the gentle Slieve Bloom mountains to the steep wooded valleys and the awe-inspiring Cliffs of Moher.' Almost all of the fourteen groups who discussed this statement recognized it immediately as tourist advertising. Consequently, they frequently deconstructed it in terms of its idealised representation of the 'real' Ireland. In doing this they drew on a number of different lenses, including a romantic and patriotic lens (teachers, unemployed, retired), the pleasured eye of remembered leisure time in the countryside (environmental managers, teachers), or the lens of returned travellers and tourists (environmental managers, actively mobilised groups, as well as teachers, commuters, students, and the unemployed group). There were two further and indeed more oppositional or dismissive lenses: those of the sceptical environmental regulators and scientists, and the Dublin-based working-class single mothers and Travellers. For the latter two groups, Dublin, and not elsewhere, represented Ireland and home.

A Romantic Image

The teachers confirmed their spontaneous romantic perspective in their response to the statement, but also raised questions about it:

1   *... it's a very romantic image of Ireland I suppose. I mean my reaction is governed by a certain amount of cynicism that the environmental debate would have engendered ... I thought the statement was talking to tourists, but in the heel of the hunt, despite all the cynicism, I feel proud of our country as a sort of, a ... beautiful place.*

Teachers

Thus, despite their awareness that the statement was for advertising purposes, most in this group agreed that, *'it's a beautiful statement as in "poetic", and I think it's talking to tourists and maybe aspiring writers and I just feel I'm glad to be living here'* (4). Again, having acknowledged its tourist intent, another noted *'... it made me kind of appreciative of the beautiful country that we do live in. Beautiful physically'* (6). Or another participant: *'It made me feel proud of the country we are living in. It also gave me a feeling of ... that we should protect what we have ... Because I feel a lot of areas could be destroyed in the whole thing of building and developing and the whole lot of it'* (7).

The first speaker elaborated on his appreciation:

1   *I think parts of this country are incredibly beautiful and they give me immense pleasure and enjoyment ... On a fine summer's day you could travel the bogs of west Mayo, for example, where there isn't a house within twenty miles – there is no place in the world like it and that's what maybe makes me think about ... the development that has happened has probably put a fair old dent on that you know, has damaged it considerably.*

Teachers

On the other hand, some of the teachers, in recognising it as a statement beamed to tourists, felt it was *'idyllic and simplistic'*, and that, in highlighting the *'peasant and raw ruralness of it'*, it represented an outdated version of Ireland that was now *'progressive, aware, affluent and educated'* (all stated by participant 3).

Some in the unemployed group, who, like the teachers, lived in the West of Ireland, also concurred with the statement at one level, while also being explicitly critical of contemporary destructive developments. In identifying with the statement, some in the group noted the beauty of the country, that it made them feel *'proud of your nation'* (8), but sad as it was being destroyed: *'tearing down trees'*, and *'housing estates going into these places'* (9). One noted:

6 *I frequently visit the Aran Islands and now even when you arrive in*
   the village where the boats land they have big houses there, and a
   shopping mall, it really takes from the whole thing. When you come
   into Kilronan, that is the name of the village, you see a big shopping
   mall; the wild island is gone. There is this big yellow shopping mall
   ... I don't think we have any pride any more in our own country.
7 *Our national identity has been taken away from us.*
5 *I don't think we are Irish anymore, we are Europeans.*
3 *Yeah, we are told that every day of the week.*

Unemployed

However, there was also considerable ambivalence about the statement,
with some rejecting it as *'tourist propaganda'* (3) for the *'gullible*
American' (9), that it represented Ireland as the *'land of the leprechauns'*
(2), and that Irish people prefer to go abroad:

3 *We don't bother, people in Ireland seem to go away to other places*
   for holidays, they seem to travel to Spain and all these places.
   Foreigners want to see these [Irish] *places. We don't want to.*
5 *We still take note of them, you would drive around them ...*
3 *Yes, but it wouldn't come to me to drive out today and have a look.*
   But Americans would love it.

Unemployed

It was members of the retired group who identified with the statement
more immediately and completely than any other group. To the agreement
of others, one described it as *'a lovely description of the country'* (1),
another *'I feel proud to be Irish listening to that statement'* (2), another that
it made him think of a *'song and relate it to Ireland'* (4), while for yet
another it brought a lump to her throat and made her *'happy and*
emotional' and proud (6).

Memories of pleasurable leisure-time experiences in the countryside
were drawn upon in elaborating a positive response to the statement. This
was the case for teachers, as quoted above, and for environmental
managers who gave a positive and generally uncritical response to the
statement. They remarked that it was *'a nice statement and factually*
correct' (2), remembering hillwalking, touring, holidaying and showing
visitors around the Irish countryside. Elsewhere in the discussion, one
participant also noted decreasing biodiversity:

2 *While we still have a lot of greenery and what have you around,*
   there's a lot less wildlife. I remember even from my own childhood

when I was working on the farm, there's considerable less variation in the birds and types of plants that I see around today and I think a lot of that is just due to, well the building boom ... and animals tend to be shy and that, they've been put into smaller areas and secondly ... the stripping of the hedgerows in farming. Now again maybe the REPS is improving this.

3   *I would say it has improved it without a doubt.*

Environmental managers

Ireland through the Eyes of the Returned Traveller and Tourists

To what extent did the focus groups respond to the statement by taking the viewpoint of others, especially outsiders or tourists, what Rodman has called 'a decentred perspective', or contrast the familiar known Ireland with experiences garnered outside it, what Rodman calls 'translocation'? Half of the groups responded to the discourse statement in this way.

Both student groups identified with the statement in a translocal manner. They noted how, on returning to Ireland, they were made particularly aware of the *'uniqueness of Ireland'*: *'When you go away and then come back in the summertime, and everything is green.* [The statement] *is truthful. It's like Clare, it's just beautiful'* (1). However, there was also ambivalence here. It was commented that the statement did not refer to the intrusion of industry, motorways and *'the people peeing on the streets at the weekend'* (1). The commuting group also commented that on returning to Ireland it was the litter they most noted.

Within the Cork Environmental Forum group some were also critical of the idealised 'tourist speak' which did not take into account the environmental destruction from forestation and timber manufacturing which had occurred in the bogs and mountains, and to the Cliffs of Moher from the proposed interpretative centre. Others identified with the statement and Ireland's *'fantastic countryside'*, *'it's absolutely stunning'* (2), while some noted that they themselves lived in beautiful places, which had influenced their lives. Added to these perspectives was that of the traveller on returning to Ireland and seeing Ireland through tourists' eyes:

7   *I was in Singapore in February and it made me realise how lucky we are to live in Ireland ... everyone there lives in an apartment in a block and nobody has any green, it's all concrete. If you want green you have to go to another island. It's amazing and I look back and if somebody could live in a cottage with a bit of garden around them, they're a millionaire in Singapore. Whereas we live like millionaires here in a beautiful country.*

- *We do.*
- *Yeah.*

CEF

The attraction of the statement to tourists was further noted:

5   *Ireland avoided industrialisation in the 50s. It's now perceived by Europe and America as being very attractive so for visiting, and you know romantic and simple. Maybe a bit of Irishness in the case of former immigrants.*

CEF

Many groups gave brief translocal references in relation either to Ireland's landscape attractions for tourists, or, in order to criticise Irish practices, in terms of what other countries were doing to protect the environment, especially their commitment to recycling. Thus, there was evidence of relatively frequent decentred and dislocated forms of response, but neither was particularly extensively discussed.

The Sceptical View of Environmental Regulators and Scientists
The DoE immediately identified the source of the statement: *'Did somebody steal that from the Bord Fáilte brochure for North America?'* (4). One dismissed it as *'romantic nonsense'* (5). Another noted that while it was not incorrect, that there were beautiful areas in Ireland, there were also the *'litter and waste problems, traffic, etc.'* (6), and another, *'when I think of the Slieve Blooms, I think of the dreadful over-grazing and the erosion and the plantations and also the transmitters on top of it'* (2).

Likewise for the environmental scientists, while one recognised that *'the essence is probably true'*, and another that it reminded him of the paintings of *'Paul Henry, and I think it is going to rain shortly'* (8), yet another noted, to laughter, that the statement conjured up for him, *'the white goods dumped in the bog,'* and, *'there's pot holes in the road and the chewing gum in the streets ... '* (7).

Dismissal of Rural Romanticism
Two groups, the young working-class single mothers and Traveller women, all of whom lived in Dublin, rejected the identification of Ireland with the rural romanticism of the statement. As noted above, elements of a similar type of criticism were articulated by some of the unemployed group living in an urban area in the West of Ireland, who noted that they would not be bothered touring in the Irish countryside and that Irish people would prefer to go to Spain for their holidays.

In the working-class single mothers' group, some rejected the rural representation of Ireland with what Morley (1980) has called a 'critique of silence'. The first participant, when asked her response to the statement, simply noted: *'I am thinking blank'*; others, *'no idea, lost'*, and *'where are the Cliffs of Moher?'* While some noted it was a *'lovely'* and a *'peaceful'* statement representing the countryside outside Dublin, and that it was like something from a holiday brochure, another strongly rejected the representation of Ireland purely in terms of the countryside, and thus excluding Dublin. On the contrary, Dublin to them was what *'we only know'*, *'If you were from the country, yeah, it's the country, but when you are from Dublin and you're reading it, it's not the thing you get from Dublin. Like if we went to a place like that we'd be – d'you know what I mean?'* (2). When asked: *'If you were to leave Dublin to go to the country, where would you go?'* the answer, to laughter, was, *'probably close to Dublin, like Meath'.* Others concurred, mentioning Kilkenny, Wicklow, or another city like Cork, or the holiday village close to it, Trabolgan. Another stated she would like to go to Maynooth as *'I have an uncle living out there and I seen this beautiful house and the cow-field in the garden, it's only like, it's still in the city like, you know what I mean* [laughs] *it's still close to home'* (7).

Some of the factors that contributed to the participants' preference for city life were the closeness of neighbours and shops, travel facilities, and just being used to it. Their pride in their city was closely bound up with the fact that this is where they lived and reared their children. When asked, *'What have you to be proud of in the city?'* their replies included, *'achieving rearing three kids'*, *'surviving in a very tough environment'* (8), and *'rearing a child in it.'*

Although the young working-class mothers dismissed rural romanticism, they, along with other Dublin-based working-class groups, the skilled building workers and the retired, raised and discussed the environment of the street – especially concerns about litter and trees – as well as the issue of the maintenance of urban parks. The latter were of particular concern to these three groups, each raising them spontaneously. The mothers' group noted of Fairview Park:

10 *But the likes of Fairview Park is getting dug at the moment.*
8   *I think that's a disgrace.*
9   *But it's the port tunnel* [... all talking ...]
–   *But they have moved the playground to another part of Fairview Park.*
10 *But it's not as good as it was. The bandstand an' all was there.*
–   *But then like they are improving as well, they are trying to cut out the*

likes of the buses and things like that, they are, I suppose, trying to improve things.

10 *Yeah, I suppose, but ...*

Young mothers

The young skilled workers made similar points spontaneously about Whitehall Park and St Anne's Park, and their partial destruction for 'development' purposes:

2 [They are] *disappearing anyway around Dublin, tell you that much.*

– *Yeah.*

2 *Portions of them taken out every year ... The Whitehall Park there, that used to be huge.*

F *And what's the land being used for?*

2 *That's the Dublin port tunnel.*

– *Taking big chunks out of that.*

– *They took part of the park, did they?*

– *Yeah.*

– *A big chunk of it.*

2 *Bleedin' lumps out of it, there's nothing left, trees and all are getting whipped down the length of the park.*

6 *St Anne's Park is the same ... parts off that as well for houses.*

2 *For houses?*

– *Yeah*

2 *And who, Dublin Corporation?*

– *Yeah ...*

– *... your heritage like.*

2 *The whole lot is gone ...We were training up there last week and there's a crane right in at the back of it, you know what I mean, but like to get in, it used to be huge like, there's nothing left of it now, you know what I mean, the houses are right into the back, but it was historical like as well, so you're not meant to be able to touch anything, you know what I mean, historically you can't go near a Georgian house, you can't change the windows in it, you can't change the doorframes but like something as old as that now and you can build ****** houses on it. Why? Money, know what I mean, the government again, money, the tax on it, get a few washers off this, get alloys for the jet or something, you know what I mean ...*

F *How do the rest of you feel about the stripping away of the park?*

– *Some of it is necessary though, you know, you do have to make way for progress.*

Skilled workers

As will be seen in Chapter 6, romantic sentiments were frequently not strong enough to hold out against the perceived demand of 'progress'. Nonetheless, the skilled workers noted:

7   *It's nice ... rambling around the Phoenix Park ... lovely, yeah.*
8   *It just appeals, there's something in you, you just can't help it can you?*
–   *Nature, you know, you just love taking the dog out or whatever ...* [laughter]
4   *... you'd walk into Stephen's Green ... A bit of green in the middle of concrete* [laughter].
3   *In the summertime you go in and chill out, just have a lunch break or whatever, take a half-hour and it's nice.*

Skilled workers

The retired group of Dublin working-class men and women also expressed their pleasure in walking on Dún Laoghaire pier, especially that it was now well-maintained and clean; and Dún Laoghaire Park *'is lovely', 'yeah, it's gorgeous', 'it is and they keep it very well'*.

Like the young mothers, the group of Traveller women, all of whom lived in Dublin, also distanced themselves from an identification of either themselves or Ireland with the rural. Discussing their occasional trips outside Dublin, one noted that when she went up the Wicklow Mountains, *'I thought I would never get down'* (8), and that the first time she saw cows she thought they were horses. An annual visit to Clare was more interesting for its fair and dancing and singing all night in the pub than any mention of the Cliffs of Moher. Furthermore, there were no chippers or McDonalds in the country. On the other hand, some also mentioned, sometimes in relation to their own childhood or in relation to bringing their own children out to the country, the sensuous pleasures of walking though fields, the smell of the grass, the salty smell of the beach, and the fresh air. Their major concerns, however, were providing for their children, even in terms of such basics as food, clothing and nappies; keeping as close an eye as possible on their adolescent sons, fearing fighting, drinking and the taking of drugs; and the time at which their men returned home in the evening.

Conclusion: Is Romantic Ireland Dead and Gone?

A romantic discourse, although articulated briefly by almost all of the general public and mobilised groups, was not a strongly elaborated discourse for the majority. In its weak form, the romantic sentiments expressed were those of pleasures that could be seen, heard and smelt, rather than a deep sense of awe, wonder or sacredness. The lack of a romantic discourse among environmental regulators, scientists and engineers, and indeed their scepticism when offered the romantic discourse statement, was an interesting difference between them and the general public who they regulate. It was possible, of course, that the context of the focus group discussion with work colleagues was not perceived as an appropriate setting for the articulation of romantic sentiments. This, however, was not a problem for teachers or returned missionaries who also spoke to work colleagues within the focus groups. It might also be pointed out that the context of discussion with work colleagues is also the context in which environmental policies and regulations are formulated. Thus, the seeming inappropriateness of articulating these romantic sentiments, which are of importance to at least some of those who are regulated, may limit the possibility that these policies and regulations will be designed in a way to capitalise on those romantic sentiments which exist and which motivate pro-environmental behaviour.

For that minority who articulated it spontaneously, a romantic discourse regarding the countryside and nature affirmed a strong sense of self and of place, as well as a deep concern at current destructive environmental developments, summed up in the image of the concrete invasion of nature by roads and housing. This was the response of teachers, walkers, returned missionaries and students, and in particular of some members of the shop workers' group. The latter articulated a classic romantic discourse, but drew on the contemporary idiom of alternative and natural therapies to do so. They thus integrated the imaginative, experiential and holistic, arguing for recognition of the beauty and potential harmony of all species and acknowledging a deep embeddedness in their local place. Indeed their environmental romanticism led, for at least one, to a biocentric perspective.

Romantic nationalist sentiments that idealized the rural and the natural landscape and identified it with the quintessentially Irish, and that expressed pride in belonging to the Irish nation were not frequently heard, despite the added stimulus of the discourse statement. The retired group of sixty-five to seventy-five-year-old men and women, based in Dublin, was the only group that agreed wholeheartedly with the statement, indicating its previous potency as a discourse in Ireland, but now much less frequently heard. Some teachers and unemployed (both based in the West of Ireland) also expressed some such sentiments and criticized destructive and inappropriate developments that encroached on previously idealised areas such as the Aran Islands. In both of these groups, however, there were others who offered different perspectives. Among the teachers, for example, some saw the discourse statement as presenting an outdated image of Ireland, which was now *'progressive, aware, affluent and educated'*.

Nonetheless, the role of teachers, in this instance primary school teachers, as carriers and articulators of a rural romantic tradition was strongly suggested by the data. A corollary of this was perhaps the lack of such romanticism among the less well-educated – for example, the Travellers and the young working-class and Dublin-based mothers. These two groups dismissed the romantic discourse statement's identification of Ireland with its rural landscape. This was not their world or their home place (see also O'Connor 1987). However, working-class Dubliners were well aware of, and sensitive to, their local environment of streets and parks, complaining of litter, tree felling and the loss of open city spaces and parks.

As the guardians of the countryside, the views of farmers were of particular interest. Dairy farmers indicated a strong identification with the natural living world, and an embeddedness in its routine time and place dimensions. The small and mainly part-time farmers, while acknowledging pride in landownership, perceived their farm-based livelihoods as under severe threat both economically and because the next generation showed little interest in this kind of farming. They were concerned, however, to maintain a peopled community and an ordered and cared-for countryside rather than, as they perceived it, a wilderness.

Regarding translocality or seeing through the eyes of foreigners, there was some evidence of this. The experience of travelling abroad was associated with an alternative comparative perspective regarding the protection of the environment, which frequently led to criticism of Ireland and Irish people's attitude and behaviour in relation to it. Regarding tourists, some saw tourists' appreciation of the Irish landscape as confirming their own, while others were more dismissive of the 'gullible American' and of the 'leprechaun' image portrayed in the discourse statement. Indeed, among environmental regulators and some of those most concerned with active mobilisation to protect the environment, such as those in the Cork Environmental Forum, there was a rather jaundiced view of the statement's 'idealised tourist speak'. It was seen as 'romantic nonsense', hiding the environmental destruction that was perceived to be taking place all around.

Overall, a romantic identification with a particular location and its natural features was spontaneously articulated by roughly one-third of the groups. The place identified was frequently that of the home place, or the place where childhood was spent (particularly a rural childhood), or particular leisure-time areas, such as the mountains for hillwalkers. A sense of place was also evident when identification with particular natural phenomena was discussed. Here participants typically cited the beauty of certain trees in particular locations and the distress caused by their destruction. However, the strength of this romantic perspective varied considerably across and within groups. Containing and limiting it were the 'realism' and 'pragmatism' associated with buying into economic 'progress' and participants' rather ambivalent acceptance of its negative environmental consequences.

5

Scientific Discourse: Trust and Power
with Brian Motherway

Introduction

The scientific tradition, which draws on an experimentally oriented science of nature, developed from seventeenth century Enlightenment thinking. It limited itself to the intensive study of what can be systematically seen, classified and theorised in nature. Nature in this paradigm became 'a system of component parts to be tended, or operated, like a machine so that its productive utilisation for human benefit could be made more effective and extensive' (Jamison 2001: 75). This scientific practice gave rise to a range of specific sciences and related professions, oriented to efficient resource use. It is often seen as strongly anthropocentric, prioritising humans over all other species, and as having contributed to the legitimation of human domination and exploitation of nature, especially as expressed in industrialisation processes (see Jamison 2001; Worster 1985; Merchant 1992).

Few people now articulate this discourse of simple domination and nature-as-machine, but a strong scientific discourse remains prevalent in relation to the role and position of science in society and, of specific relevance here, its potential role in making decisions about environmental protection and sustainable development.

The heart of the discourse is the assumption that environmental problems and their solutions can be fully known and scientific solutions found, and that science should thus be given a special place in decision-making about such issues. In knowledge terms, then, the scientific discourse claims that issues are fully knowable in a *scientific* way, meaning that facts can be established in one situation (i.e. the laboratory), applied to another (i.e. the 'real world'), and definitive technical answers found. This discourse also claims that science is, or at least can be, free from political or social contextual factors and that scientific knowledge is absolute and not contingent on such factors. It asks for a privileged position in decision-making, where it can be trusted to make informed, independent judgements and find the best solutions to problems.

Several aspects of the discourse can be identified for analysis: the role of scientific knowledge in decision-making and environmental and risk issues; the characteristics of scientific knowledge in terms of generalised, abstract application; the possibility of knowledge independent of interests and other social and political influences; and the question of trust in science and experts.

The Place of Science in Risk and Environmental Issues

Ulrich Beck's *Risk Society* (1992) offers one of the best-known analyses of the role of science and politics in the development of contemporary environmental discourses. Beck's thesis is that contemporary industrial or 'risk society' is characterised by a level of man-made risks, especially environmental risks, previously unknown to society. It is also characterised by the perceived inability of social institutions, whether related to the state, economy or science, to control or deal with these risks. Beck would particularly emphasise the risks associated with the nuclear industry, genetic engineering and chemical pollution. These risks frequently cannot be limited in terms of time or place; they are global, long-term threats. He further argues that society's capacity to deal with these risks and the insecurity they engender has been weakened by other social changes. These include labour market changes and occupational mobility which have undermined a sense of secure class and occupational identity, as well as changes in gender and familial roles so that the family is no longer a secure place into which to withdraw. All of these lead to individualisation, each individual having to negotiate his/her own career path as well as gender and familial identities.

However, he also argues that the recognition by society members that social institutions are unable to limit and deal with environmental and social risks has led to a fundamental questioning of what sort of society we have created. Thus, 'risk society' becomes a self-critical, reflexive society, reflecting on the character of modernity and its ecological and social nature. This has led to ecological questions becoming a focus of political mobilisation and conflict, and ecological problems being seen as originating from the kind of society that now exists.

The role of science in risk society is highly ambiguous. Applied technology is seen as the cause of modern risks, yet the identification of risks is frequently dependent on science to offer either a solution to these risks or a specification of an 'acceptable level' of risk. Beck argues that in this context, scientists themselves tend to become self-critical, and this, along with many other factors, has contributed to the growth and mobilisation of environmental movements, or what Beck calls, sub-politics. Moreover, there are two further responses to risk. One is the establishment of centralised state agencies to take responsibility for curtailing environmental degradation; the second is the establishment of green business and the promotion of green consumption. Together these form ecological modernisation policies, which will be discussed in Chapter 6.

The risk society thesis is relevant to a discussion of scientific discourses for two particular reasons. Firstly, in the risk society, the place of knowledge is elevated. Many environmental hazards are knowable only through information and awareness, not through our bodily senses (Beck 1992: 73); and some of the greatest risks in today's society are associated directly with our bodies in the sense that we feel endangered by what we take in through eating, drinking, inhaling, touching, etc. The invisibility of the risks we face leads to our suspecting everything we consume. We cannot, for example, detect the level of radiation present in the water we drink, nor tell if the food we eat has been genetically modified or chemically sprayed. We are thus forced to trust 'experts' to judge what is safe (Halkier 2001: 801; Schifferstein et al. 1998: 120).

Secondly, science and expertise are seen as part of the set of modern institutions, such as contemporary industry and government, accused of undermining health and safety and exposing people to so many risks, and thereby undermining trust. However, the need for scientific input into seeking solutions is recognised. Paradoxically, then, science is seen as both part of the problem and part of the solution.

The increasing questioning of science is but a part of what some social theorists see as a movement from modernity to post- or second modernity, or to use Beck's earlier term, 'risk society'. Tovey (2002) has raised the question of the extent to which, in Ireland, we have made this move from development as 'progress', with its relatively unquestioned belief in science as a major instrument in this developmental project, to risk society. The latter society is characterised by the perception of the environmentally destructive nature of 'progress' and a questioning of the scientific and technocratic knowledge on which it is based. Bauman has further characterised this move as 'a shift from certainty to ambivalence – from legislated orthodoxy to the relativism of multiple interpretation – across a wide set of cultural spheres, including those of aesthetics and of morality' (quoted in Tovey 2002: 27).

Tovey argues, drawing on the example of the response to the outbreak of foot-and-mouth disease in Ireland and across Europe in 2001, that the ready acceptance of the policy of 'aggressive strategic slaughter' (to quote the Minister for Agriculture) of some 55,000 animals in Ireland (not to mention the 4.5 million adult animals in Britain), as well as the public's ready compliance with the limitation placed on their right to movement, indicated that the Irish state, scientists and the public in Ireland have not moved to a post-modernist perspective of ambivalence and a questioning of the role of science. Rather, as a policy, it 'reconfirmed technocratic models of expertise' without 'any sustained public debate about the causes of the epidemic or the appropriate way to manage it' (Tovey 2002: 26). A major reason for this, she argues, was the desire to protect the interests of the food industry, while also reconfirming its attitude to animals as disposable objects.

However, the findings of the research project outlined in this book indicate that unquestioning belief in science cannot always be assumed. There was evidence among the focus groups of a considerable ambivalence towards science and its role in environmental issues, especially those issues based at the local level. Beck's 1990s risk society thesis and his discussion of the public's environmental concerns focused on potential catastrophic events such as global warming and the collapse of biodiversity, and the global growth of nuclear energy and GM crops, for which citizens must rely almost totally on scientific knowledge. These were not the major environmental concerns of the Irish focus group participants who spontaneously raised issues that were much closer to home: waste, landfills, incineration and dumping, litter and plastic bags; water pollution; and road building.

While the commitment to continued economic growth and 'progress' remained steadfast among the focus groups, as will be seen in the next chapter, there was also a questioning of science. This questioning, as noted by Beck, among others, is related to an increasing recognition that science is not context- or value-free, that it does not offer purely objective knowledge, and that it is influenced by the 'interest-constituted attitude' of the knower, which is itself influenced by such social and economic factors as funding bodies, science–industry linkages and indeed by science itself as a social institution (see Lash 2000, Latour 1987). This is also the perspective of the sociology of science (Irwin and Wynne 1996; Irwin and Michael 2003) and of Wynne's research in particular, from the 1980s to the present (see, for example, Wynne 1996, and Wynne et al. 2000), which has made connections between the sociology of science and the sociology of the environment.

Drawing on empirical research, Wynne (1996a) argues that criticism of science arises from the lay public's increasing recognition that the findings of scientific knowledge are limited by the context (usually the laboratory) in which they are established, and furthermore, that the interests of those who fund the research and apply the findings can bias the way these findings are presented to the public and used to legitimate decision-making, for example, in the areas of industrial or farming production or regulatory action. Much of the lay, or non-scientific, public's knowledge and judgement regarding risks is based on their own local, everyday experiences and what they perceive as 'common-sense knowledge'. The argument here is not that the lay public dismiss scientific knowledge altogether, on the contrary, they may seek scientific knowledge to bolster their own environmental case, but they also feel that the facts can be manipulated by those in power against their local interests and own common-sense knowledge.

Thus, there are two components to a discussion on scientific discourse. Firstly, there is the use of scientific language or paradigms to describe or explain and, secondly, there is the use of science as the basis for decision-making. This chapter will examine both, with the latter the more pervasive theme articulated by the focus groups. The role of science, and other forms of technical expertise, is at the centre of many environmental issues and is also a key component of the politics of environmental issues, local development, and broader questions of decision-making and democracy. Beyond specific talk in scientific terms, this data set included considerably more talk about these wider environmental and political issues, and the place of science and expertise in them. These elements were often very revealing of attitudes towards environmental politics and its place in wider political questions. Before these issues can be discussed more fully, however, it is necessary to first consider what are claimed to be the special characteristics of scientific knowledge and expertise as compared to other possible inputs or approaches.

Scientific Knowledge and the Lay Public
It is clear that science holds a special place in decision-making about environmental questions. A number of factors have contributed to this, including science's role in alerting society to environmental problems and providing a language in which to discuss them (Macnaghten and Urry 1998: 50). It is often assumed, perhaps particularly by environmental regulators, that scientists are the most appropriate people to solve the problems associated with the environment.

What is scientific knowledge? The core claims are for its independence and purity in finding the 'truth', and for its ability to disconnect from local specifics, to be universal, generalisable, and hence to 'travel', i.e. to be similarly applicable in many different places. According to Clarke and Murdoch (1997: 42, 43), it is the ability to travel and act over distance that defines scientific knowledge and gives it its power.

The role of sociology is to recognise that there are different systems of knowledge at work in society, and to step outside them in order to describe and analyse their dynamics. If a system of knowledge can offer the attributes of independence and an ability to apply solutions found in one place to many other situations, then its attractiveness in solving societal problems is clear.

However, these claimed attributes are not universally accepted at face value. Researchers in the sociology of scientific knowledge have amassed considerable evidence to show that the accumulation of scientific knowledge is no different from any other human endeavour in being subject to many social and political influences (see, for example, Knorr-Cetina 1981; Knorr-Cetina and Mulkay 1983; Latour 1987).

In terms of generalisation and non-local specifics, the characteristic of treating all situations as the same is a key theme in both criticisms of science as well as its defence. Forcing laboratory conditions on real-world situations and a refusal to take account of local conditions or local knowledge are seen by many as weaknesses in the scientific approach, especially when applied to environmental problems at the local level.

An illustration of this tension can be seen in Wynne's (1996a) research into the effects of nuclear fallout in the aftermath of the Chernobyl accident on sheep farmers in Cumbria in mid-1986. In the aftermath of the Chernobyl accident, windborne radioactive matter fell on the uplands of Cumbria. The effects of this fallout on the sheep in the area were immediately played down by scientists and politicians, but restrictions on movement and slaughtering of livestock were nonetheless imposed. In order to establish the effects of the fallout, scientists conducted experiments which the farmers correctly predicted from the beginning wouldn't work because of false assumptions. The farmers came to understand how poor science could be because of its failure to adapt to local circumstances (Wynne 1996a):

> What was not lost on the farmers ... was that the scientists had made unqualified reassuring assertions that had been proven mistaken, and [they had] not even admitted making a serious mistake. Their exaggerated sense of certainty and arrogance was a major factor in undermining the scientists' credibility with the farmers.

While the farmers' prior attitudes to science and experts are not known, it is clear that by the end of the process there was a complete absence of trust and confidence. From their perspective, the farmers were essentially told that their own knowledge of the situation was of no value, and they had to do what they were told by the 'experts', even though the farmers could clearly see the failings of these experts.

Local knowledge often clashes with scientific perspectives in this way. Burgess et al. (2000) conducted research in the UK using a focus group methodology to examine how the universalistic perspective of professional conservationists (including scientists) was perceived and questioned by farmers drawing on more local perspectives. The research also explored how the conservationists perceived farmers. Farmers were perceived as being 'non-scientific', their knowledge of nature being based on the specifically local and particular. This type of knowledge questioned the assumptions of conservationists, their more generalised knowledge, and their institutionalised power.

Burgess et al. (2000) also discuss some of the policy dimensions of local perceptions in their study of farmers. Here, farmers' attitudes were again contrasted with those of the conservationists (the 'experts'). The debate between the two groups was over the most effective way of managing the land. The farmers, who had specifically local knowledge and understanding of the environment based on their experiences of farming, saw themselves as being good managers of the land and wildlife (Burgess et al. 2000: 9). This view was supported by the fact that none of the farmers had to significantly change their farming practice after the conservationists had carried out their study. However, conservationists saw themselves as the experts, and were backed up by administrative power and the ability to demand changes in farming practices.

The local basis of the lay public's environmental knowledge and judgements has also been highlighted in research into their perceptions of 'dirty industries', such as chemical factories situated in their neighbourhoods (Walker et al. 1998). This research indicated that perceptions of risks were influenced by one's social relationships in the community and also by more general views about the government, factories or business in general. Thus, although 'experts' may make claims regarding the safety or risk associated with such enterprises, people form their own judgements about them according to other criteria, particularly their local knowledge and relationships. This highlights a very important point, that the generalised nature of science also devalues sensory experience – abstract facts are more valued than personal experience. To scientists, this is the strength of the paradigm, but to many others it is the core failing. This, as will be seen, is a very common theme in people's discussions about risk, the environment and scientific knowledge.

A report by Wynne et al. (2000), *Scientists Reflect on Science: How Scientists Encounter the Environment-Risk Policy Domain*, examines the views of British scientists. This report documented scientists' awareness of their lack of knowledge of how the general public perceives their work, and also revealed a lack of motivation on the part of scientists to open up such a dialogue or a lack of understanding of how this might be done (Wynne et al. 2000: 20, 22, 25). It highlighted the 'public deficit' model of science, whereby the public are seen by scientists as lacking the necessary understanding to fully contribute to these kinds of debates (see also Owens 2000). It also noted their uncertainty and the difficulties they felt in bridging the gap between the scientific institution and society, but suggested that many of the constraints were more at the level of the scientific and other institutions within which, or for which, they worked, rather than under the control of individual scientists.

Divisions between types of knowledge also pervade environmentalism itself. As already noted regarding environmental mobilisation in Ireland in the 1980s and early 1990s, Tovey (1993) has argued that there was a distinction between two broad types of environmentalism: the more urban-based, top-down, expert-oriented type as against the more rural, local version, which was often connected to farming issues or emerged in response to particular local environmental conflicts, such as pollution. The former was immersed in scientific discourse, the latter, while not exactly in opposition to it, was much more ambivalent towards it.

In these discussions, there is a difficulty with the language of 'facts', 'truth' and other such terms. This will be seen in particular when the topic is how to get at the 'truth' and the place of science in this, as discussed by the focus groups. Across the data set, for any given environmental issue or debate, discussions revealed a strong desire to get to the 'truth' of the situation and to allow this truth to arbitrate on the necessary response. It was clear from the data that people did believe in 'facts' and 'truth', but that they did not necessarily see these as emanating just from scientific knowledge processes, or from the proclamations of scientific experts. Most saw a place for local input, the weighing up of contextual factors, and the negotiation of outcomes. It is in this light that scientific knowledge seemed inflexible and dictatorial. It has become common, for instance, to hear calls for a more 'democratic' form of science in many environmental and knowledge disputes, such as that over genetically modified foods (GMOs). Proponents of scientific knowledge in its pure form would see such changes as corrupting and undermining the core value of the scientific paradigm. On the other hand, as will be seen from the data set, many 'lay' people see a more democratic or consultative form of scientific knowledge as the missing piece of the puzzle that would make science meaningful to the issues that concern them.

Whose Interest?

Experiences such as those of the British farmers mentioned above have had a knock-on effect on how the public treats claims by experts. As well as objections to the claims of generalised truth, research within both the sociology of science and the sociology of the environment has found that there is much scepticism among lay people about the supposed absolute and independent nature of such knowledge. To many, science is not seen as being objective, but instead heavily influenced by other bodies, particularly government and business, which fund the research. Research on public attitudes towards GMOs in the UK, for example, has found that the technology is widely seen in terms of 'patterns of oligopolistic ownership, technological opaqueness, and potentially irretrievable side effects and unknowns' (Grove-White et al. 2000: 7). There is an increased questioning of the motivations for undertaking scientific research, and of those funding it, with a related ambivalence about the findings of such research. Focus group research indicates that the central questions asked are: 'For whose benefit is the research?' and 'Should it be trusted?' A view frequently expressed is that the force driving society is commercial profit – a force that overrides the health or environmental concerns of the population and the public's own needs and views (Marris et al. 2001). The important point is that people ask broader questions than simply 'Is it safe?'

Discussions with scientists also indicate their own lack of clarity or agreement about where the research should be directed and by whom:

> In many cases there exists a pervasive ambiguity as to where scientists' responsibilities lie (e.g. are financial imperatives more important than knowledge-based imperatives for conducting more research?) ... Scientists are unclear whether the research agenda is, or should be, science-driven, user-driven, industry-driven, policy-driven, budget-driven. (Wynne et al. 2000: 25)

In addition to this, there is evidence to suggest that scientists in Britain are encouraged by funding bodies, particularly those in the policy area, to make definitive statements where, scientifically, uncertainty exists (Wynne et al. 2000: 12). This may result in certainties being disseminated to the public, with the resulting erosion in trust documented below.

Trust

UK focus group research indicates that the privileging of scientific knowledge in decision-making has resulted in greater scepticism and mistrust towards it (Marris et al. 2001 and Wynne 1996a). People question scientific knowledge, drawing on their own context-dependent knowledge and on their previous and negative experiences of the large institutions of industry, business and government which sponsor scientific knowledge. This is true particularly in relation to public perceptions of risk.

Recent examples include the issues of BSE (bovine spongiform encephalopathy) and GMOs. Reilly (1999) examined the British public's understanding of BSE in 1993, following the initial crisis of 1990, when the government (and by extension scientists) had claimed that there was no risk. This was then followed up with further research in 1996, following the CJD (Creutzfeldt-Jakob disease, human-variant BSE) announcement. She found that people were comfortable with the notion of uncertainty, indeed that they routinely live with uncertainty, risk and unknowns (Reilly 1999: 135). The scientific claims of certainty had in fact undermined the public's trust in the experts.

Trust in science also relates to the phenomenon of people feeling disempowered by its elevation in decision-making. The use of scientific discourse in an exclusionary way has often been seen as a way – deliberate or otherwise – of excluding non-elite groups from decision-making.

There is a body of research in Ireland documenting how people have felt sidelined in decision-making by the power given to science and scientific experts. Both Keohane (1998) and Taylor (1999) have analysed the first ever oral hearing by the EPA on an integrated pollution control (IPC) licence, held in 1996 in relation to the proposed development of a toxic waste incinerator at a pharmaceutical plant, Roche Ireland Limited, in County Clare. Locals had reacted angrily to the company's proposal to install the incinerator, and the issue was characterised by controversy long before the oral hearing was announced. The hearing itself was procedural and quite legalistic in format; one person presided as chair, recorder and decision-maker, and each 'side' presented its 'case' in turn. Only agreed representatives could speak, along with the 'witnesses' called. The dominant discourse was that of scientific evidence and technical solutions. While this may have been appropriate for the subject of the discussion, the local protesting communities saw it as exclusionary and found it difficult to participate.

Both Keohane (1998) and Taylor (1999) make similar observations as to the shortcomings of the process from the local community's perspective. The most important of these were the community's negative perception of the professionalism of the procedure and the seriousness with which the issue was being treated; the dominance of technical discourse to the exclusion of other discourses and actors; the limited breadth of discussion allowed (failing to discuss the company's poor compliance record in other countries, for example); and the lack of transparency regarding the basis for decision-making. The discourse of the hearing may have been entirely appropriate for the issue being discussed, but expectations of a wider debate had been created, and were left unfulfilled.

Similar experiences are reported by Peace (1993) in his analysis of a famous An Bord Pleanála oral hearing into the proposed Merrell Dow Pharmaceutical Development in County Cork in 1988. Again, taking a local community perspective, people came to the hearing with a range of issues to discuss, but found the inspector drawing a sharp line between what he defined as 'facts' as against 'opinion', and ruling out much that they wanted to discuss about their sense of community, what they wanted for their area, and their 'gut feelings' against the development. Instead, the language was scientific, and the focus was on what would minimise (not eliminate) pollution from this proposed factory. Thus, community representatives found themselves in the midst of negotiations about compromises on factory design that would reduce negative impacts. In this context their 'no factory under any circumstances' line was seen as a radical, intransigent position, and they found themselves marginalised. Local community members came away feeling that they had been defeated by narrow procedure and clever, manipulative opponents, and that science had been the instrument of this manipulation.

Interestingly, an almost identical experience was discussed in one of the focus groups conducted for this research project. One participant had participated in, and observed, an oral hearing of a planning appeal, and his reactions have remarkable resonance with the above cases:

> *The set-up is completely against local people. For example, An Bord Pleanála, you cannot put in concerns for health – which seems crazy. You can ... I actually went over and gave a presentation and they said 'What are you going to talk about?' and I said 'I am going to talk about ethics', and they said 'There's no place here for ethics', and I said 'Could you minute that please?'. Anyway, the man in charge of that particular ... he actually ... although he's an engineer himself and pro-incineration said 'This is not the place for it', ... so there's a feeling, and it would be mine, that the EPA and An Bord Pleanála have been set up as quangos and that they are basically pushing through ideas from government, particularly the PD [Progressive Democrat] side of government ...*
>
> Returned missionaries

It is important to remember in this regard that this kind of experience represents what Giddens calls 'access points' between the public and powerful institutions, where people acquire their experiences of expertise and experts. He notes that 'attitudes of trust, or lack of trust, towards specific abstract systems are liable to be strongly influenced by experiences at access points' (Giddens 1990: 90). In other words, the small number of direct experiences that people have with expert institutions influences their perceptions of, and level of trust in, these institutions and the wider system for a long time.

None of this is to suggest that there is no place for scientific analysis in such processes and indeed it may well be the case that it is correct and necessary to prioritise expert inputs over more general inputs. It is probably fair to say, however, that if a balance is sought between expert inputs regarding technical information and scientific solutions and local inputs on contexts, priorities and values, it is often not achieved, and local knowledge is often inadequately regarded. In addition, the above discussion illustrates that when different discourses meet and one is given ascendancy over others, there are risks of unmet expectations and of damaged trust. If people feel they are being manipulated – with expertise being used as the tool of this manipulation – relationships are damaged and the legitimacy and credibility of both the powerful institutions involved and the scientific discourse itself are lost.

This overview of the issues relating to scientific discourse and its place in environmental matters looked at what it means to speak in terms of science itself, but, more importantly, at discussions about the place of scientific thinking in addressing environmental problems and related questions. Scientific thinking, and scientific and other technical experts, tend to hold dominant positions in the analysis of environmental problems and in decisions about their resolution. This obviously recognises the central place of science in such questions, but does not address concerns relating to the limitations of a scientific analysis which fails to take account of local context, priorities and values. The dominance of science in such discussions also risks the exclusion of other discourses and, hence, the many people who wish to include these discourses. It seems clear that trust in expertise is not what the experts feel it should be, and that the simple model of independent and 'certain' expert analyses informing decision-making is not an accurate reflection of what actually happens.

This is the context for an analysis of how these themes were discussed among the focus group participants. Aspects of these themes came up frequently in every group, illustrating their centrality to the questions of environmental concern and appropriate responses. The following sections detail the patterns of these conversations and discuss what they illustrate about attitudes towards the place of science, its role in environmental debates, and the connections made between these themes and wider issues of power, trust and democracy.

Scientific Discourse Themes Articulated by the Focus Groups

The literature review on scientific knowledge would suggest that an idealised version of scientific knowledge is characterised by the use of very scientific language to describe nature, by the perception that science offers solutions to environmental problems, and by a belief in science as truth or absolute knowledge. While none of the focus groups articulated a scientific discourse in these ideal terms, some groups did tend to use scientific language more frequently than others. This was especially so for two of the mobilised groups – the anti-incinerator group, and to a lesser extent, the Cork Environmental Forum (CEF) – and the dairy farmers. It would appear that the mobilised groups, especially the anti-incinerator group, worked in an atmosphere where they felt the need to establish their knowledge credentials. It is relevant to note that the anti-incinerator group pointed out a specific experience they had had in interactions with other expert groups: *'They thought we were a shower of fools.'* The following is an example of how strong their own use of scientific terms is:

> – *But it's a scientific fact that dioxins are poisonous to human beings, that is known to man, and yet they bring out these laws, the EPA and people like them, to allow, okay a fraction of one per cent or whatever is safe, but no particle of it is safe, they just bring out the regulations to allow the industry to operate,* [saying] *'We will allow this much into the air.' But really ... they are poisonous, none of them should be allowed into the air.*

Anti-incinerator group

This is a particularly interesting quote in the light of Beck's discussion of differences between local groups who perceive themselves to be at the receiving end of pollution and science-informed regulators, who attempt to establish 'acceptable levels of risks'. Beck notes the difference between what he calls scientific and social rationality in the definition and acceptance of risks, and that it is in this definition that *'the sciences' monopoly on rationality is broken'* (Beck 1992: 30, italics in original). Regarding nuclear facilities, he notes that while scientists work within a framework of a quantifiable and mathematically established probability of an accident occurring and the technical manageability of such, for the general population a mathematical calculation means little if life or health is at risk. Thus the two groups talk past each other.

In the focus group discussions, scientific themes were likely to be referred to both in relation to the identification of an environmental problem and in relation to a proposed solution. An example is the CEF's discussion of a group's efforts to get an area designated as a Special Area of Conservation:

> 1   *It's a wooded laked area on the Lee and it contains areas of primeval oak forest, so it's actually a biogenetic reserve. They hope that when and if we start rebuilding the biodiversity of Ireland,* [the biodiversity will spread from there] *because it's got unpolluted biogenetic material ... there was a biologist and an ecologist involved in the environmental group and they just started writing letters to everybody about it and got some scientists interested from all round ...*

CEF

The CEF also noted the time voluntarily given by locally based scientists and how they linked up with international specialists. In relation to one environmental group (CHASE), which was exploring alternative ways of dealing with toxic waste and had brought over an internationally respected scientist from the Massachusetts Institute of Technology, they had '... *pooled their resources with his on a voluntary basis to go around the pharmaceutical companies in Cork and see how they can reduce their toxic outputs'* (7).

Dairy farmers also drew on science to offer potential solutions to environmental problems:

> – *Like it has been proven that if you run waste or soiled water from farmyards through a reed-bed system, a properly constructed reed-bed system, that the actual reed beds will filter the nutrients from the water and what you get at the end of it is a drinkable product.*
>
> Dairy farmers

The focus groups of environmental scientists and managers were the other two groups most likely to use scientific language, usually acknowledging both the wider organisational and political definition of the environmental problem as well as the need to try to resolve the environmental problem itself. The environmental managers spoke of putting stringent regulations in place regarding local river pollution by both farmers and industry, and linked this to concerns about global water resources:

> 3 *... and when you look at it ... of all the water that's in the world there's only actually 3 per cent of it that isn't salt water and of that 3 per cent there's only something like another 3 per cent that is actually available for drinking water, so I mean the amount of water, even though we think we've loads of water, the amount that's available to the world on an international basis is extremely small, and we're continuing to pollute rivers on a constant basis ... It just has to be addressed, because without water we will die and it's as simple as that, it is an issue that's becoming more and more important.*
>
> Environmental managers

Environmental scientists noted regarding the pollution:

> – *I think the major pollution issue ... would be ... the one in the rivers and lakes; this phenomenon of eutrophication, which is excess growth of plants in rivers and lakes due to discharges of phosphorus and nitrogen from sewage, animal waste, that type of thing, that seems to be the biggest pollution problem.*
>
> Environmental scientists

The recognition that science's perceived role was to explore and explain the reasons why certain natural phenomena existed, and could thus offer 'proof' and 'the truth', was widely articulated across the data set. For example, the commuters noted:

8   *I think there used to be a lot of cancer kind of scare-mongering, and I think people don't take that as seriously any more.*
F   *Why not?*
8   *Well, because it's probably been proved not to be so serious like, you know.*

Commuters

The implications of scientific knowledge were likewise acknowledged. In the following example, dairy farmers discussed the scientific claim regarding the dispersion of dioxins over a radius of thirty kilometres, and the consequences for them of the nearby siting of an incinerator:

8   *Yeah … like the dioxins … [given] off when you have incineration, I think there was a figure bandied out that it could travel up to thirty kilometres, or something in that region, if we were to fall within that radius it would certainly concern us. And like there was a statement made there at one stage that down the road, like if this was to happen, if there were dioxins in the milk, a lot of milk could be rejected from farms, say within a thirty kilometre radius of the incinerator. So that would impact on my livelihood.*

Dairy farmers

The common underlying theme here was that facts about the natural world can be explored, explained and proven by science and thus truth established. On the other hand, there was also plenty of scepticism about the use of science and expertise to resolve or close issues, which will be discussed in more detail below. However, in general, it seemed that in this scepticism people were not questioning the possibility of the 'truth' and definitive answers, but rather highlighting the possibility of abuse in establishing or using scientific truth, thereby diverting attention from the 'right' answers.

In this context dairy farmers criticised what they perceived as the biased nature of a scientific study into the well-known case where the illness of a farmer's animals was attributed by many to emissions from a local factory:

5   *And they are blaming the aluminium plant at Aughinish … and they have fair proof that it's Aughinish, but they are getting no backing …*
2   *Because you have to have money. There is a reason why they are getting no backing …*

5 *But the EPA brought out a report on it and blamed the farmer for it, and it cost three million pounds ...*

6 *The EPA spent three million ...*

2 *Whoever had the most money wins. You have to take on the authority; you have to pay money to take on the authority.*

Dairy farmers

As can be seen in the above discussion, the processes of decision-making were seen as politicised and money-driven, but the possibility of establishing the 'real' proof was itself not questioned. This contextualising of how science and expertise were used by power holders was the predominant perspective on science among the general public groups, the mobilised and the farmers; it was also frequently acknowledged by the scientific groups themselves.

Other Scientific Discourse Themes

Science and expertise featured in many discussions within the focus groups, including discussions about how environmental risks are assessed, how priorities are established, and how decisions are made and who makes them. From these discussions a number of key themes emerged regarding what people said about expertise and its role in environmentalism.

A widely discussed theme, one at the centre of all the discussions on the role of science, was an exploration of the role of science in the making of environmental decisions. The dominant role of science in decision-making was more often challenged than supported, and even scientific, regulatory and business focus groups were quick to acknowledge that decisions should be, and probably most often were, made on wider bases. An important part of this challenge to the dominance of science among the general public, farmers and activists was a rejection of its value in determining issues where 'common sense', personal sensory experience, or local knowledge were seen as equally, if not more, valuable.

As well as quite subtle arguments about these various types of knowledge and their value, many groups were also quick to articulate the distinction between how science is claimed to be used or might ideally be used and what actually happens in practice. There was considerable scepticism among environmental activists, farmers and the general public about what was perceived as the misuse of science, whether in terms of questioning the independence of experts and their inputs or suggesting that scientific argument was often used as a smokescreen for other decision-making bases. One place where such scepticism was to the fore was in reactions to the two scientific discourse statements read to the groups to prompt discussion (see p. 130).

One discourse theme that was in many ways the converse of all of these themes, and one of the few places where science was strongly supported, was what the literature refers to as a discourse of 'public deficit' among scientists and policymakers. In this discourse, experts see science as perhaps the most important source of environmental knowledge on which to base environmental policy and behavioural decisions and are critical of the general public in their ignorance about what are seen as the 'true facts' of a given case. Since scientific and policy institutions are often accused of such ways of thinking and talking, both in the literature and by focus group members, it is of value to examine this new data set for instances of this discourse theme and its context and usage.

Science, Local Knowledge and Decision-Making
At the heart of most scientific discourse is the debate about whether science alone should be the basis for making decisions about environmental issues. The perception of many in the general public, farmer and activist focus groups was that scientific thinking dominated such decision-making to the exclusion of other important considerations. It is useful to consider this issue by looking in the first instance at the ways in which people rejected scientific claims when they arose. When science as a basis for decision-making was discussed, there were two principal ways in which people challenged it. One argued that science contributed to the making of bad decisions (because it is too rigid, too general, etc.), another that, although decisions were purportedly based on science, other influences dominated.

Regarding the first challenge, when focus group participants suggested that science makes bad decisions, they were usually either talking about its inflexibility and detachment (from the local context), or they were specifically stating a preference for the local or the sensory. One example of criticism regarding the inflexibility or generality of science was voiced by the dairy farmers:

5 *You see you have bureaucrats, they fail to realise that actually farmers are probably the most educated environmentalists in the world. You know, we have to work with the weather, the elements … You know, there are times when you don't use nitrogen, you are dealing with ground temperatures and all that.*
– *You know there is a lot, it's a wide science, and basically what you have is, you have bureaucrats trying to cram it down on paper, you do this on this day and you do that on that day.*

Dairy farmers

However, environmental scientists were aware of the difficulty of generalising from particular instances and tests. With reference to attempts to introduce nutrient-management planning into farming, especially given concerns regarding the (over)use of slurry, they noted:

7 *... it depends on the P concentration, Morgan's P* [6] *concentration in the soil and if they are deficient in P or if they have assimilated capacity they can take it but it's a question of where the P test is being done and then follow-up measures for that and you won't always know the slurry is going to be delivered and how it's going to be applied, etc.*
2 *Oh yeah, it's a very difficult area.*

Environmental scientists

The difficulties of controlling what actually happens at the local level were thus recognised by environmental scientists themselves: *'We can give a licence based on what* [applicants] *submit in terms of a land bank, but in the long-term it's very difficult for us to control what they actually do use ...'* (5). They also noted the farming practices that contributed to the overuse of slurry:

7 *It can be done very well. Why it's not being done very well is usually down to a few very small factors or a few small reasons. One is that the farmer's tank fills up so he has to get rid of it anyway, regardless of whether the conditions are ideal or not. Two, they get a sub-contractor in to do it who is paid on a per load basis, so he's going to spray it out at the most convenient place for him. So these* [are the reasons] *why* [the farmer] *may not be adhering to the best environmental practice and it goes on like that. The problem is that a lot of the slurry disposal is seen as a waste disposal rather than a nutrient application; throw it in there, Boss, like.*

Environmental scientists

A further instance of a preference for those with local knowledge and expertise was reported by teachers:

3 *We've an expert coming to the school now on Monday and he does the schools in* [name of local area, his name and reference to the fact that he was not a qualified scientist] *... He's the expert and since he's arriving in the school for the last number of years, all the so-called experts have bowed to his expertise. He's an invaluable resource.*

---

6 Morgan's Phosphorus Test – soil test

4   *Because he's out there and his head is inside of the burrows and inside of the nests. He is really into nature.*

7   *And is an expert ...*

3   *In a nice way – as opposed to say the stereotypical eco-warrior. I suppose we can trust ... I don't know, he's nice and he's trustable and he's local and all that. He doesn't have a mission or an agenda besides honest care for the environment.*

Teachers

Here the word 'expert' was used several times to reinforce the contrast between local knowledge and outsiders. Here the 'expert' is the insider.

Many among the general public and mobilised groups noted the importance of local knowledge; indeed it was one of the most common themes in the discussion of science in the data. However, environmental scientists also acknowledged the importance of local contextual factors, which influenced, for example, agricultural practices, although not necessarily the validity of local knowledge *per se*.

Regarding the second common challenge to science in decision-making – that science was being used merely as a cover for other less justifiable decision-making grounds – this was voiced by activists, farmers and some of the general public groups. When focus groups rejected the place of science in decision-making, it was often the case that they questioned whether those in powerful positions who claimed to make science-based decisions were not in fact simply using science to justify themselves. This suggestion, made frequently throughout the data set, was that 'the powers that be' made decisions for self-interested reasons and then sought to argue that the decisions were the result of scientific analysis. In other words, science (and expertise) was part of a 'conspiracy of elites'.

A common argument in this context was that it all came down to money. However, it was interesting that this was often articulated by environmental scientists and regulators as well as other groups. Participants in the DoE group commented in relation to the economic value of environmental protection and eco-tourism:

'Yeah, there has to be self-interest, but I think that I'd be inclined to very much agree with [participant's name] *comments, ok, there are consequences of it, but profit is the end product'* (4).

There was also the acknowledgement that scientists might support either side in an environmental conflict, thus offering environmental protestors support and ammunition. Regarding the safety of incineration, the shop workers stated:

7 *... like the incinerator thing, like, sure* [the government] *are trying to prove that* [incineration is safe] *and they have their facts and everything, but it's the government, you know, don't believe them ... whereas, like, the local people and the scientists have their information but they are saying, no, it's not safe.*

F *Do you see the scientists on the side of the locals?*

7 *Yeah, a lot of them are, yeah, it's the government that are corrupt because* [they] *can invest and make so much turnover on it.*

3 *Scientists are looking more towards the environment.*

7 *Yeah, they are not looking at the money side of it.*

Shop workers

As noted above, despite the wide range of objections by locally based groups to the place of science in decision-making, it seemed to be very much the case that the objections were to how science was actually being used, not to how it theoretically could be used. There was a rejection of what were perceived as current models of the use of science and expertise in decision-making, especially decisions taken by those who resided outside the local area and imposed upon it, but not of the existence of facts themselves. The scepticism was about current ways of getting to the facts rather than whether such facts could ever be reached. For instance, when the retired group objected to bureaucracy and difficulty in accessing information, they still referred to the *'true facts'*, which they had difficulty sourcing: *'The big thing about it is, where do you go to find out all these things? You go to some people and they just keep pawning you on, "That's not my thing, it's so and so down in the next office", or whatever. It's very hard to get the true facts off people'* (5).

In the light of research on scientists in Britain, as reviewed at the beginning of the chapter, it is of particular interest to note the extent to which Irish scientists and regulators recognised and articulated how local dynamics contribute to problems in establishing 'the facts' on the ground. They were also aware of the difficulties in monitoring the enforcement of environmental regulations at the local level, and the underpinning of environmental protection and related scientific investigations of it, by economic motives. It is difficult to know if Irish scientists are more reflective than the existing research literature on British scientists might suggest, or if both are now more reflective than the literature has recognised.

Common Sense and Personal Experience

Participants often rejected science as a basis for decision-making because they gave priority to their own sensory and long-term experiences, or to what they called 'common sense':

4   *Now I'm not saying that locals always do know best but I have seen,*
     in the area where I teach, for example, the County Council developed
     a road through a bog and a very uneducated elderly man said at the
     time, 'It's madness what they are doing – that road is going to sink.'
     Now that man hardly saw out primary school and within fifteen years
     of his prediction, the road sank. So you know, there is a lot of
     common sense ...

                                                                    Teachers

Likewise, the shop workers criticised decisions regarding pollution made
by experts who did not live in the area: *'Yeah, and like the people that live*
near it, they are the ones that have to put up with the smell from it every
day, but experts don't have to put up with it, so what do they know?'
    The general public, the mobilised groups and the farmers looked first to
their own experiences or those of local peers in deciding about an issue,
and, in comparison, the abstract nature of science was seen as a drawback.
One teacher expressed this when asked who she might trust on such issues,
saying *'but I suppose it is first-hand experience of your own environment*
that you would be, I suppose, the expert on really'. Similarly, one member
of the returned missionaries' group rejected the suggestion in one of the
discourse statements that responses might be postponed until there was a
better understanding of the issues, arguing for more immediate action: *'I*
mean you can see things about the environment and just things you can do
... like today, you don't need any study.'
    An interesting example of the use of common sense that, paradoxically,
turned into a call for scientific investigation, came from the anti-
incinerator group. They pointed out that if environmental scientists visited
what they saw as their already polluted local area, they would find, in every
second home:

6   *... somebody with some kind of sickness, like diabetes after coming in*
     [name of local area] *recently. Now it mightn't have anything to do with*
     it, but you would love to do a survey like that and see. There's a lot of
     people, young people, after dying with cancer down our road, you
     know, maybe it's nothing to do [with it] *but you would love to sort it out.*
                                                          Anti-incinerator group

This was one of the most common themes in the data set relating to
scientific discourse: the comparison of expert, abstract scientific views
with local knowledge, said to be rooted in either common sense or
personal, sensory experiences. The following are further examples:

6   *I would say in general the farmers are the most, are the best keepers of the environment ... They are more conscious of what damage can be done and you farm, you can't damage your own land because you are depending on your land to live off, it costs you.*

Dairy farmers

3   *You know I think it is important – that there is a lot of expertise in local areas and you can't ... dismiss that with the people who are being ... have only just looked at it one day and said 'this is what should be done'.*

Teachers

These quotes also illustrate the perception of expert knowledge as dictatorial, trying to impose itself in situations where people feel it is inappropriate. There was also a strong discourse of travel in the talk: expert knowledge travels from somewhere else (often Dublin) to try to dominate in 'our' locality.

This sense of science imposing itself from elsewhere paralleled the very common view that political decisions were generally made too remotely from the local context. It was also linked to the contrasting of local understanding and intelligence with outside inflexible bureaucratic thinking that does not travel or adapt well:

3   *I mean there are a lot of scientific experts that are just sent different places and doing different tests and everything like that, but they wouldn't have been living there for a number of years or something, so they don't actually really know what a thing is like or how a thing affects different things. 'Cause they have only been doing tests or carrying out small studies and stuff like that.*

Shop workers

It was illuminating to compare some of the general views on asthma, a topic of discussion in many groups, with expert versions. The general views were:

1   *There are so many people now suffering from asthma and bronchial-type stuff that never did before.*

Young mothers

2   *It does, you know, if you're walking through town now, if I was shopping like that, I'd have to stop and use the inhaler.*

Travellers

5   *Just the pollution, smog and the bi-product of smog that causes*
    asthma and stuff. There are a lot of diseases that weren't particularly
    prominent before and now everyone is allergic to something and
    loads of people have asthma.

Students 2

Environmental scientists were more circumspect about the evidence,
saying that: *'There may or may not be a gradual increase in asthma*
incidents, it's very difficult to pin it down with the statistics and the
reporting, we really don't have figures to make the same kind of concrete
statement about air quality and the effect on health' (8).

Scepticism about the Misuse of Science
As seen already, the themes of trust and mistrust were very prominent in
discussions of science and expertise. Most people seemed to take for
granted an attitude of mistrust of 'the powers that be'. Science and
expertise were usually seen as part of this system and hence as part of the
domination and manipulation processes.

A common view existed that science was often used as a smokescreen
to legitimise decisions made for less meritorious reasons, producing
considerable cynicism:

4   *You can distort figures to suit your own advantage …*
–   *Twist and manipulate them.*
F   *Who does the distorting?*
4   *Whoever is making a buck.*

Dairy farmers

There was, however, an important recognition by some groups of the
difficulty in establishing 'cut and dried' facts about particular issues.
Already noted above were the shop workers' recognition that scientists
often worked on behalf of environmental activist groups, and in the chapter
on radical political discourses (Chapter 3), the recognition by consultant
engineers that these activist groups used science to promote their own
interests, often, in the engineers' eyes, 'misrepresenting' the facts. Also
quoted above was the environmental scientists' recognition of the difficulty
of making 'concrete statements' about asthma. On the same theme, the
teachers commented:

6   *I suppose some issues are fairly clear-cut and some aren't. I mean,*
    oftentimes we'll say like the North Sea issue which I know nothing
    about, the scientific case isn't always very clear-cut. I mean, people

*who have loads of money can generate research ... to prove their
point and I mean you really don't know what to believe. So it's not
always issues of ... very cut and dry.*

Teachers

While many were cynical about how science is used, it should be noted that
faith in the role of such knowledge in theory usually remained. The general
impression was that the facts were obtainable; it was just that the processes
were open to manipulation.

This theme of vested interests, corruption and greed was very common.
Another dairy farmer, when discussing a local authority's lack of interest
in a particular reed-bed technology for waste disposal, even though he
claimed its efficacy was well-proven, explained its opposition away as,
*'They must have a vested interest why they won't allow it, allow these reed
beds'* (5). In another group, a young mother equated such vested interests
with wider political cynicism, stating of politicians, *'They all have one
thing on their mind, the money and they want to be voted in, the power'* (7).

This cynicism was widespread:

3 *That goes back to the government, they don't follow up anything.*
9 *They don't follow up.*
3 *All they want is to have tribunals about discussing this person and
  that person; they don't care what is happening to anybody else. They
  are robbing everybody.*

Unemployed

7 *So I don't know if that sort of protest* [environmental protest
  regarding the building of roads] *works anymore. Especially when
  there's a lot of money to be made in roads and re-zoning lands and
  there's a lot of power.*

Commuters

Once again, connections were made between decision-making, the
deployment of knowledge, and wider politics, issues which will be further
addressed in the chapter on environmental regulatory discourses (Chapter 6).

Responses to the Scientific Discourse Statement: the
Discourse of Cynicism

Very similar themes arose in response to the two scientific statements.
Because of this, the discussion below is brief. The two statements read:

- Sometimes you just have to accept what scientific experts say about an environmental problem. But sometimes, for example, if it is a local environmental issue, local people may know as much or more about it than the experts do.
- Before doing anything we should be sure we know everything about the problem. We need more facts and figures.

Regarding the first statement – the need, on occasions, to accept scientific knowledge – there was some reluctant support, especially regarding issues for which no direct sensory experience was available. The commuters noted: *'I mean if you are talking about the ozone layer or something like that, there's no way you'll have knowledge about that so you just have to take the evidence that's given ...'* (7).

However, as might be expected from the analysis of spontaneous discussions outlined above, the statements generated further discussion related to cynicism about experts' trustworthiness and a preference for local knowledge or sensory judgements. Regarding the first statement it was noted:

7   *It's like someone telling you, 'Well I know that I have had a problem for the last ten years because somebody has been throwing this onto my land,* [and] *the government saying well that is not possible because A + B = C', and that is the way it is, and that is the way it has always been.*

–   *But the farmer down the road knows, I know my cows are dying, like that man that took the case, he knew there was something wrong and nobody was believing him.*

Anti-incinerator group

The case referred to in the anti-incinerators' quote was most probably that of a Tipperary farmer who pursued a local factory for damages in relation to sick animals on his farm, claiming that emissions from the factory were the cause. This and one or two other high-profile cases were the subject of several references across the groups – already quoted from the dairy farmers above.

For the second statement, rejection was also often related to cynicism, such as:

–   *I would see it* [the statement] *as something that could be said* [by someone when] *they realise they are after making an unmerciful boo-boo and then they come along and use this bland stuff, we need more facts and figures to find out what the problem actually is.*

- *And they are fobbing you off like.*
- *A con job.*

Dairy farmers

There were also some challenges to the second statement on the issue of waiting for more information before taking action, such as the following spontaneous articulation of what is known as 'the precautionary principle' within a sustainable development discourse. The DoE participants noted, *'You should take a precautionary approach without necessarily having absolute scientific evidence of the effects'* (5).

Overall then, the pro-science aspects of the statements tended to be criticised, accused of being nothing more than excuses for inaction, or being used strategically to justify business as usual. This pattern confirmed the earlier finding of a link between attitudes about the role of science and wider socio-political views – those who were cynical about centralised power and decision-making tended to see expertise as part of the same powerful manipulation process. Furthermore, those who felt that decisions were being made too far from their specific circumstances (probably the majority view), saw the remote, abstract nature of science as part of the problem.

Public Deficit Discourse Articulated by Experts

One particular discourse, which was only articulated by the regulatory, scientific and business groups, related to how they saw the wider population. Such groups are often accused of holding a poor opinion of the wider public, perceiving them as ill-informed or reactionary. This is often referred to as the discourse of 'public deficit', and was mentioned earlier in the chapter in relation to Wynne et al. (2000) on how scientists perceive the general public. An example of this discourse can be seen in the following extract from environmental scientists:

3   *I think it causes more hysteria when* [the public] *see a stack* [factory chimney]. *When you see pollution in a river you can see what's happening and you know what's happening, whereas a stack you just see it going into the air and dispersing and you don't know, the average person doesn't know what's happening, they just perceive chemicals coming out of this facility or whatever. I think that causes people to panic a bit more and to be a bit more wary about things like that, whereas they may not be all that interested in whether the local river has got a little bit more algae in it. They're far more interested in the fact that you know there's a stack that may or may not have chemicals coming out of it or whatever.*

Environmental scientists

It was, however, the consultant engineers who spent most time discussing the issue of the public as a 'problem', as they saw it, when they objected to large building or infrastructural projects. The tenor of the conversation was that many such objections were spurious or even mendacious, and invariably based on ignorance or self-interest. The lengthy interchange on the topic quoted below ended with the point, also made by members of the environmental scientists' and DoE groups, that the general public did not take responsibility for their own environmental impacts:

6   *Also, they don't see themselves as part of the problem, if you take waste, they'll object to something to do with waste or something to do with electricity.*
–   *Yeah*
5   *But they're using energy, but they don't see that ... It's a real us and them.*
1   *They don't make that connection.*
5   *Yeah, it's their problem and it's ...*
6   *They're contributing, everybody contributes in some way.*
–   *Yeah.*
6   *Through the waste or the energy use ... Yeah, but they don't see that when they make the objection.*
5   *They don't see that.*
      ...
6   *They just see this monster coming but don't make any connection with their own personal lifestyle or their community.*

Consultant engineers

However, some within this group also spoke with empathy regarding the environmental problems faced by some of the general public, although still within a public deficit model:

2   *This is not being ... I'm not saying this from my work point of view, it's just an observation I'm making. I think that this Rio convention that we're meant to be actively sustainable so we need to take a social and environmental and economic viewpoint and the big thing about that is consultation and I think, historically, that there's not really been consultation, it's just giving out information and I feel sorry sometimes and I know somebody who had a landfill was going to be put next to them, and I felt sorry, they were just a local person who had no background in, technical background, did not really know what they were up against in terms of the information that they'd need to know and I felt very sorry for them. You know, I felt*

more sympathy for them than I did for the consultant who was preparing the report and because, unlike what you said there about them thinking that they're not part of the problem, they understood that they're part of the problem but they'd see the government as not doing anything, not providing any recycling facilities, not doing enough so as this problem doesn't arise in the first place, and they would love to be part of the solution but they don't want a landfill next door to them. I felt very sorry for them, and it has educated me more than any ten years' or twenty years' working.

Consultant engineers

It is interesting to note the speaker in this last extract challenged the dominant view in the group that people do not make connections between their own behaviour and its environmental consequences, but still did so very much within the public deficit paradigm, expressing regret about people's ignorance of the technical information.

Although there were examples of regulators, scientists and business groups describing people in the language of public deficit, it was by no means the dominant discourse in the data set, and indeed there were many examples of experts expressing considerable empathy with, and understanding of, the frustrations and concerns of communities affected by their policies and actions.

Conclusion: Science, Trust and Cynicism in the Construction of Environmental Realities

Views on science and expertise tended to be part of a wider discourse based on the polarities of distant versus local, abstract versus sensory, and power versus disempowerment.

How power was conceived and constructed was a strong theme. Most of the general public, farmer and activist groups considered themselves to be subject to some degree of domination, or at least manipulation, from 'the powers that be', generally defined as a conglomerate of politicians, business interests and experts. Science was perceived, in the main, as part of the power structure, a tool of spin and domination, and experts were associated with government and business as the dominators.

The position of scientists was, for the general public, part of a construction of 'they' or 'them' – the outsider, the powerful, the remote, and the interloper. They were not seen as independent (*'Well, who is paying the experts?'* Commuters 7), but as part of a state/big business group, a conspiracy almost, which used scientific findings and consultants' reports as tools for getting their own way.

This created a sense of need for self-reliance, where the 'outsiders' were, at best, no help and, at worst, to be resisted and opposed. The opposite to 'them' was both the 'I' of personal senses and experiences, smelling odours, knowing the area, or seeing 'how things really are', and the 'we' of the local community. The general public invariably trusted their own personal senses and experiences (the 'I') more than the pronouncements of others, particularly scientists and experts from outside the locality.

This unfavourable contrast between the scientific take on an issue and their own local knowledge, sensual experience or common sense also affected the public's views on wider environmental risks. It is quite difficult to characterise the paths by which particular issues become popular concerns, but in general, the general public tended to think about local, quality-of-life issues much more than abstract, global concerns. This possibly means that a global problem may only become of salient concern to citizens when it actually becomes local – when people are told that they are at a direct risk from something, such as toxins in food, emissions in the air, or unwelcome local development. Science as the purveyor of knowledge from a distance compared weakly with people's trust in their own judgement based on local knowledge and their own senses. Science alone will find it difficult to raise awareness regarding climate change or provide solace regarding GM crops. It is particularly hampered by the view that it can only play a role in finding solutions when its manipulation by outside forces is ended.

The scientists, regulators and business groups acknowledged the role of science, but also recognised its contextual rather than universal or absolute nature. They also recognised the broader context, rather than the purely scientific one, in which environmental decisions were made. Nonetheless, environmental scientists and engineers also felt that environmental groups used scientific knowledge in their own interest, rather than adhering to 'the scientific facts', and shifted the grounds of their complaint when it suited them. The general public was also seen as, at times, lacking in environmental knowledge, as well as being willing to act in an environmentally irresponsible way – an accusation which these 'expert' groups also levelled at themselves.

It seems quite possible that 'expert groups' do not acknowledge the conditional and limited nature of their knowledge when it is in direct conflict with that of local groups and when other interests are involved and are being protected. It is possible that a focus group setting of discussion with one's peers provides a sufficiently secure social context for weaknesses in one's own 'expert' arguments to be declared. It also indicates the possible capacity and cognitive basis for moving beyond an adversarial 'them' and 'us' situation in future discussions with local groups and for seeking sufficiently acceptable or compromise solutions regarding difficult and conflictual environmental issues.

It should also be noted that mediating between the theme of scepticism articulated by the general public groups and the farmers on the one hand, and the theme of the public's knowledge deficit, as articulated by the scientists and technical experts, on the other, was a recognition by some on both sides of the difficulty faced by science in offering definitive 'cut and dried' findings and solutions, and that, furthermore, scientists could be found on both sides of environmental debates. This bridging of an absolute 'them' and 'us' divide would appear to offer grounds for further discussion and understanding but, undoubtedly, the different power positions, especially the perceived power of those at the centre, and how the centre operates, would need to be acknowledged and opened up to discussion if a *modus operandi* is to be found.

To conclude, virtually no one, not even among the expert scientific groups, spoke about the environment in a purely scientific way. Even those who used scientific language or seemed to process their views in scientific terms almost always spoke of it within a broader social and political context. In particular, talk about science and expertise and their place in environmental debates was connected to questions of trust, power, and concepts of 'them and us', local versus distant, lay versus expert.

Trust in scientific expertise was generally quite low among the general population. People saw experts as biased in favour of their paymasters, with science used as a tool of domination for reasons of profit or control. This theme of domination resonated particularly with the image of outsiders imposing solutions on local communities, without either local knowledge or interest in local values and concerns. In the context of this constructed contrast between local and elsewhere, the importance to people of their own personal experiences in forming their positions cannot be underestimated. This orientation also influenced which issues were of most concern to most people, i.e. those of a local or personal nature.

However, the data clearly suggested that this pervasive cynicism about expertise, as it was currently seen to be employed, did not for the most part equate to scepticism about the possibilities of scientific input into issues of concern. People sought a system in which scientific knowledge is balanced with appropriate local inputs of knowledge, context and values, thus acknowledging a potentially strong role for science, once current patterns of misuse were addressed. The general public, as well as scientists and regulators, seemed to believe that the facts were out there to be found, and saw a place for science in this. But two things would have to happen if a new way forward is to be found: the addition of local, negotiated inputs and the removal of corrupting, interest-driven distortions and abuses. This opens up many difficult questions, ranging from the epistemological to the political and institutional. The extent to which this critique was carried over into regulatory discourses is one of the main themes of the next chapter.

6

Regulatory Discourse: Economic Growth and Environmental Protection

Introduction

A regulatory discourse regarding the appropriate role of the state in mediating between rapid economic growth and its negative environmental consequences was the most predominant of the five environmental discourses spontaneously articulated by the focus groups. Two major regulatory themes were raised. Both are central to a sustainable development or ecological modernisation discourse. The first related to how best to align economic and environmental goals, and the role of the state and environmental policy in this alignment. The second and related theme was a discourse on the implementation of environmental regulation in Ireland, the difficulties involved in this, and its democratic responsiveness – or not – to local concerns.

Both of these themes, as discussed by the focus groups, were strongly embedded in broader socio-cultural and political discourses regarding democracy on the one hand, and, on the other, the extent of participants' support for the project of modernity, in which modernity is seen as synonymous with 'progress' and economic growth. Group participants in their discussions also drew on personal experiences of the environmental regulatory regime in Ireland. These experiences were based on either occupational position – especially important for regulators, private business groups and farmers – or participants' everyday local experiences of what was seen as a necessary but highly imperfect environmental regulatory regime. It was seen as imperfect both in its inadequate delivery of a service and in terms of its democratic deficit and marginalisation of local voices. These latter themes were particularly important for farmers, active environmental groups and the general public.

Ecological Modernisation – the Alignment of Economic and Environmental Goals
In Ireland, the high-profile local environmental protests of the 1980s, frequently regarding the siting of industrial facilities, contributed to two

trends in the 1990s and into the new century. One was a significant increase in awareness, talk and policy initiatives on environmental issues. A second was a move, especially at a policy level, from a perspective that placed the protection of the environment in opposition to economic development, to one in which 'sustainable development' was promoted.

In the international sphere, sustainable development as a discourse has been articulated and promoted by the UN in its Agenda 21 and conventions on climate change and biological diversity, and by the EU in its translation of these policies into firm commitments. In Ireland, sustainable development as a policy theme grew strongly in the 1990s, culminating with the publication in 1997 of *Sustainable Development – A Strategy for Ireland* (DoE 1997), plus a range of other policies that drew heavily on the language of sustainable development, including the *National Climate Change Strategy* (2000), the *Green Paper on Sustainable Energy* (1999), *The Planning and Development Act* (2000), and several others. Even policies with much less direct environmental connections, such as *The Programme for Prosperity and Fairness* (2000), made significant mention of sustainable development, though whether these sorts of references are substantially more than rhetoric is a matter of debate.

The political and institutional changes or modernisation required to promote the sustainable development agenda are frequently termed 'ecological modernisation'. This is a reformist, regulatory discourse that emphasises scientifically developed technologies, managerial controls and the modernisation of state and economic institutions in order to protect the environment, while still maintaining economic growth. It subscribes strongly to a proposed synergy between environmental protection and economic development, and the positive-sum game this is assumed to offer all social groups. This is to be achieved through stringent government environmental policies which ensure that the environment is no longer considered as 'external' to economic growth, but given detailed consideration in decisions regarding economic development through, for example, the undertaking of adequate Environmental Impact Assessments before committing to major projects and product development. Pollution is seen as a matter of inefficiency. Environmental controls on pollution are seen as encouraging technical innovation and the diffusion of new, cleaner technologies (clean cars, safe incinerators, green energy) and, if pollution continues, the polluter pays. Environmental Impact Assessment (EIA), Integrated Pollution Prevention and Control (IPPC), and the Rural Environmental Protection Scheme (REPS) are all core policy elements of the ecological modernisation approach in the EU and in Ireland. Furthermore, the general population as a whole must be mobilised to pro-environmental action, especially in its waste and consumer practices. The paradigm is reforming but not radically so. It does not fundamentally challenge current political and economic institutions, but calls for their modernisation and adaptation to new priorities through integration and realignment. (For examples of sociological discussions of ecological modernisation, see Hajer 1995, 1996 and Spaargaren et al. 2002.)

The three strands of the ecological modernisation paradigm are environmental protection as efficiency, with economic growth and environmental goals aligned; environmental management as a technical project, with technical expertise at the centre of most solutions; and recognition of the economic opportunities created by environmental protection, through both enhanced efficiencies and new business growth areas, e.g. in waste management. All of these themes can be seen in the Irish political and institutional response to the environmental imperatives of the 1990s. The policy document on the subject, *Sustainable Development – A Strategy for Ireland* (DoE 1997: Foreword), states:

> Continued economic growth is essential to meet people's legitimate ambitions for a better life and to provide the resources for implementing environmental protection measures. But we should not tolerate development that is inefficient, that is excessive in its consumption of natural resources or that unduly pressurises the environment.

Many researchers examining other economically developed societies as well as Ireland have argued strongly that, despite four decades of environmental protest regarding what are seen as the destructive forces of economic growth and development, the modernist project of equating societal 'progress' with economic growth continues. They would argue that the sustainability and ecomodernist policies which have incorporated some of the more moderate goals of environmental protection have in fact contributed to weakening the critique of modernity and its prioritisation of economic growth. This critique, offered by environmentalists in the 1960s through to the 1980s, strongly criticised industrialisation, continuing economic growth and the exploitative and environmentally destructive practices on which, they would argue, it is based. However in the 1990s environmentalism as a social movement became less radical, as its goals were co-opted and weakened in the process of the development of government environmental policies. Noting this pattern, de Paiva Duarte (2001: 105–6) concludes:

> Mainstream environmentalists of the 'New Millennium' no longer propose to 'save the planet' for its own sake, but tend to share the policy-maker's preoccupation with the rational management of the Earth's

resources for economic development. As a growing number of nations adopt economic rationalist policies in order to survive in an increasingly globalized economy, ecocentric globality is marginalized, as it is perceived by the guardians of the status quo as a threat to economic 'development'. Saving the planet for its own sake implies heavy regulation of and restrictions on the activities of corporations, which is anathema to the current climate of economic rationalism, where 'the market' determines outcomes … [This pattern] illustrates the resilience of the modernist project of progress-as-affluence, and the significant effects it continues to have on social behaviour.

Aspects of a radical social and environmental critique have been picked up again by the anti-globalisation movement. The generally negative response among focus group participants to this narrative has already been examined in Chapter 3.

In Ireland, Skillington (1997, 1998) has examined the way in which environmental discourses have been marginalised by the predominance of an 'economics-centred', pro-growth perspective, even when the environment itself was the apparent issue. In her examination of the discourses and storylines articulated during the Irish National Recycling Conference, 1993, which hosted most major stakeholders, as well as in her study of the reporting in the *Irish Times* of transportation and urban re-development issues between 1991 and 1995, she found that the master frame of economic growth continued 'to enjoy a pervasive degree of cultural and social anchorage' (1998: 461). The predominance of this frame led to the failure of more radical voices to gain media coverage, while, during the conference, the alignment of policy actors and business interests marginalised environmental groups. She also notes (1998: 466–67) that even oppositional actors 'did not subject the philosophy of development and growth embodied in modernity's dominant cultural code to an ecological critique'. Indeed, she argues, the construction of the nation as a whole was expressed predominantly through an economics-centred frame.

Peillon (2002) has also argued that the Irish state's historical role of promoting and animating economic growth has continued and indeed strengthened in the 'new' economy of the 1990s and into the new millennium. This economy includes not only industry and agriculture but a services sector which has experienced phenomenal growth and employment creation in the 1990s, so that the current Irish economy might be characterised as 'post-industrial'. In this new economy the state nonetheless continues to define economic growth as its highest priority, to define the national interest in terms of promoting Irish and transnational firms, to incorporate the potential dissent of oppositional economic forces such as the trade unions through its neo-corporatist policies, while at the same time dissolving the boundaries between the state and the business class. He further argues that the state has successfully colonised previously relatively autonomous cultural spheres such as education. Its capitalist project has also been strengthened by the weakening of institutional sources which might have offered a significant cultural critique, such as the Catholic Church and those offering a nationalist cultural perspective. Lacking organised sources to articulate a critique, Peillon argues that 'the negative has buried itself deep into the fabric of Irish society', expressing itself in 'sceptical and possibly cynical distance', in subdued and uncommitted forms which do not appeal to broader values and principles, and 'an individualised sense of welfare and, possibly, a pleasure-seeking orientation that introduces a wedge between the individual and society' (2002: 53). Glimpses of these themes have already been in evidence in previous chapters, especially Chapters 2 and 5, which examined moral and scientific discourses.

Regarding the relationship between economic growth and the protection of the environment, the questions which were asked in relation to the focus group data collected for this project included: In what terms did the participants discuss the possible alignment of economic and environmental goals? Was there evidence of a movement towards decreasing the prioritisation of economic goals, given increasing economic wealth since the 1990s? Was environmental management seen as a way of mediating between the economic and environmental priorities raised and discussed? Were there differences in perspectives on this central issue between policymakers, business groups, farmers, mobilised environmental groups and the general public? What do the discourses articulated on this theme tell us about reflexivity in Irish society, that is, to what extent did discussions on these issues articulate a concern regarding the future direction of Irish society?

Ecological Democracy – the Environmental Regulatory Regime and Civil Society

A second major theme articulated by the focus groups was in relation to environmental policy formulation and particularly implementation. Many participants perceived these as weak and as lacking democratic responsiveness to local concerns. With a view to understanding the context in which these discussions took place, some relevant aspects of the governance structures within which environmental policies are formulated and implemented in Ireland will be reviewed briefly below, as will the role of democracy in the broader sustainable development project. Also discussed briefly will be the strength of support for democracy within Irish political culture, a theme drawn upon by both the mobilised and general public groups to criticise what they saw as state ineptitude in listening and responding to the concerns of civil society.

Some researchers argue that ecological modernisation offers a weak model of sustainable development. A more robust model, it is argued, is offered when ecological modernisation is extended to include ecological democracy. Ecological democracy takes seriously the role of civil society in the drive towards greater sustainability and argues for the need to modernise political institutions if sustainability is to be delivered. Such institutions are characterised by a greater emphasis on partnership, with stakeholders and citizens involved in both policymaking and implementation. They require greater openness, transparency and a willingness to involve other interested groups in environmental policymaking and implementation. The goal of these processes is what is sometimes referred to as discursive democracy, characterised by the existence of healthy *public spaces* for discussion and debate, where consensus, or at least acknowledgement of the reasonableness of differences, is built over time through accessible and transparent interchanges. Ultimately, policymakers and institutions retain legitimacy by being seen to be responsive to these debates, acknowledging the expressed preferences of the active public. Comparative studies indicate that the form of state practices most conducive to the development of sustainable development are those that are democratic and participative, including some forms of corporatist, partnership or stakeholder arrangements between, for example, the state, economic, local and environmental interests (see Jänicke 1996, Dryzek et al. 2003, and Meadowcroft 2004).

In his study of twenty-four environmental policy 'success stories' Jänicke notes in particular the importance of modernising state institutions, meaning a move from public institutions characterised by a closed culture to institutions committed to freedom of information and public access. Such institutions are also characterised by intra-policy co-ordination in the environmental policy sectors, as well as inter-policy co-ordination between environmental and other policy areas (Jänicke 1996: 76). They actively include economic and environmental interest groups in policy discussions and policymaking. There is also a mechanism for including these groups in longer-term planning. Facilitating the work of such institutions is a consensus-oriented political culture rather than an adversarial one, a co-operative and flexible planning style and a shared language or paradigm regarding both environmental issues and policy practices. Jänicke (1996: 83) concludes that '… the more ambitious goals of sustainable development (as enunciated, for example, in the Rio

Declaration and Agenda 21) can only succeed if the capacities for communication, bargaining and learning are further expanded.'

While emphasising the importance of participatory democracy at national and local levels if sustainable development is to be achieved, the role of central state institutions remains crucial. As Meadowcroft (2004: 186–7) concludes:

> ... the extension of participation does not mean that the role of government is in any sense diminished. On the contrary, governance for sustainable development depends first and foremost on active *governments* that place this goal at the centre of the political agenda; clearly define the substantive orientation of environmental policy; and establish legal and organisational frameworks to facilitate appropriate participation. In this context, the basic institutions of political rule – including elections, the party system, and the hierarchy of decisional bodies with the constitutionally and traditionally defined separation of powers – remain essential for deciding just what sustainable development implies.

Whether Irish state institutions have the will and capacity to take sustainable development seriously and facilitate democratic forms of participation remains an open question. Researchers have noted that, while at the national level, environmental legislation may be passed in response to, for example, EU Directives, actual implementation tends to be weaker, in response to particular business, agricultural or local authority agendas (see Flynn 2003; Taylor 2001, Taylor and Horan 2001, Boyle 2002). Furthermore, they would argue, particular groups, such as business and agricultural interests, frequently have strong links to other government departments, so that a co-ordinated push at state level to deliver robust policies of environmental protection does not exist. In the Department of the Environment itself, as Flynn (2003: 139) notes, there exists 'only a small dedicated environment policy bureau' and indeed the 'regulatory enforcement capacity of the Irish State appears essentially weak'. Within the neo-corporatist institutions or 'social partners' of employers, unions, farmers and the community and voluntary sector, which exist at national level and where environmentalists are not represented, economic development is prioritised over the environment, reaffirming the agenda of business and pro-economic growth groups.

Boyle (2002), in his examination of the role of the state in formulating waste management policies in Ireland between 1996 and 2001, argues that these policies are further evidence of the Irish state functioning as a 'flexible developmentalist state'. Such a state is characterised by strong alignments with national and international economic interests and by policies that prioritise economic growth and the maintenance of profitability. Required by the EU to initiate a more rigorous waste-policy regime, the Irish government instituted a regional waste-management policy which not only decreased the role and influence of local authorities and hence local democratic voices regarding appropriate methods of waste disposal, but also attempted to distance the central government from decisions regarding the highly contentious siting of incinerators and 'super-dumps'. The proposed new Planning and Development (Strategic Infrastructure) Bill (2006) is further evidence that central government is attempting to override local protests regarding large infrastructural projects to ensure that its national economic agenda is fulfilled.

Regarding the role of elected local authorities, Lafferty (2001), concluding a comparative analysis of the implementation of Local Agenda 21 (i.e. local sustainable development policies) in European states in the 1990s, argues that local authority autonomy, in terms of both finance and local environmental policy implementation, is an important structural feature conducive to the formation of partnerships and sustainable development. Regarding Ireland, he states that hindrance to the implementation of Agenda 21 'arises because of a strong tradition of local dependency, originally with respect to the national government, but more recently vis-à-vis the EU' (Lafferty 2001: 289, see also Mullally 2001). He also notes that this lack of local independence and firm financial footing in local authorities within what he calls the Anglo-Irish tradition is increasing (Lafferty 2001: 273) and has 'resisted the general European trend of increased administrative independence in recent years' (Lafferty 2001: 274). Lafferty concludes that 'by most indications ... high autonomy in local authorities, coupled with a history of environmental concerns and actions, provides a solid base for LA21 involvement' (Lafferty 2001: 245). While by 2003, one-third of Irish local authorities had adopted a Local Agenda 21 plan, there is as yet little sign of a strong institutionalisation of sustainable development policies (see Motherway 2002).

As with Local Agenda 21 plans, there are signs of attempts to increase local involvement through the establishment of locally based partnerships, such as City/County Development Boards (CDBs) and local authority Strategic Policy Committees (SPCs), where strategic thinking is encouraged within forums that include community representatives as well as locally elected and executive officials. The jury is out as to how representative these may be or to what extent they may facilitate discursive democracy (see Motherway 2002: 3; Broderick 1999).

Payne and Stafford (2004: 4) in their analysis of two urban regeneration case studies in Dublin in the late 1980s and 1990s note that they excluded local authority representation and were established by the Department of the Taoiseach and reported to that Department:

> The case studies ably illustrate the curious clash between Ireland's traditional centralised, hierarchical and clientelistic political culture and the growing call for greater participation at all levels of the political process in Ireland. However, instead of strengthening the existing local authority structures, new institutional bodies or quangos are established which report to a central government Department … The selected representation of interests is defended as being derived from shared interdependencies around the specific project, rather than the formal requirements of institutional representation. The research suggests an emergent model of partnership around urban regeneration, which is driven by informal, networked participation rather than rigorous democratic accountability.

They note in particular that such partnerships can sideline local authorities, and do not tend to alleviate the broader problem of 'enhancing the resources, management capacity and policy remit of democratically elected local government' (Payne and Stafford 2004: 31).

Thus governance structures related to environmental and development issues in Ireland are characterised by a lack of clarity and by contradictory tendencies, between, for example, the roles of central government, local government, and regional planning areas; and between an emphasis on partnership and stakeholder involvement on the one hand and top-down direction on the other. A further layer in this governance structure is the EU.

While the establishment of area-based partnerships has been influenced by the political agenda of the European Commission, which has strongly supported a multi-level system of partnership-based governance under the Reform of the Structural Funds, the EU has also been important in instituting and supporting top-down discourses regarding the environment, in particular a discourse which sees the rural as an environmental problem to be managed through environmental regulations. The EU has been a central force influencing environmental policies and practices through its Common Agricultural Policies (CAP) and, more recently, through its monetary support for the Rural Environmental Protection Scheme (REPS).

The introduction of the REPS has been studied sociologically by Tovey (1996, 1998) as an example of ecological modernisation and as a top-down discourse. She argues that from the 1950s to the 1980s a coalition of the state, agri-business, agricultural scientists, large farmers and, from the 1970s, the EU through the CAP, upheld a productivist and developmentalist definition of agriculture and of the rural society in which it was based. In the 1990s, however, a coalition of the EU, the Department of the Environment, tourist interests, conservation environmental groups, as well as urban-based 'experts', contributed to redefining the rural as an environmental problem to be managed.

The REPS was introduced in 1995 to encourage farmers to switch from intensive to extensive farming. Intensive farming, based on chemical and technological inputs, it was argued, lowered the quality of the rural environment (by, for example, the overgrazing of fragile environments by sheep), led to a lack of attention to pollution by agricultural wastes, and lowered the quality of food through the overuse of pesticides and chemicals. In the REPS, farmers contract with the Department of Agriculture, for a cash payment, to farm in an environmentally sensitive manner, to reduce pesticide and fertiliser use, and to preserve and protect natural features and those of historical or archaeological interest. Additional funding is available to farmers whose land is in a Natural Heritage Area or Special Area of Conservation (SAC), where farmers are required to draw up acceptable plans regarding conservation, environmental protection and stocking regimes. Thus the rural is defined by state agencies both in terms of a countryside characterised by sustainable agricultural development and as 'natural heritage' open to the tourist gaze, with the farmer as its managing guardian.

As in ecomodernisation policies in general, the REPS is perceived as a positive-sum game for farmers and the environment. Two-fifths of all farmers, mainly in the small-farm areas of the West and Northwest, have joined up. Remaining outside, however, are large-scale farmers and agri-business, with the result that intensive production, which is responsible for most farm output, continues. The REPS is a centralised and bureaucratic scheme, with little evidence, Tovey (1997) argues, that it encourages reflexive thinking about either agricultural production or consumption generally. Nor does it encourage social change. In contrast, the organic farming movement, at least for some, is characterised by strong locally based discourses and a questioning of the effects of intensive production on both human society and the natural world.

The redefinition by central government institutions of the rural as 'natural heritage' in need of conservation became increasingly prevalent in the 1990s, frequently under pressure from EU directives. Possibly the most controversial of the EU's environmental policies has been the 1992 Habitats Directive regarding the designation of SACs. Ireland was not alone in failing to meet its deadline in designating these sites. As Laffan and O'Mahony (2004: 13) note in their study of the transposition and implementation of this top-down directive in Ireland, it marked 'a decisive shift for the conservation authorities from protecting wild life and fauna on state owned property to demanding habitat protection from private owners', and hence contributed to potential conflict with landowners. They examine the strong politicisation of the issue as farmers sought compensation, mobilised at the local level, and lobbied the national government; while conservation NGOs groups, which, in Ireland, are limited in both membership size and financial resources, sought assurance, especially from the EU, that the directive would not be watered down. Local authorities and An Bord Pleanála, the researchers note, 'found themselves in a difficult position as they were the bodies nominated to protect designated SAC sites in the planning process and were at the same time under considerable pressure to facilitate economic and rural development' (Laffan and O'Mahony 2004: 33). Thus the government itself was under pressure to revisit the implementation measures.

However, despite top-down attempts to redefine the local, or more likely perhaps, because of them, the local in Ireland has frequently been the site of environmental protest and mobilisation. The mobilisation of groups and citizens regarding environmental concerns is central to an ecological democracy perspective. Here a central question is, what is the role of civil society and environmental movements, especially in relation to the two powerful poles of state and economic interests, in the formation and implementation of environmental polices and practices? While business associations have tended to be increasingly willing across the EU generally to be involved in the discursive forums required by LA21, this is not the case for labour groups or trade unions (Lafferty 2001: 284). Representatives of environmental movements differ in their willingness to become involved with state and business interests. Some non-governmental environmental organisations may willingly play their part in environmental policy formulation and implementation; others may remain more sceptical of their ability to fundamentally change environmental polices and practices through partnership arrangements with state and business. Research indicates that environmental groups may be con-siderably weakened over time and lose their critical edge through overly intensive 'ecocorporatism', as they become incorporated into policymaking with government and industry, becoming in the process more elitist and losing contact with their grassroots members (see Dryzek et al. 2003). On the other hand, by involvement or partnership with the state they may see the implementation of more pro-environmental policies.

In Ireland, environmental movements have been important in pushing forward the environmental agenda. The anti-toxics environmental projects of the 1970s and 1980s placed environmental issues firmly on the political agenda at a time when Ireland was undergoing state-sponsored dependent industrial development, which encouraged the establishment of large transnational corporations often in rural and small-town areas. These protest movements, which were often locally based but with nationally based networking, contributed to ensuring that Ireland is nuclear-free and, by placing industrially generated toxic pollution on the political agenda, have been credited with contributing to the establishment of the Environmental Protection Agency (EPA) in Ireland, before such institutions were established elsewhere in Europe (Taylor and Horan 2001). It has been argued that the early anti-toxic movement was not only a protest against toxic fumes, but a broader protest against the kind of society that Ireland was becoming, especially a protest against dependent economic development (Baker 1990). The lack of consultation by the state or large businesses regarding the usage of local areas led to considerable local protest in the past and indeed continues to do so – as anti-waste dumps and anti-incinerator protests, among many others, testify. However, Baker noted that the significance of the anti-toxic movement of the 1980s should not be overestimated. It was not always successful; community groups were often divided and the movement failed to win the support of the trade unions.

Tovey (1993), in her analysis of different forms of environmentalism in Ireland in the 1980s and early 1990s, argues that a very different ethos pervaded centralised and often Dublin-based environmental organisations from those at a local level, which were often organised to protest against specific environmental issues. She characterised the centralised groups as often 'expert' oriented and elitist, and their different perspective on environmental issues from those of locally based groups as part of a broader societal conflict over the future direction of Irish society. Most recently, in advance of the Johannesburg World Summit, a group of environmental and community groups came together to produce a publication called *Telling it Like it is* (Earth Summit Ireland, 2002), documenting what they saw as the failures of Irish environmental policy, implementation and enforcement. The core of the argument, presented through a set of case studies highlighting environmental damage or management failure, was that any progress in environmental policy has been both patchy and weakly applied, so that the extent of ongoing damage remains larger than any gains.

Regarding the attitudes of the general public, survey evidence indicates that environmental concerns are increasing among the general population (see Motherway et al. 2003). The increased vote for the Green Party in the 2002 general election, albeit from a very low base, also shows some evidence of this. Patterns of voting indicate that its voter strength lay in its capacity to project itself as an oppositional party with centre-left positioning, and its pragmatic strategy of taking up locally based issues of housing, transport, planning disputes and quality-of-life issues (see Taylor and Flynn 2003).

The core values in a society's political culture will fundamentally influence how the state's environmental regulatory regime is perceived and discussed. A core value in Irish political culture is a commitment to democracy. Coakley (1999: 54) suggests that the strongest evidence for this is the very survival of the democratic institutions created in difficult circumstances in 1922, even during the 1930s when democracies were collapsing elsewhere in Europe. Survey evidence for the 1970s through to the 1990s confirms this commitment. However, trust in parliament and in political parties has declined in the 1990s, to a level relatively similar to the EU generally (Coakley 1999: 56). Survey evidence from the 1990s also shows popular support for government intervention in the economy, and for egalitarian policies regarding the distribution of resources (Coakley 1999: 60–1).

However, other scholars have questioned how well the institutions of the Irish state are serving democracy at the present time. O'Cinnéide (1998: 42) notes that:

> There are three main things wrong with the system: the government and civil service has become too powerful, weakening the role of the Dáil and Seanad; neocorporatism ties in major economic interests with that of the government; and bureaucracies have become less accountable.

As a result, he argues:

> ... a lot of people now feel excluded from the political process and are cynical about the whole system. Divisions between the haves and the have-nots, between city and country, between believers and unbelievers, between those who are 'in' and those who are 'out', are probably widening. Political representation, the bedrock of democracy, is perceived as being biased, corrupt or irrelevant.

Even if trust in democratic institutions has been weakened, the core value, or what some might call the 'meta-discourse', of democracy has remained and can be called upon to criticise and mobilise. Skillington (1998: 462) concludes from her mid-1990s research on the media coverage of transportation policies that, while 'a discourse of environmental protection was conspicuously absent ... the cultural theme of mistrust featured very strongly ... with episodic moments of moral revulsion at establishment practices'. There was also:

... a wider meta-discourse on democracy. The latter was the primary vehicle through which strategic actors revealed the weak institutional basis of a participatory discourse on Dublin transport and government's loose commitments to discursive principles. Several accounts of bureaucratic inertia, blighted administrative procedures and factionalized pursuits of private-interest agendas arose ...

The extent of trust in powerful institutions, the belief that they are acting – or not – in the common interest of all, and belief in the efficiency and honesty of governments will influence willingness to subscribe to the environmental policies and sustainable development practices proposed by the state.

Some of the central themes which arose in the focus groups' discussions on environmental regulations were related to these questions of trust and democracy. This was particularly so for the environmentally mobilised groups but also for some of the general public groups. They raised the question of the relationship between government institutions and major economic interests, the lack of responsiveness to local community interests and the difficulty in having their voice heard. Groups were also eager to discuss the implementation or, more accurately, the lack of implementation and enforcement of environmental regulations, and the negative political and social forces undermining this regulatory project.

Analysis of Focus Group Data

Of the five discourses this research was interested in exploring, the regulatory discourse was the one most frequently and spontaneously articulated by the focus groups. This may be partially due to the way in which the focus groups were introduced to the topic for discussion, which stated, 'This research is part of a research study on environmental attitudes, values and behaviour in Ireland.' It would appear that most participants associated the statement with the regulatory emphasis on the need to protect the environment. If the research team had referred to attitudes to 'nature' instead, a different response might have been elicited, for example, a more romantic discourse. However, the focus groups' emphasis on the regulatory was also undoubtedly due to the public's anger regarding perceived governmental arrogance and weak implementation of environmental policies and a wish to express this.

Much of the focus group discussions and the quotations drawn upon in this chapter were spontaneously articulated. Few new perspectives were brought up in response to the 'regulatory' or 'ecological modernisation' discourse statements. These statements and the groups to whom they were presented are set out in Appendix 1, Table A1.

The structure of the remainder of the chapter reflects the differences in how the five sets of focus groups articulated the two major themes within a regulatory discourse. The next section examines how the regulators perceived and discussed, firstly, the existing alignment of economic and environmental goals, and, secondly, their perspective on the environmental regulatory regime and its democratic responsiveness to civil society. This is followed by a sequential analysis of how each of the other four groupings – business focus groups, the farmers, mobilised groups and the general public – discussed these two themes. As in previous chapters, it is evident that 'the environment' is never discussed as a stand-alone concept; it is always embedded in broader discourses about the nature of Irish society and culture. As Lukács (1971: 234) famously noted, 'Nature is a social category.'

Elaboration of Regulatory Discourse Themes by Regulators

Alignment of Economic and Environmental Goals

The regulators, who included the DoE group, heritage officers and environmental scientists, articulated and supported a strong ecological modernisation discourse, while also clearly recognising the difficulties they faced in implementing such practices. Regarding the policy of sustainable development, the DoE focus group noted its rapid development as a policy in the 1990s and its linking of the economic, the social and the environmental. They pointed to two factors, however, which militated against its easy implementation in Ireland. One was the priority given by the public to continued economic growth, and the second was 'the lack of a strong environmental lobby'. Regarding the former they noted:

2 *It's just that people's priorities are, you know, when the politicians knock on people's doorsteps before the elections, they're not saying, 'I'll vote for you if you clean up the air or reduce noise or whatever.' They're saying, well, 'We want more jobs, we want more schools, we want more houses', this is a problem, people have themselves to blame because the politicians will basically do what the voters want, and we will do what the politicians want, so the only thing is to provide good leadership.*

5 *But I think as policymakers here we have a role to put forward our agenda rather than looking at the end user and saying you should do this, do your bit.*

2 *To provide leadership, yeah, that's right.*

DoE

The demand for further economic growth was reinforced by experiences at local level, especially in disadvantaged rural areas. Here the popular perception of locals was:

3   *... we don't have enough people and [...] we don't have enough development. And I haven't come across yet any real opposition to roads. People want more roads and they want the railway service expanded and they want the towns to get bigger, they want the villages to get bigger. There's this terrible feeling that we* [the local community] *were very much bypassed by the national development plan, so ...* [they are] *still sort of at the development at any cost kind of level, any sort of development.*

Heritage officers

Given that any attempt to limit economic growth was seen as a non-runner, the ecomodernist goals of aligning economic growth and environmental protection through good environmental management and regulation gave the regulators a focus and an agenda. Thus, a strong emphasis was placed on managing the environment. In response to the question, 'Is it possible to have economic progress and protect the environment?' heritage officers replied:

3   *Yeah, in many cases the only way you could protect it would be by managing it.*
F   *And is it possible to have a balance between the two, do you think?*
−   *Yeah.*
−   *Yes.*
−   *Oh yeah, of course it is.*
5   *Yeah, it's called sustainable development! That's what we do all day long.* [laughing]
4   *That's the whole point of the heritage plans.* [laughing]
3   *If you don't protect the environment, ultimately your economic progress will collapse.*
−   *Yeah.*
−   *Yeah.*
−   *It's essential in fact.*

Heritage officers

Heritage officers work directly with local authorities and have immediate contact with those responsible for the implementation and delivery of many environmental services. They recognised the daily impact the practices of local authorities had on heritage and the environment and their role in facilitating the development and implementation of plans that would manage the environment in order to conserve it. They discussed the term 'conserve' rather than 'preserve', noting that, *'conserve means managing in a good way rather than preserve, which means putting a line around it saying, you can't touch this'* (6). They also noted that in the constant and immediate role of local authorities in relation to the environment, the routine possibility of breaching environmental legislation was always present, thus their role in trying to ensure that council workers were not, for example:

5   *... running around milling through hedgerows in the season that you're not allowed cut hedges and all that sort of stuff. I mean the council, because the council, the work of the local authority involves so many different aspects of heritage ... So we have a huge job there to raise awareness and education within the local authority, right down from the man who holds the Stop-Go sign right up to county councillors and the county manager.*

Heritage officers

Environmental Regulatory Regime, Democracy and Civil Society

In relation to establishing a robust environmental regulatory regime, it was not just the general public or local authorities who were seen as posing difficulties, but the lack of co-ordination and commitment among government departments. With regard to developing polices on climate change, it was noted that:

8   *... from an international perspective and the policymakers' perspective, climate change is the major challenge to Ireland at the moment. We're way, way above our binding Kyoto targets ... It's not as tangible as recycling facilities, but it will have a huge impact on the economy trying to reduce emissions and become more eco-efficient to comply with the Kyoto commitments. We're way, way, way above it at the moment and I think from a policymaker's perspective at the international level that's really the major challenge of climate change and to try and engage with the stakeholders who have influence over industry, NGOs, IBEC, people like that, other government departments, the Department of Finance, to get other civil servants to engage or to integrate environment policy into their activities. For example and for instance, in the Department of Agriculture ...*

DoE

They were concerned about the under-resourcing of the DoE and its ongoing marginalisation in favour of other departments:

1   *We never manage to show real clout, either at official level or international level or sort of at political level. Why should the*

environment, why should the Ministry for the Environment be less important than the Ministry for Agriculture? Now don't give me the obvious reason for that because I don't buy it, because the environment is going to be always with us but the agriculture thing is going to contract … But classically in an argument you will find environment losing to agriculture, classically.

– [and to] *energy, transport and finance.*

DoE

Local authorities likewise faced difficulties in implementing environmental legislation:

6   *I think, just coming back to lack of resources, it's not just within the Department, I think the other thing with regard to lack of resources [is at the] local authority level. I mean, we're very quick to blame local authorities for not doing x, y and z or we get a phone call from a member of the public and we say, oh well, the legislation is there but it's the local authority that enforce it. They're in the same boat as well, they're getting more and more responsibilities and tasks to do and not being resourced either, so it's not just to say that we're the only ones that are under-resourced, I think at local level as well.*

DoE

Nonetheless, as might be expected, the lack of implementation and of policing the laws caused considerable frustration:

7   *It's lack of policing, I'd say, that's probably, for me anyway, that's the most frustrating part of it … it's a part of the national psyche … we bring in a law and to hell with it, forget about it, that solves the problem. There's a law there to do that, so therefore that problem doesn't exist anymore. There's no policing of it.*

8   *That's part of what we are …*

Environmental scientists

Difficulties in policing the pollution caused by industries and farming were noted. Regarding the former, environmental scientists felt that negotiation, 'give and take', was often the best policy. Regarding farmers' use of fertilisers, they noted:

7   *That is one of the deficiencies of the current system … that we can't police it, certainly in the agricultural area it's quite apparent that they can do more or less as they want to.*

8   *Is there not a financial constraint? Surely it's costing a fortune for all this fertiliser ... why are they so willing just to throw extra money all over the fields if it's not needed?*
6   *It's not outrageously expensive per acre.*
–   *It's the fear of loss of crop yield.*

Environmental scientists

The nature of Irish political culture, or 'the national psyche' as quoted above, was referred to on a number of occasions by regulators. In particular, the reluctance to address and attempt to resolve our own problems and the expectation that others would do so for us:

1   *Ireland has classically, as a country, avoided decisions in the past, when we had problems with our people we exported our people, when we had difficulties with abortion because of our wonderful Catholic religion, no problem if it happens in England, it didn't happen in Ireland ... We produce 100s of 1000s [tonnes] of hazardous waste, we're happy if somebody else burns it for us. Now the day is coming rapidly where they're going to say, 'To hell with you lot in Ireland, you're producing it, you fix it', and I don't see why we shouldn't fix it ...*

DoE

In its ideal form, ecological modernisation encourages consumers to buy green and mobilises citizens not only to comply with environmental regulations but to actively support them. In the regulators' view, Irish consumers and citizens fell down on both counts. As was analysed in greater detail in Chapter 2, on moral discourses, the public's prioritisation of economic growth above all else was seen as making them 'selfish', and their self-interest had to be appealed to in order for them to willingly comply with environmental regulations; alternatively, they were penalised for non-compliance. Regarding recycling, it was noted:

6   *I suspect there's a sense though that the people who are good are very, very good, the others don't give a stuff. The people who are recycling are probably giving an inordinately large effort, whereas there's lots of people haven't changed their ...*
1   *I think people will only recycle largely if they have to, if there's a penalty for either not doing it or a reward for doing it or both ... That's the position that [exists in] Germany or Austria ... everything, organics and paper get segregated and they get penalised when they don't.*

Environmental scientists

Mobilising voluntary compliance was a major difficulty, especially given the public's scepticism regarding authority figures:

1   *… it's a basic message which has to be got across, that there's not a big issue here, it's not as big as you think. But convincing people is our problem here and I do accept that the voice of authority and indeed officials like ourselves don't wash very often with the general public, I don't know how …*
–   *The great unwashed.*
1   *How we're going to convince them with phosphorus-free detergents as well, by the way, is another story, it's a difficult one, it's going to be just a constant battle …*

DoE

Not only was there a problem with individual compliance, but also with the mobilisation of communities and environmental groups against particular policies, for example, incinerators. The lack of a willingness to take ownership of environmental problems was particularly referred to, and the complaints and mobilisation against incineration were noted:

1   *Down in Ringaskiddy and of course here in Ringsend, they're all campaigning and giving sort of lectures to their TDs. And the state has tried by, for example, giving responsibility to county managers instead of council officials to respond, to make somebody responsible, but ownership is a problem, nobody wants to take ownership of the issue. You can make a difference, I can make a difference, but nobody wants to make a difference because you can throw it in the bin and it's somebody else's problem.*

Environmental scientists

Some of the environmental campaigning and lobbying, as was noted in previous chapters, was seen as both dishonest and as shifting the grounds of the complaint in order to suit the campaigners' own interests:

8   *A lot of the campaigning too is, I think, frankly dishonest, where they start off with, you might say, scientifically difficult areas to pin down, like there may be a dioxin problem or there may not, and when that's dispensed with because of scrubbers and so on, they say, well, there'll be a lot of trucks going down the road so we don't like that either. If you get down to it there are problems, there are lots of problems but the shifting argument makes it very difficult to decide what do you really want to solve, it's very difficult …*

Environmental scientists

Nonetheless, there wasn't a blanket condemnation of environmental NGOs and protest groups. Indeed there was an acknowledgement of the need for protest in order to move environmental issues up the political agenda.

The attitude of the public to paying for environmental services, which was regarded as a government tax rather than payment for an environmental service, was perceived by the regulators as strongly negative:

4   *... there's going to be a lot more obligation on people to actually pay for things, I mean, the issues of, say, even just paying for your own water and paying waste charges is a big thing for a lot of people, they don't understand, they don't think it's something that should be done*
    ...

6   *But they view that, they view paying for things as a tax rather than an environmental measure ...*

4   *They see it as a right ...*

7   *They don't relate the payment to an environmental* [measure], *they relate to it more as a tax, another scam or whatever by the government.*

Environmental scientists

The regulators' difficulties in putting an effective ecological modernisation regime in place were strongly emphasised. However, they also saw some positive moves in this direction, albeit somewhat puny when compared with the difficulties noted above. Among the positive developments noted were Ireland's late economic development and hence the avoidance of the earlier industrial pollution experienced in other countries; EU directives as the main driver of environmental legislation; the possibility that new technological developments would be adopted by green businesses; the provision of high quality environmental information through the EPA and ENFO; the establishment of an Office of Environmental Enforcement; and the success of the plastic bag levy. The DoE's stated positive attitude to partnerships with local communities will be further discussed below.

Elaboration of Regulatory Discourse Themes by Business Groups

It became apparent in the analysis of regulatory discourses that the two business focus groups, the consultant engineers and the environmental managers, were somewhat differently positioned regarding the promotion of pro-environmental actions because of the different kinds of firms for which they worked and their position in them. With regard to the environmental managers, it was evident that those working for large pharmaceutical companies saw these firms as having already established rigorous environmental regulatory practices as required by EPA licences. They expressed strong occupational commitments to the promotion of good environmental practices within their firms and saw themselves as attempting to push the environmental boat out further, while also acknowledging the constraints of profitability and competitiveness.

The group of engineers was occupationally in a rather different position. Members of this group were mainly employed by engineering consultancy firms, which worked as consultants for major construction firms, building roads and other infrastructural projects, or for manufacturers seeking environmental licences from the EPA, or, on occasions, for government departments wishing to develop energy or environmental strategies. Co-ordinating work on the preparation of environmental impact statements (EISs) for clients was frequently part of their job. However, they were not employees of these client firms. While the environmental managers identified with the firms in which they were employees, and with their own role as environmental managers concerned to promote good environmental practices within these firms, within the limits of profitability, the engineering consultants were more distant from the construction firms for which they acted as consultants, and had less of an occupational vested interest in promoting environmental practices beyond those strictly required by legislation. The discussions below exemplify some of these differences.

It might be noted that the differences between the two business focus groups regarding environmental protection occur not only in Irish businesses but also those located elsewhere. A review of ten years of research into industry and environmental protection in Britain has shown that while progressive and larger companies have adopted a more proactive attitude to the environment and sustainability, the greening of industry 'is not universal and is a much more problematic process than may be expected' (Berkhout et al. 2003: 20). Differences in the production and trading conditions of firms both nationally and globally, non-compliance and opposition to environmental regulations, and lack of clear trade-offs regarding environmental protection and costs are among the factors contributing to these tendencies (see also Schaefer et al. 2003).

Alignment of Economic and Environmental Goals
With regard to the prioritisation of economic growth over environmental goals, participants in the two business groups offered a range of perspectives. Some prioritised growth; others noted that economic goals, in particular job creation, need not take as high a priority as in the past,

when economic growth in Ireland was weak; while a further perspective was a felt need to find a balance between environmental regulations and continued profit-making.

Regarding the first of these points, one member of the engineering group noted that, *'...there has to be growth for society to progress, that's my view of it'*. However, an environmental manager nuanced the argument somewhat:

2   *I honestly believe one of the fundamental things that has changed is, twenty, twenty-five years ago, this country wanted jobs at any cost, I think we've now matured as a country to a point that we are economically secure, as a country, and that we are now demanding standards to go with that level of development, and I think that's one of the crucial things, that we don't, we don't have to take jobs at any cost today, whereas twenty years ago ...*

Environmental managers

Regarding finding a balance between growing their industry further, ensuring continued profit-making and environmental protection, the environmental managers emphasised the need to keep an eye on 'the bottom line'. Drawing on a discourse around using 'the best available technology not entailing excessive cost' (BATNEC), they stated:

3   [BATNEC], *it's one of these terms that the EPA use, but I mean, let's say taking, looking at a water-treatment system, there might be particular elements in it that you might want to take out or pollutants in it that you might want to take out, I mean because we're a company, because we have to be economic ... we want to make money, every company wants to make money, at the end of the day that is.*

F   *The bottom line.*

3   *Yes, it's the bottom line. So if you were to be leader* [in environmental management] *and really push the level forward you would be buying in the best technology available to take out whatever pollutants there might be in your water treatment plant, but because you mightn't be able to spend, because you couldn't justify spending a million pounds or a million Euro on a particular type of equipment, you're going to buy the one that probably isn't as effective but will do, and will get you within the level that's required by the EPA, and that might only cost €10,000 or €20,000, whatever the case may be, but from that point of view we can't really, you'd be a hypocrite if you said you're really a leader* [in terms of environmental protection] *because on the*

bottom line you want to make your company as economically viable as possible and you will look at all solutions and you will probably get the most effective and the most economically viable solution to that problem. If you were to be a leader you would be buying the top technology, you would be using the top technology regardless of cost.
Environmental managers

Some managers noted the ecomodernist point that being environmentally friendly could be more economically efficient. After initial investment, businesses could stand to make considerable savings on running costs, thereby increasing their profit margins. A drawback to this was that, because savings were not necessarily immediate, environmental protection could be an expensive option in the short term. Asked if the pro-environmental initiatives in his/her firm were for economic or environmental gain, a manager replied:

5   *Both, it's a double benefit ... You get both, which is great because a lot of the environmental initiatives*
–   *Are costly.*
5   *Are costly, yeah, and they take investment; but now it's, well certainly I find in* [name of company] *anyway it's got to the stage where we're starting to save money.*
Environmental managers

Likewise, another participant in the same group noted the initial expense but the longer-term insurance benefit:

3   *There are no economic returns, in fact there's probably an economic loss by actually having an environmental department, but in the long term if you were to do damage in some form, the consequence of the clean-up cost would probably be enormous altogether, so it would far outweigh any good that we're actually doing.*
Environmental managers

There was discussion in both groups as to the extent to which they could be proactive on environmental issues, providing leadership and encouraging businesses to move in the direction of pushing up the standard of environmental protection. The environmental managers in discussing this point noted:

5   *Well, that's leadership because you're pushing up the standards.*
–   *Yeah, and you're pushing the standards.*

2   *Exactly.*

5   *All the time, and that's what environmental management is about, it's continuous improvement and it makes, the economic side of it, makes you look at it even harder to see how you can improve without costing too much and without costing the environment, so I definitely agree with ...*

Environmental managers

The environmental managers noted that different industrial sectors were at different stages in terms of applying for, receiving and implementing IPC licences, as well as going beyond the strict requirements of their licence. In what they regarded as companies with 'a mature [environmental] management system in place', the emphasis was to move beyond the requirements of legislation and the licence, in particular by drawing on technological advancements:

2   *I mean our emissions, our licence would be, we're below 4 or 5 per cent of what goes out on the licence at this stage but our management system is still looking at ways to improve that, economics come into it, they've had to come into it, but there are things, there's always things you can tweak and improve, new* [technologies are] *coming into play, sometimes they're actually cheaper than the old ones that existed and that's where I would claim leadership for that, because then those standards that are economically achievable, certainly put in place and other industries follow suit.*

Environmental managers

Some felt that the government and the EPA did not sufficiently encourage technological improvements. They noted that there were many companies, including some of those in the focus group, that had gone beyond the stage of simply fulfilling their licence requirement, and had:

1   *... gone from the reactive side of things to the proactive side of things. Now I don't think the EPA have followed suit and I don't think the government have actually followed suit with actually providing incentives to industry to actually go out and do stuff or to try stuff out; they're losing out on a huge amount of capital because there's a lot of goodwill there.*

Environmental managers

However, the consultant engineers were clear that, in general, it was not their job to be proactive on behalf of the environment:

1   *I don't think our role, I'm not sure if I'm being clear, but our role is not necessarily to be proactive in promoting the environment, that's my view. We have a duty of care which I think we discharge fully to our developer clients and we need to make sure that we address all the issues that are generally imposed upon us by legislation, Kyoto or whatever. But the nature of the work we do does not involve us in going out there and saving the whales, without being flippant ... it's just we're doing a different type of work with due care and attention, that's how I would see it.*

Consultant engineers

As another engineer stated, they were 'not the World Wildlife Fund'. 'Progress', which in this instance was epitomised by the development of new roads, was impossible without some environmental impact, so their job was to limit these adverse affects:

2   *In our role as consultant, we are on behalf of the development identifying what needs to be done to adhere to legislation rather than, we're not out there to protect the environment, that's not our job.*
F   *Is that not your job to protect the environment?*
2   *Our job is not to let the project to do anything ...*
5   *To minimise the impact.*
–   *Yeah.*

Consultant engineers

Along with this some noted that it was advisable to keep an eye on ensuring that the clients' economic interests were protected:

2   *I think we are proactive sometimes, in terms of, we would have a role, a professional role to advise our clients to do, not just the minimum, to do the best possible, which we do. You very rarely see a professional consultant recommending the very bare minimum to any client, so we have professional ethics and we try to, that's the way we approach our work, so I think we have in a way ...*
4   *I disagree with* [name of previous participant]. *See I mean, you know, if your clients want you to do something and you know in the back of your mind it's not quite right, they're not going to go along with you, they'll find somebody else ...*

Consultant engineers

Both the engineers and the environmental managers noted the ecomodernist point of needing to keep an eye on technological improvements that would protect the environment, for example, a product that would reduce the amount of CO_2 in the making of cement, and the increasing imperative to do this, particularly in relation to climate change.

Environmental Regulatory Regime, Democracy and Civil Society

Environmental managers spoke of the pivotal role the EPA had played in reducing industrial pollution:

5   *What you're saying about the reports from the EPA that it doesn't seem to be as bad now, but I do think that the EPA licensing companies is definitely, you know, it's improving or stopping some of the pollution anyway ... and they are doing monitoring and they're required to do it and legally obliged.*

Environmental managers

Nonetheless, they felt that industry was an easy target for regulatory controls because of its clear visibility; a much more difficult subject to regulate was the car driver, for example, given that *'we all like to drive our cars'*. They also felt that their job would be facilitated if so many different regulatory groups did not exist – if the regulatory process was streamlined.

To the consultant engineers the major problem area was physical planning rather than industrial pollution, which had in the main been addressed by the EPA. Indeed the environmental regulatory regime for the consultant engineer in this area was seen as having grown exponentially in the last decade, making very extensive and expensive demands on them and the planning process in general. Consulting with regulators in the formulation of an EIS was very much part of the job, and:

1   *... in terms of the practical way to move things forward it is very much an interactive thing. [The EPA] do not dictate, they will tell you what they're doing and you can get on great with them and so on and so forth, but the practical way to get things done, I think, is to listen to them and try to implement what they want as long as you think it's reasonable. There's no point in writing an EIS contrary to what you expect them to accept. The real problems come ... when it comes to publishing the EIS and dealing and defending it at the oral hearing. The real problems come from the third party and they go looking for loopholes in the justifications you give, which by definition might call into question some of the decisions that you've arrived at ...*

F   *And who would they be, who would be the third party objectors?*

1   *Landowners, for instance, if you're putting in a new power line, over-head power lines across the country, and you've four families living locally and they're worried about electro-magnetic radiation and so on and they will find any objection they can to the thing, just don't want it, not in my back yard.*

3   *The same with waste ...*

1   *Absolutely. Waste, incinerator now in Cork ...*

3   *There's a huge local lobby group.*

1   *So these are real problems ... these are where the greatest amount of difficulty arises ... And these are people who will take on their own highly paid professional advisers to look for the loopholes in the applications that are being made and if necessary take it all the way, to the highest court in the land.*

6   *And they don't see themselves as part of the problem.*

Consultant engineers

The engineers, seeing themselves as one of the main targets of local mobilisation, were more critical of environmental groups than the managers. The managers felt that environmental mobilisation in the past had helped to place environmental issues on the political agenda, and put in place a regulatory regime which they, for the most part, now favoured. Furthermore, they felt that Irish people in general were becoming more environmentally aware. The engineers in general were far more sceptical, seeing the situation as *'a real us and them'*. On the other hand there was recognition by some that the public may have a point and that more time should be given to local consultation, a point discussed in Chapter 5 on science and expertise. It was also felt that there should be a greater willingness by the construction firms who employed them to pay for this consultation process and not just the dissemination of information.

However, while some in the engineering group appeared to be moving, at least potentially, in a more participatory direction, and indeed to note that the environmental demands of their current job had made them *'think more about things'*, including everything from archaeology to rare insect habitats, the more general feeling was that local environmental mobilisation caused significant problems for them, and that Irish people were not willing to take responsibility for the environmental problems associated with the kind of society which they themselves had created.

Farmers' Regulatory Discourses

The two farming focus groups, small farmers in the West of Ireland and large dairy farmers from the Midlands, were, in economic terms, positioned quite differently. The small farmers, most of whom were part-timers, were economically dependent, generated only low incomes from farming and lacked a sense of empowerment or efficacy within the declining agricultural small-farm sector of which they were part. The large dairy farmers were more robust in their own defence and sense of efficacy, while sharing with small farmers a distinct antipathy to what they saw as bureaucratic environmental regulations.

Alignment of Economic and Environmental Goals

Regarding the ecomodernist ideal of aligning economic and environmental goals, small farmers noted the need for 'balance' between the two, but tended to prioritise the economic side – taking, as they saw it, a 'realist' stance in favour of 'progress', but also recognising the role of environmental protection:

> 1   *And you have to balance one against the other, you have to, we would love a nice clean environment but you have to live in the real world. Somebody said one time you can't eat the scenery. We have to live. And in living we create a certain amount of pollution. That is what we try to reduce and do the best we can.*
>
> Small farmers

They also noted regarding radical environmental protesters that, not only were they not successful but, *'You can't stand in the way of progress.'* They were also clear that they had not joined the REPS for environmental reasons but for:

> 1   *Money.*
> –   *Money.*
> F   *Money, okay, is the money good?*
> –   *Not great but it's a help.*
> –   *It's a help.*
> 4   *It was £50 an acre five or six years ago and it's still only the same now. The value of it is not going up, like, you know.*
>
> Small farmers

They were also clear that they would not still be farming except for the economic support they received:

> 1   *We wouldn't be farming if there wasn't some kind of help. There wouldn't be farmers here in the West of Ireland.*

5   *It wouldn't be a viable enterprise. No way. It wouldn't be farmed. We*
      are competing on a world market now.

Small farmers

With regard to the alignment of economic and environmental forces, large
dairy farmers spoke of good farming as being sensitive to getting the
'balance of nature' right. As such they spoke of it being in their own
economic interest to protect the environment:

4   *But it's in our own interest to protect the environment.*
–   *Yeah, it is.*
4   *Our income is derived from part of the environment.*
5   *We have to* [get the] *balance of nature right in order to have a*
      successful farm ...You know what I mean? Animals won't thrive if you
      have the balance of nature out of control.
4   *Like we pollute the water supply on our own farm, we are feeding*
      that to animals and expecting the animals to produce.
–   *Like it's not healthy to give them polluted water so why would we do*
      it?

Dairy farmers

Environmental Regulatory Regime, Democracy and Civil Society

Both of the farmer focus groups took a highly critical stand regarding some
environmental regulations designed to protect the environment, regarding
them as instigated by 'bureaucrats' who knew little about the everyday
lives of farmers, and who offered inflexible regulations in an area which
required a high level of knowledge as to the variability of place and
climate. It was this flexibility which characterised, in their eyes, good
farming practice, as farmers adjusted daily to, for example, varying
weather and local conditions:

3   *I think* [name of member of focus group] *made a very good point*
      about the restrictions they put in on spreading [slurry]. *If you get the*
      month of January and it could be a lovely month, and February
      comes it's raining, and by that time the tanks holding the effluent and
      slurry and everything it's now filled and you can't put it on the land.
F   *What do you do with it?*
3   *I think that is one thing that is wrong if you like. But there is no way*
      out of that. It's just driven by the EU and the government, that is it.
2   *It all seems to be decided by guys with their feet under the desk, you*
      see.

Small farmers

The larger farmers, while equally critical of 'bureaucrats' and experts, were more forthright in stating that they acted on their own knowledge and judgement, and in their own economic interest in protecting their lands. In this they justified the regulators' perception of farmers, *'they can do more or less what they want to'*. They noted that *'we ignore half of it* [environmental regulations]*'*, and *'we make up our own minds on it anyway'*. They thought that regulators regarded them as 'ignorant', but saw themselves as highly knowledgeable about the particularities of their own farms and their own economic interest in maintaining it and farming profitably.

As already noted in Chapter 5, they emphasised in particular their everyday knowledge of the land and farms as the primary source of their expertise, rather than depending on 'expert' or Departmental 'rules and regulations':

4   *We know more than we are given credit for ... We are living in the middle of it sure.*
–   *We are observant.*
8   *... you read the rules and regulations that are brought out and some of these have never been on a farm in their life.*
5   *We are observant, we are living, we see things growing every day. We are there every day. 365 days a year looking at it.*
4   *And we have to make a living by keeping the thing right.*
F   *How do you feel about these rules and regulations?*
8   *Some of them are good.*
F   *Are some good?*
8   *Some good, but some are pure ridiculous.*

Dairy farmers

To support the point, they noted incorrect advice and regulations in the past:

5   *Yeah, and that is always the case, that people that are not involved in the active work and day-to-day work of farming make decisions and enforce decisions, which are not in the best interest of the farming, the environment or rural communities, you know. That is what I would be coming at you know. To build slurry pits up against rivers, like I mean that was all done through the 70s. You wouldn't get planning permission to build a slurry pit unless it was able to go into the river.*
    ... [laughing] ...
5   *That is what was done.*

Dairy farmers

Small farmers also noted mistakes in the farming advice they had been given in the past regarding the use of fertilisers. Discussing the reasons for the introduction of the REPS, they noted that it was in order:

5   *To protect the environment was one, to promote good farming practice.*

F   *Was there a need for it, were farming practices bad?*

5   *Overuse of certain fertilisers and stuff, sprays and things.*

1   *Farmers were getting bad advice over the years.*

F   *From whom?*

1   *... the advisory service ... the Department ... and farmers have been blamed for the pollution of the lakes ...*

–   *So it was bad advice.*

1   *The farmers take all the flack for the pollution ... but they were only following advice.*

F   *Do farmers need advice?*

1   *They do.*

3   *Common sense advice.*

7   *The pollution isn't always ... you are not always able to see pollution. The actual run-off of phosphates, like, you can't see that if it was right there in front of you. That was going on for a long, long time.*
    ...

2   *The finger was never pointed to them [Teagasc] ...*

1   *Then agriculture is the culprit. We are not really the culprit. It's the advice. They are the culprit. Farmers aren't.*

F   *Acting on the advice they were given?*

1   *Correct.*

Small farmers

In the broader environmental context other than farming, they also distrusted 'expert' advice because they felt it was tainted with, and favoured, powerful economic – especially industrial – interests. Small farmers noted:

2   *These masts for the mobile phones, a lot of people didn't agree with them in their area, and all that. But even though they tell you that they are no harm, I don't know, you wouldn't believe them.*

F   *Why wouldn't you believe them?*

2   *Because we don't know who is calling the shots like ... [laughs] ...*

F   *How much trust do you have in people who make the rules, we are saying here we need rules and regulations but how much trust do you have in those rules?*

5   *They might be following their own agendas.*

2   *Yeah, you would be very wary about them. You see people, it happens*
    that kids get, people get leukaemia, so many kids in a certain area
    getting it, there has to be a reason. Even if they say they do no harm,
    but why are people in that area getting leukaemia?

Small farmers

They continued, saying that they felt they had little power to influence
decision-making, that *'it's us against them'* (5) and that *'multinationals*
can come along and do this, that and the other' (2) while they could not.
In reply to the regulatory discourse statement regarding *'turning a blind*
eye to rules and regulations when it suits', there was laughter and the
comment, *'it's the Irish way I think'*.

Dairy farmers also voiced their suspicion that regulators were aligned
with industrial and other vested interests and did not play fair with farmers.
Furthermore, civil servants were felt to know *'nothing about rural*
Ireland', and regulators such as the EPA were deemed not to follow up on
the implementation of pollution licences with industries, as well as being
limited by their inability to ensure that local councils did not pollute:

3   *I have a neighbour who has a dump, well not a dump, he has filled*
    in a bog and it's all clay that is going into it and he was reported to
    the EPA and somebody from the EPA came out and said, 'What is
    being thrown here?' And he said it was only clay and rubble. And this
    [EPA representative] got fairly narky with him and said, 'This will
    have to be taken out.' 'That is fine', says he, 'it was the council that
    threw it in there, they can take it out.' And [the EPA representative]
    said nothing, just walked away.

F   *Why do you think ...?*

3   *Because the power, [the EPA representative] is not going to go*
    against the council, yet he can make an eejit out of this lad, why not?

Dairy farmers

The strongly anti-authoritarian discourse of the dairy farmers and their
growing anger at their decreasing autonomy and status was evident in the
above, as it was in the following:

8   *There was a time when you were a farmer you were your own boss.*
    Now we are governed from Sir up there.

3   *Stooge of Europe.*

Dairy farmers

Mobilised Groups' Regulatory Discourses

Alignment of Economic and Environmental Goals

A major goal of the representatives of environmental groups who constituted the CEF focus group was to seek to explore and clarify what sustainable development in an Irish context would mean and to discuss and consult with the three other major sectors, local authorities, industries and farmers, in an attempt to get these policies implemented. However, they felt that little headway had been made by the government in terms of actually clarifying such policies and pursuing them. For example, they argued that, *'... we have been given instead a national development plan which nowhere in it has the word sustainable, we've got planning acts which are constantly reformed and use the term, still with no understanding of what it means'* (8).

The Forum's function was to explore and examine a range of sustainable policies, and to mobilise and lobby on behalf of the environment. They saw their role as:

7 *To teach ourselves about it* [sustainable development] *first of all and then to raise public awareness so that in a democracy with the government that we have, we can get a groundswell of educated opinion in order to lobby our elected representative and that's what we have been doing in Cork and they are listening to us but unfortunately the government is going to overturn them* [i.e. the local council].

F *Why do you feel that?*

7 *Well, the government has passed a law specifically to overturn our Cork County Council, for example ... so that whatever they say about incinerators they're going to have it overturned, well if that's what ...*

F *That's an example is it?*

7 *That might be a little bit strong.*

10 *Well, that's the ultimate effect, I mean what it means is that a decision about the waste management plan will be made by the county manager alone, whereas prior to that it was made by the councillors who were elected representatives and could be lobbied, whereas you can't lobby a council manager* [laughter].

8 *And he's not elected, he's appointed by the Department.*

CEF

They pointed out that it was a central role of the government to regulate business and corporate bodies in the interest of the environment and for the common good. This included, *'... protecting the environment and protecting life for future generations, not just for the common good.'* (5)

Neither the CEF, the anti-incinerator group nor the walkers questioned the possibility of aligning economic and environmental goals as aspired to in sustainable development policies. However, some in the returned missionaries' group took a more radical stand in challenging the ecomodernist assumptions regarding the protection of the environment while at the same time continuing with increasing economic growth. Questioning the discourse statement, 'Is it possible to have economic progress and protect the environment?' they asked, whether by economic 'progress', economic 'growth' was meant, and if so:

8   *If you had said 'economic growth', absolutely not, you couldn't have economic growth* [and protect the environment]. *We have a finite planet and ... if you focus on the annual growth, you are doubling your growth every twenty years. The present growth has destroyed the air, water, soil, the lot – so if you double that you just ... we have a finite planet – that's the problem. We would need about ten planets.*

6   *... if all the Third World was living even as we are living, I don't know the statistics but the planet wouldn't survive. As Americans we wouldn't survive ten years ... We have to sacrifice if we are going to protect the environment ... How we are going to do that is another question.*

Returned missionaries

Others in the returned missionaries' group also noted the need to limit the excesses of productivist agriculture encouraged by the CAP in the past, because it was *'out of proportion'* and *'against nature'* to have *'cattle producing 1,900 gallons a year, and they are just machines, you know?'* (6). Thus, again they integrated a moral perspective.

Environmental Regulatory Regime, Democracy and Civil Society

An aspect of ecomodernist thinking that was articulated strongly by the anti-incinerator group was the precautionary principle, especially as it related to incineration. It was also placed within a discourse on rights:

7   *Like, you can't bring out a drug without it being proven to be safe, you can't administer drugs unless you can prove that it's safe, but you can go ahead and put stuff into the air until something happens. That is crazy. They should prove that it's not going to hurt you before they should be allowed to put it in the air, they should have definite proof this definitely won't hurt anybody then you can put it into the air. Otherwise it's crazy putting it into the air.*

F   *Who do you think should be responsible for monitoring for it?*

7   *The government, definitely. The government.*

– *It's all down to the government, isn't it?*

7 *There should be zero tolerance in anything that is poisonous at any level. Unless they can either prevent it, or prove that it doesn't hurt you, before it should be allowed into the air. Otherwise what rights have we? We have no rights, they have the right to poison us if they feel it's okay for them.*

Anti-incinerator group

This discourse of the democratic rights of local people being usurped by an alliance of political and business interests was very central to these activist groups. Their protests regarding both developments which impacted negatively on the local environment, and the non-enforcement of environmental policies, were not being heard. Immense frustration and anger at this lack of local consultation and hence democratic disempowerment were voiced.

The difficulties they faced with both national and local government included:

(1) what they saw as its too-close alignment with the interests of big business, and the consequent lack of trust this engendered
(2) the lack of strong, clear and consistent environmental policies, and deficiencies in implementing environmental measures
(3) the government's disregard of scientific research findings even when offered by research teams it had itself established, and the advice offered by its own officials when these were contrary to government interests
(4) the lack of responsiveness by government to strong local concerns regarding the environment, which left no option but to appeal to the EU.

The walkers articulated these concerns. Talking about a proposed incinerator for animal waste, they noted:

6 *I don't have any problem with an incinerator at all if its properly supervised and policed. Again, like I said it to you at the start ... we have a very corrupt government, they're for it, they're against it, they're for it, against it. Now they've given them a licence to incinerate bonemeal for the next three months, but they haven't put in any people there to supervise, government officials to make sure it's burned off properly and that's where the problem comes in, do you know what I mean? Like we have to get rid of our waste, we just can't sweep it under the carpet, waste has to go somewhere, so we're going to have to accept incinerators eventually or some type of it, like it's costing the taxpayer unreal money sending it out foreign at the*

moment to have it incinerated elsewhere and that like, so we're going to have to do it ourselves eventually and people are going to have to stop and wake up to the fact that it's costing the taxpayer a fortune. Give people like [name of company] *who are speaking about it now a licence to do it, but make sure that they're supervised properly in doing it, again back to policing.*

Walkers

Talking about incineration in other countries, such as Austria, they pointed out political differences between it and Ireland: *'Yeah, but the thing about it is, other countries, people don't have access to politicians in other countries like we have here, politicians are too easily got at by big business in this country'* (6).

They recognised that waste was a problem, that it was generated by consumers as well as industry, that something needed to be done about it, and that this was the responsibility of all. They were critical of what they perceived as a lack of concern among the general public and their NIMBY (not in my back yard) attitudes to waste and incineration, especially their perceived lack of a sense of responsibility. Talking about a discussion with neighbours about a proposed dump in their area, one noted that his neighbour said to him:

7   *'... Jesus did you hear about the dump up the road, they're opening a new dump, they won't open a new dump here, I'll pay hundreds, I'll get solicitors and I'll do this and I'll do ...'. And he was going to do so much to stop it, and I said like, 'And what do you think should be done with it, John?' 'I don't give a ****, they're not having it here and that's that', you know what I mean?*

1   *Illogical.*

6   *Just no alternative.*

–   *Not his responsibility.*

–   *Yeah.*

6   *Completely irresponsible like, you know what I mean? If people only look around today and look at what's coming out of the supermarket in trolleys and one thing and another, where do they think it's going like? It has to go somewhere, it just has to go somewhere.*

Walkers

Mobilised groups were not only disillusioned with the public but also with the government and the environmental regulatory regime. The anti-incinerator group noted:

3   *What she was saying there, who is responsible? I am beginning to have zero faith in the government, the EPA forget it, they are just working for the government ... The government set up research with the Health Research Board ... Their findings were that incineration and all the rest does cause a potential threat to human health and the government ignored it and granted planning permission to this place ... And the inspector of An Bord Pleanála, wasn't it, who attended the oral hearing for that incinerator, advised his board to say 'no' to the planning permission, and the rest of the committee went against him and granted it. And he attended the oral hearing and listened to all the people's fears and concerns and he suggested that they vote against it, and they went against him and voted for it. I just think, I just don't have any faith in these officials or these government departments any more.*

–   *They are sitting up in Dublin, they have no idea what ...* [talking over each other].

3   *It's down to big business and industry and that is really what it's down to and we are a small group left fighting ... And the EPA have said so many times that* [name of company] *was the second worst run* [meat] *rendering plant in Ireland, I sat and listened to* [name of EPA scientist] *saying that down in Johnstown Castle and yet they told the Department of Agriculture about a month ago that they could see no reason why* [name of company] *couldn't render SRM* [specified risk material]. *So I just feel, I think, disillusioned with all these people that are supposed to be running these things and protecting the environment.*

1   *These are the watchdogs.*

3   *Yeah, they are the watchdogs.*

5   *Who's watching the watchdogs?*

Anti-incinerator group

The returned missionary group noted the fact that practices authorised by the local authorities themselves were sometimes contrary to their own environmental regulations. In response to the discourse statement, regarding turning a blind eye to environmental regulations when it suited, the returned missionaries noted how the county councils themselves did this:

8   *A very good example of it is, you know the destruction, like the bird population – the small birds have fallen here by one-third in the last ten years, so they have brought in this thing, you can't cut* [the hedges] *between April 15 and August 30, you can't cut the hedges.*

The county council go and get private operators to go and cut the hedges and not a single ... there hasn't been a single prosecution in the last six years. So that's a very good example of it ... And they look the other way and it is your finches are going down, your thrushes are going down, larks, basically the birds that live in hedges – a perfect example.

5   *You can't cut the hedges only in certain times of the year.*

8   *That's what I am saying ... I remember two years ago going home to ... and counting fifteen trucks out for cutting hedges and I stopped at a few and asked what they were doing, 'Oh sure, we are doing it for the North Tipperary Co. Council.'*

4   *God, they have a lot of hedges in North Tipperary!*

F   *... What were you going to say?*

2   *Well, I was sad because evil is being allowed to happen.*

Returned missionaries

They were also concerned at the lack of democracy represented by the setting up of such quangos as the National Roads Authority: *'The same is true of the roads thing, the National Roads Authority. In other words, all these quangos are undermining democracy and people are getting less and less ... We break our guts at it and yet nothing will happen'* (8). Another participant confirmed these concerns, citing an instance when a county council's vote was overturned by An Bord Pleanála: *'So then democracy like ... our representatives coming down in favour with the people, and Bord Pleanála overthrowing their decision, and we have no say on who goes on this board ... '* (1).

In contrast, they were highly supportive of environmental initiatives coming from the EU:

F   *Can I bring you back to the EU and the EU directives? What is your understanding of the EU's role in this debate?*

8   *Well, some of them are very positive. We wouldn't have anything on drinking water; we wouldn't have anything on waste management – I mean toxic waste is one ... and we are actually in breach of something like nine out of the eleven EU environmental ... directives and we have been fined by the European Court for the one on the water so ...*

Returned missionaries

Some members of the CEF described their moves to inform the EU of Ireland's environmental problems. One such complaint was about the protection of a bird habitat:

4 *We've taken on the city council in one particular issue and discussed the preservation of a habitat, you know, a sand martin colony ... What happened was that it was zoned as an amenity area and last year the city council decided to rezone it for housing ... Well, we found out that they had breached a European Council directive so we had to write to the European Commission and that's what we're in the process of doing at the moment ... Like, it just highlights the general problems in Ireland which we're talking about, it's environmental law which is ... I'd say, in relation to other European countries, very underdeveloped.*

7 *We, our government does flagrantly breach undertakings. I mean, we're breaching Kyoto at the moment, we're breaching the Stockholm Agreement on persistent organic pollutants, we're breaching the best available technology regulations. It doesn't seem to matter, does it, they just are. For example, the Kyoto agreements, we're all going to have this carbon tax quite soon, we know that but at the same time the government is going to put up these incinerators which are going to vastly increase the carbon emissions because for every tonne of waste burned you're getting another tonne of carbon dioxide emissions, so how can they square that?*

CEF

They were also highly cynical about the will of the government to act on environmental issues:

7 *And it's so easy for the government to have an enormous* [impact]. *I mean, that An Taisce suggestion to Noel Dempsey to put a tax on plastic bags, that was so easy and it has raised enormous amounts of money and it has saved I don't know how many 100s of millions of bags going on the environment, and at the stroke of a pen they can do that, at the stroke of another pen they could stop all the four million milk bottles from going on the dump every day ... There are so many easy little measures that they can take which will have an enormous impact but they don't seem to have the will to do it.*

2 *Well, I mean the fact that it took so long to just get the plastic bags' one should actually make you realise that we'll all be long dead and buried before they get to the serious ones.*

– *That's right.*

7 *But that has been a success.*

2 *Yeah, but they're now living off the credit ...*

– *Off the glory.*

7 *And glory and they will live off the credit and glory of that.*

CEF

A Way Forward?

Despite this stated cynicism regarding the existing regulatory regime, the CEF focus group, which consisted of a wide range of representatives from the voluntary sector, were willing to continue participating in the forum whose brief was to provide an arena within which the different sectors (local authority, industry, farming and the voluntary sector) could come together to discuss common environmental problems, and indeed were very positive about the opportunities it offered, not only for small environmental groups to come together, but also the partnership it offered with local authorities and other interest groups. They saw their role as listening to different interest groups in these terms:

> 11 *What you're really trying to promote is the understanding of why different sorts of people have different sorts of solutions to environmental issues and problems, and by listening to each other hopefully the compromise can be found which everybody can identify with and take ownership of and work towards a common good.*
>
> CEF

In order to do this effectively they needed to organise, inform and lobby. They needed to explore alternative solutions, *'because if people don't know what alternative solutions are, or are not available, they feel helpless and we don't want to promote a sort of council of despair'* (10). Having prioritised the most urgent problems, they mobilised:

> 7 *by a lot of hard work, arranging public meetings locally and also e-net, e-mailing, networking on the computers, getting people to pass documents from one to another, information that we're getting from other countries and that opens up a groundswell of information in the community and we just need sufficient numbers of people who are able to lobby the public representatives, but it is a lot of hard work, but it's immensely important that we do it and I do believe that we can have success if we continue with this work.*
>
> CEF

They felt that they offered *'talent, ideas, examples'* (9) to the forum, and that they had tenacity, *'you have to damn the begrudgers'* (2). They were no longer afraid of mobilising and felt that within the forum, *'there has been a certain amount of empowering'* (2). Furthermore:

> 2 *... the degree of respect accorded to the forum is because it has held its head and avoided being dragged down the hysteria road, which is*

always so tempting when you, I mean, because fear is, fear is the driving force for a lot of environmentalism. It's either a deep-seated long-term fear or an immediate fear, it's fear for your children or for the future, and fear promotes anger and then you're in trouble because then we're shouting at each other.

7   *Well, then you can't get creative solutions.*

2   *You can't get creative whereas the forum has that advantage, and you get to an audience and it has increasingly done that, and that's the huge value of the forum. It can be a very difficult one, but that to me is the empowerment that the forum has given.*

CEF

They felt that the city and the county councils had found working in partnership with them to be *'a very positive thing, and in fact we can offer a tremendous amount'* (11), bringing information about community needs to the councils, and being a bridge back into the community when environmental policies, such as waste facilities, were being delivered.

Partnership arrangements were also commended by the DoE focus group. When asked by the facilitator to point out a policy area that they felt was working well and of which Irish people could be proud, they noted not only the work of ENFO (Information on the Environment), but:

4   *The environment partnership fund, where local community initiatives are funded by the local authority and significantly funded by local communities, have taken positive actions to address environmental issues in their local community and then it becomes a sense of ownership because, 'We've done it, nobody is going to screw it up on us.' If the local authority of the state does it, that's theirs, but if we do it, it's ours and you find in many communities, it's like tidying up the town for the tidy towns' competition, God help whoever drops litter. It's like the local youth club who paint their own youth club. If someone comes in and uses an aerosol spray on it, they'll kill him.*

DoE

Protest Discourse in Action

Presented below is a brief case study of the reasons why local people organised to protest against an incinerator being sited in their area.

The anti-incinerator group's lack of trust in central and local government and in environmental monitoring has already been cited. Added to this was the fact that the company that was seeking planning permission to build an incinerator was not trusted and was seen to have had a weak pollution record in the past. However, the discourse articulated by the group was not simply an environmental one, but one about power, about 'them' and 'us', with politicians both from central and local government and large business interests being seen as aligned against 'us', local people, 'little people'. Potentially, scientific knowledge might mediate these differences, but was not being listened to by those with power when it did not conform to their interests and policies. Local politicians were seen as Janus-faced. It was recounted, when a meeting to protest against the incinerator was held, that:

3   *The greatest thing they* [local politicians] *did was they all came to the meetings and all stood up and said how they were against incinerators and then they went to the county council office and voted for the waste management plan for the region which includes incineration. That was just after the election. Just after the election rather than before it* [laughing].
6   *So we don't know who was telling what.*
4   *It's very frustrating.*
–   *Yeah, frustrating.*
4   *Then you go out and you are asked to vote all the time and you have these people calling to your door and the next thing ... you know. The next thing you have an issue like this and it's really important on the community and the people around, it's not the people in Dublin, they aren't going to have to be sitting down here.*

Anti-incinerator group

If the campaign had any capacity to be heard by those with power it was because a major local business with considerable financial and international backing had rowed in behind it, not because the voices of the local campaigning group had been heard:

4   *But it's very frustrating because, as you say, what can you do, you know? What can the people do? They are doing everything they can but their voice is going unheard. And the powers that be really don't care. That is the way I feel at this stage, it's like this lady said, you get so disillusioned with the government.*

Anti-incinerator group

They felt that if they had not got the support of a major local business – 'the money' – they would have been completely ignored:

3   *But if the money hadn't been there we would be just a voice in the wilderness.*
8   *A waste of time.*

3   *And you would be looked on as cranks.*
–   *Yeah.*

Anti-incinerator group

The lack of care and lack of democracy deeply offended and angered them:

7   *But what amazes me is that living in a democracy and the whole area can say 'no', and the government can still say you are getting it anyway.*
–   *Yeah.*
–   *That is it.*
7   *I can't get over that.*
6   *There was seemingly a thing that if you had over 20,000 signatures, that that would swing it a good bit ... that public opinion is supposed to sway it and we had well over 20,000.*
8   *We had 22,000 signatures.*
–   *Yeah.*
6   *That alone is that many people not wanting it in a small area. But that obviously doesn't make any* [difference] *you know.*

Anti-incinerator group

They faced what was regarded as a formidable alliance of political and business interests:

2   *But big businesses had a tendency a few years ago just to brush off the little people, just a bit of a flea scratch.*
7   *But that is what people were, they were the little people and they didn't say a word and they couldn't take on the bigger people.*
2   *They weren't listened to.*
8   *They were afraid to say anything. They would lose their job or the brother would lose their job, or it would come back on them some way.*

Anti-incinerator group

They did, however, see a possibility of becoming more empowered. When asked if the above situation had changed, they replied:

2   *Slowly changing, the information definitely.*
8   *The amount of information that is there now, and access to information, you said you got most of the information from the Internet.*
2   *But money talks, definitely.*

Anti-incinerator group

They recognised the need to organise together and to help other local communities who faced similar problems:

3   *... it makes you aware of others.*
–   *You would because of it.*
7   *Yeah, you now realise how much help you need to go against the status quo ... to fight against what you don't want. So you would be thinking of the others, saying, 'God, we will help them out because what we had to go through.' I think you would be more aware of the help that is needed. To help the little people to fight against the powers that be, that have the say. And they [the powers that be] seem to take the same view, you like it or not, which is wrong. And it's terrible.*

Anti-incinerator group

Regulatory Discourse of General Public Groups

Regarding the balance between economic growth and the protection of the environment, a range of perspectives was articulated by the groups drawn from the general public, but for the most part the economic remained the priority. Regarding discussions of environmental regulations and their implementation, all groups accepted the need for regulations but many also spoke of their frustration at weak implementation. Some also articulated distrust in the government, questioning its will to make the necessary changes and whether it had any real concerns for local interests.

Alignment of Economic and Environmental Goals
On the possibility of fulfilling the joint goals of ensuring continued economic growth and protecting the environment, groups might be seen as being placed along a continuum, from those emphasising a need to establish and maintain a balance between both by adequate environmental management and regulatory procedures (nurses and shop workers), and those who emphasised rather more that the protection of the environment should not be allowed to hinder economic growth (commuters, young working-class mothers, working-class retired). The students and young male skilled workers articulated an intermediate, negotiated position. Only the unemployed group mounted an explicit critique of economic growth *per se*.

The nurses, in response to the question, 'Is it possible to have economic progress and protect the environment?' agreed tentatively:

7   *I do, with caution ... You have to, like, when you make your decision to progress, you have to like [do] an impact study, you know, or*

*something to see the consequences of it. If you are going to progress,
then you have to say what will this achieve? Who would it affect? You
know what I mean. So we really need to have it organised. Not just
shoot something up and leave it, you have to work it out first.*

Nurses

They felt that, with the economic growth of the recent past, not enough
time had been given to examining the environmental consequences. As in
many other groups, they exemplified this by discussing traffic levels and
the building of new roads:

1   *A few years ago in the Celtic Tiger, a boom here, that all of a sudden
the roads were just chock-a-block with cars. It was unbelievable; it
seems to happen over night ...*

6   *We are trying to play catch-up now; we are trying to fix it now with
motorways and everything. We are following our tail in a way really,
we did the progress but we didn't set out the environment, you know
what I mean? There wasn't enough thought put into it.*

−   *No there wasn't.*

F   *So, you are talking about integrating them?*

7   *Yeah, planned properly. There was just no planning at that time. Just
get in the cars and go for it. No direction ... Dublin was saturated.*

Nurses

They also felt that it was necessary to have some political group ensuring
that this was done, and which *'was determined to look after the
environment'* (1) and noted that *'the Green Party should be there to keep
them on their toes'* (4).

Shop workers likewise felt that an eye had to be kept on the environmental
interest and, if trees were cut down to make a motorway, then:

7   *Lay their motorways and let progress take place and the whole lot,
but replant them and don't take every space ... and fill it with
concrete. That is what they are doing. Let them reforest the place
elsewhere. And, I mean, they put preservation orders on some places.*

Shop workers

The young skilled workers and students differed among themselves and
were less likely to be consistent regarding what they felt might be the most
appropriate relationship between economic growth and environmental
protection. Asked about this relationship, a student group noted:

3   *I don't think it's a choice we can make. We always need to find a way of growing the economy. Even in global terms, if everybody has to look after their environment then we will all be in the same restrictions.*

8   *I think it's realistic ... It's what sustainable development is. The Irish people and government have little concept of short-term pain for longer-term gain.*

Students 1

It is of interest to note that this was the only participant among the eleven general public groups to mention the term 'sustainable development'.

The Dublin-born and -based young men with skills in the building trade also tended to move back and forth between favouring economic growth while also noting the need to protect the environment. Having noted with some regret the recent use of local and historical parklands, and the knocking down of trees in St Anne's Park to make way for houses in Dublin, a participant noted that: *'some of it is necessary though, you have to make way for progress'* (8). When asked:

F   *What about, say, roads, you know, land being used for roads?*

8   *How often do you hear people giving out about the traffic? There's no way here and there's no way there.*

5   *Sure the farmers are getting paid plenty of money for their land.*

9   *The ones we have are too dangerous anyway.*

1   *You've got what, two roads, the M50 and the M1, and you go off anywhere else and there's bleedin' ...*

7   *The N7, down the N11, down into Wicklow, they've got so much. They were death traps before; people were losing their lives every ****** week.*

Skilled workers

They had no time for the *'tree huggers'* who protested against the road widening of the N11 at the Glen of the Downs, seeing them as *'a crowd of wasters'*, *'all dossers and ... from the south of England, these kind of gypsies'* (7). Rather, they saw the road works as essential, and furthermore:

4   *They* [the road builders] *did not do much damage when they built the road anyway ... there is still plenty of green around it like.*

    ...

6   *And they replanted the trees.*

Skilled workers

When presented with the ecomodernist question, 'Is it possible to have economic progress and protect the environment?' these skilled tradesmen talked about learning from other European countries, especially Germany, which was seen as *'looking after all their waste and they're sort of up on it'* (5). They were the one group interviewed after a controversial waste advertisement sponsored by the DoE had been transmitted. One participant brought it up spontaneously, noting:

2   *Have you seen that ad? The waste ad, the landfill ...?*
–   *The new estate of ...*
–   *The rubbish just starts flying up the street and the kid is standing there looking at it.*
–   *Rats and all ...*
–   *Rats and all coming over.*
–   *It's a nasty ad.*
–   *It's very good.*
–   *I haven't seen that.*
     ...
–   *Yeah, on RTÉ, the government, your man was going on about it, Cullen is it? Going on about it and saying it's a bit hard hitting. It is.*
–   *That's the whole point of it, isn't it?*
–   *Full chickens and all that.*
F   *And what's the point of the ad, what's the message that it's trying to get across?*
–   *Recycle.*
–   *If you recycle ...*
8   *If you're not going to take care, it needs to be taken care of, waste can't be just thrown away because this is what happens, it will overload.*

Skilled workers

As noted above, three groups, commuters, young working-class mothers and the retired, gave rather more emphasis to economic growth even at a cost to the environment. The commuter group discussed *'the need for infrastructure'* and its *'unavoidable'* environmental consequences, which, while *'a shame'* had to be accepted: *'Ireland is progressing a lot and if you want to, like, reap the benefits of that you are going to have to accept some of the downsides'* (7). When asked to respond to the statement, 'Economic progress in Ireland will slow down unless we look after the environment', they noted the increased cost this latter would entail for industry, which in turn would be passed on to the consumer, and that, furthermore, *'people aren't going to give up their jobs for the environment'* (8). They brought up the issue of making the polluter pay, especially if this would operate as a preventive measure:

7   *But it should be like preventing the damage being done in the first place, and I don't know if we are prepared to pay for that. We don't seem to have a sense ... In Europe, like, there's a very different attitude to it, a more responsible ... I don't think we have.*

Commuters

Young working-class mothers did not in general give priority to environmental issues. Regarding new motorways, they described these as:

2   *Fantastic.*
—   *Yeah, I love them.*
2   *They are great.*
3   *Brilliant.*
F   *What do you feel about the motorways being built on land, cutting down of trees, using up fields?*
—   *It's progress.*

Young mothers

However, this group also included one participant who was more environmentally mobilised, who voiced support for the anti-roads protest in the Glen of the Downs, and who was active in being energy-efficient:

8   *My next step would be to buy an energy-efficient fridge, now I have to say, definitely I would.*
F   *Why?*
8   *Again because it's probably, you might pay that bit more, but at the end of the day if it works, I am helping the environment but it's also helping me, I am not paying as much using the electricity. I'm being honest with you, you know, because it's only benefiting me ... I will do it. And again I don't have the money to keep going out constantly buying bags every week. That is why I choose to bring the bags with me when I am shopping.*

Young mothers

While other young mothers listened and did not disparage, neither did they lend support to these sentiments.

The working-class retired group also prioritised economic growth:

F   *But for politicians and people in the government, can they pursue protecting the environment while at the same time making sure that the economy grows or are those two things in conflict?*
4   *They should be able to do it.*

3   *It falls on the government. ... [The] Department of the Environment
     in conjunction with the other departments to make sure that although
     the Department of the Environment wants to protect the environment
     they should not impede progress of the country.*
5   *Yeah, that's true, yeah.*
4   *Yeah, very true.*
1   *Can't stand in the way of progress.*

Retired

The retired, however, did articulate a strong anti-waste discourse. This was based not so much on concerns regarding the protection of the environment but on a criticism of contemporary lifestyles based on a level of waste that would have been unknown until recently. They described with considerable satisfaction previous practices of saving buttons and zips, turning collars, ripping jumpers and knitting the wool up again, and the present-day response of their children to these practices: *'Throw them out, Mammy'* (7). They also placed a pro-environment discourse in the context of patriotic concerns. One described how recently on the television she had seen a programme about:

7   *replacing trees and buying trees and you can invest in buying trees
     and all that, now ... if you had a few spare shillings you should be
     putting it into that, for Ireland's sake. You say it but ...*
–   *You don't do it.*

Retired

Interestingly, it was the unemployed group who spontaneously offered a critique of economic growth in terms of resource depletion and the possibility of catastrophic collapse. They noted the cutting down of rainforests to serve short-term human needs such as creating employment and providing profits in Latin America and indeed that:

9   *Every country and every government, because of greed, they are
     exhausting their resources. Oil, sea, fish, cutting down forests, that is
     taking away from the world what the world is. Fifty to one hundred
     years from now it will be a different place. If it's still here. That is the
     big issue at the moment.*

Unemployed

They noted global warming, the depletion of the ozone layer (participant 3), the depletion of fish stocks nearer home (8), and a documentary regarding erosion on a small island due to the felling of trees, and how *'the island died because of the way it was treated, you know'* and only regenerated *'once it was left alone by humans'* (7).

Regarding Ireland, one noted that the current economic growth rate was too fast, while another felt that there may need to be a major catastrophe *'for people to wake up or governments to wake up'* before something was done (7), and that it was the government's responsibility to do something. It was felt that *'if they started now ... it's probably not too late now, if they started now it might stop all the people of the world paying for it later. We are starting to pay for it now, I suppose, in different ways'* (3).

The unemployed group and the returned missionaries were the only two of the twenty-two focus groups to offer a discourse that was directly critical of economic growth *per se*, thus articulating one of the central critiques of modernity. In contrast, most groups equated economic growth with 'progress', which was then discussed as good in itself. There was little evidence of a move towards 'risk society' sentiments. The threat to the environment, which economic growth entailed, could be 'managed' through good environmental regulations, although some groups questioned the public's willingness to carry the cost of this regulation. Whether Ireland was perceived as having such an environmental regulatory regime is an issue to which we now turn.

Environmental Regulatory Regime, Democracy and Civil Society

Two themes characterised the public's discussion regarding the environmental regime in Ireland. One was the weak implementation of environmental regulations. The second was a sense of disempowerment and lack of trust in the government. The weak implementation of regulations was particularly articulated around the lack of provision of recycling facilities and the lack of prosecutions for violating environmental regulations. Frequently noted – drawing on the experience of the plastic bag levy – was the possibility of changing environmental behaviour rapidly with proper government encouragement, planning and the provision of appropriate facilities. The teachers discussed the levy in these terms:

1 *The plastic bags were the greatest example of what can be done by just making the right move, you know.*
– *Yeah.*
3 *But I think that was a penalising aspect. It was the carrot and stick, but the carrot was the charge aspect and it was the same with the penalty points system for the driving. So there has to be a penalty aspect, it seems, for something to work in this country.*
5 *For recycling to be effective, it has to be convenient. You shouldn't*

have to drive either; it should be as convenient as even having recycle compartments in every village. It has to be convenient for it to be effective. You can't be driving around in circles with trailer-loads of paper. So, to follow your point, like, it has to be there on your doorstep.

Teachers

The lack of convenient recycling facilities, especially kerbside collection of recyclable materials, was frequently pointed out, while, to add insult to injury, along with the very inadequate facilities that were provided, charges for bin collections were being levied. The need for regulations was acknowledged by all groups, but the lack of follow-through was felt to be frustrating and counter-productive.

The young working-class mothers agreed. In response to the regulatory statement, 'We need environmental regulations to protect the environment, for example waste disposal, but we are also turning a blind eye to these same regulations when it suits us', they replied:

1 *If they provided the facilities you need in order to do what they want you to do, then you would do it. Like they are telling you there are bring centres and all, but as the girls were saying, not everyone is going to start lugging plastic bottles and whatever else you can bring. If they provided you with the stuff you need more people would be willing to participate and do their bit.*

Young mothers

Students likewise felt the need for a clear system to be put in place so that it would become second nature to recycle:

5 *It is not ingrained in us that we should do things like that. We know we should, but it needs to be a sort of habit. Everyone knows that they should do certain things and I can't think of an example bar putting away the things in the bin, but sometimes stuff gets left and it doesn't get put in the bin or doesn't get put in the right bin. It needs to be sort of stamped into us.*

2 *I would say, unless there are recycling bins within your arms' reach you are a lot less likely to recycle. You need to have everything kind of mapped out.*

Students 2

The shop workers, retired, unemployed, nurses, and commuters expressed a very similar range of attitudes. The commuters noted that the success of the plastic bag levy *'shows how easy it is to change your ways if there's a little bit of planning or whatever'* (2). The students and retired commented that the success of this campaign also heightened awareness generally regarding recycling and litter. The pleasure shown in the success of this regulation and the consequent lack of litter seen on the streets, hedges and trees was shared amongst almost all groups, including regulators, business, farmers, mobilised and general public groups. Two groups who commented on difficulties and inconveniences it had caused them were young mothers and Travellers. Traveller women responded to the question of the facilitator:

F *What about the plastic bag levy, has that affected you in any way, you know, when you go shopping and you're charged?*
6 *That's stupid ...*
5 *It's ridiculous.*
2 *It's ridiculous.*
– *When you buy food they should give you bags free.*
5 *You're not going to keep bringing your bag.*

Travellers

Some explained that they bought black bags and used them to both carry their purchased goods home and to subsequently put their rubbish into. Some wondered why the levy had been introduced, to which another replied: it was to stop them *'blowing in the roads and all, I think that's why they done away with them'* (8).

Participants in the young mothers' group were divided in their opinion of the plastic bag levy. Some felt it was a good idea and that the streets were noticeably cleaner and that people were becoming more aware. Others felt it was an inconvenience having to remember to bring bags, if one forgot, this entailed a cash cost at the check-out when money was already in short supply, and furthermore, they discussed a concern not to be laughed at because of violating local shopping norms:

5 *I hate when they say, don't forget the bags, I don't give a *****
   ...
9 *They cost me a fortune. I am always buying them. I would be embarrassed walking up the road with a bag with bags in it [laughing].*
– *A bag of bags.*
– *All empty bags.*

Young mothers

They noted that, in the past, one of the reasons they would not have brought their own bags was because:

11 *Everyone would have something bad to say about you – 'A hungry *******'*

– *That's exactly.*

1 *I have seen on maybe two or three occasions, couples, before this came in, getting out all their plastic bags, all crumpled up, bashed up, taking them out and I hear them* [others in the queue] *saying 'the ... *****' you know what I mean, bringing the bags back down!*

10 *They always seemed to be old people.*

– *They'd bring a shopping bag with them.*

Young mothers

Despite most groups agreeing to the importance of environmental regulations, many groups also agreed with the discourse statement regarding the public's willingness to turn a blind eye to regulations when it suited, and a lack of a sense of personal responsibility in these matters. Some in the commuters' group emphasised personal responsibility particularly strongly:

F *Are the authorities leading by example in your eyes?*

4 *No.*

2 *But, like with the plastic bags and the recycling bins, like we have to start somewhere.*

7 *Yeah, you can't blame them without blaming ourselves – it's like when we were talking about traffic, it's like people in cars, it's their decision to go out and buy a car and then drive to work and go on their own and just little things like that can be done at a personal level and community level that's not being done.*

8 *Yeah, people sit back and blame the government for everything that goes wrong.*

– *I think they have to make changes themselves as well.*

Commuters

Because of this lack of personal responsibility, regulations and their reinforcement were even more important; as the Travellers noted, *'There's a lot of laziness in people'* (9). The Travellers, young mothers and the retired group all gave examples of their own disregard for environmental regulations when it suited them, while none of the groups held themselves up as paragons of virtue in this regard.

Contributing to a sense of a lack of personal responsibility was the lack of a sense of empowerment among the general public groups, a sense that their voice was not being heard and that decisions were being taken by the government and others in the interests of those with money and power, and with little concern for ordinary people. Shop workers, skilled workers, students, commuters and the unemployed all expressed explicit concerns in this regard, often drawing on their own experiences regarding developments that they felt harmed the environment in which they lived or worked. The following are some examples:

Students 1, regarding housing developments:

F   *What can you do about it?*
3   *Not a thing. We signed petitions and all that, but nothing.*

And regarding developers:

2   *I think it's just money. I think eventually it'll come out that they were given backhanders to make decisions.*

The retired discussing how it was easier to get things done in the past:

6   *You don't have the confidence in them* [the government] *now like you used to ... because you're thinking the smaller things they don't want to be interested in, I think, it's only the bigger people with the money seem to get more ... out of the government, not the little people, the bigger you are the more you get done in that respect I think, no matter what it is.*

Skilled workers talking about builders:

2   *It's about money, it's about making money ... It's not about the environment.*

Conclusion: Economic Growth, Weak Regulation and a Local Democratic Deficit

There was little evidence of a lessening in the priority given to economic goals despite increasing affluence, with only two of the twenty-two groups, the returned missionaries and the unemployed, articulating a critique of economic growth. Underpinning this prioritisation, in the opinion of regulators (DoE), was an alliance of political and citizen commitment to the project of modernity, or progress-as-affluence. In comparison, environmental protection played a side-line role. It was further weakened in the eyes of the Department by a lack of both cross-departmental support and local authority resources and capacity. Thus, the master-frame of economic growth as progress continued to enjoy a pervasive degree of political, economic, social and cultural anchorage.

An ecomodernist or sustainable development discourse argues that the goals of economic growth and environmental protection can be achieved simultaneously, through good environmental management, regulation and technical solutions. A discourse on environmental management was articulated favourably by regulators, environmental managers in industry, most mobilised groups and by some of the general public groups, but none argued that it was strongly institutionalised in the Irish regulatory regime. Indeed only one of the eleven general public groups actually used the term 'sustainable development' in what were relatively lengthy two-hour focus group sessions on the topic of the environment. However, a sustainable development discourse did appear to give regulators a shared idea of what they as regulators would like to deliver and on which they would like to provide leadership. They, however, were under no illusions as to the difficulties they faced in doing this.

The discussions on the environmental regulatory regime in Ireland were dominated by pretty scathing criticism of the weak implementation of environmental law. This theme was articulated by many of the regulators themselves, especially the DoE, mobilised environmental groups and the general public. It was much less frequently heard from the business groups, especially the engineering consultants, and the farmers. On the contrary, the latter disparaged environmental regulations, which they perceived as coming from 'bureaucrats', 'suits' and experts out of touch with the everyday life and the necessary flexibility of good farming practices, as they saw it. With farmers it was very much a 'them' and 'us' conflict.

For environmental managers who were self-selected from large industries, it was often in their own interest to be occupationally committed to promoting good environmental practices in their firms, although always within the context of ensuring their continued competitiveness and hence profitability. The consulting engineers, who worked on large-scale infrastructural projects which had major environmental consequences, were in a less strong position, as the firms that hired them ultimately called the tune. While observing environmental regulations, most did not see it as their job to push the environmental boat out further, while the hiring firms' ever present concern was the bottom line of profitability.

If the majority of the mobilised and public groups did not offer a critique of economic growth or articulate a 'green' agenda, what they did articulate was a discourse on local democracy, or more accurately, its absence in what they perceived as entrenched and powerful interest alignments between politicians and major economic interest groups. This was a discourse strongly influenced by the experiences of environmental issues in their local areas regarding, for example, roads, housing and waste, and by a sense of frustration at their inability to be heard by those with power and thus a sense of disenfranchisement. It was also underpinned by a lack of trust and by a strong discourse on democracy which remains embedded in Irish society and was readily articulated by the mobilised and general public groups. It was a discourse which pitted 'us', 'the little people', against 'them', 'the big boys', 'the money', especially used to characterise perceived alliances between political and economic interest groups. This alliance was seen as corrupt, and as inhibiting the possibility of participatory democracy, of being listened to and heard. It included a discourse on rights, in which those of the local community were seen as overlooked. To quote again the anti-incinerator group: '... *what rights have we? We have no rights* ... ' It was used to claim ownership of the local area against those who wished to use the area either in 'the national interest' in terms of, for example, national governmental environmental waste policies or the introduction of industries which were not wanted. It was used to mobilise at the local level, to emphasise the community 'we'. It was not necessarily a pro-environmental or green discourse, but could be used across a range of local issues. It was a discourse that was used very effectively to raise awareness about issues across a local community, to claim the moral high ground, to bind and organise, to inform oneself and others about issues, and to network this knowledge to other communities that wished to protest or move the environmental agenda forward.

While many of the general public groups felt disempowered and angry, others used this anger to carve out a relatively autonomous space for themselves, for example large farmers, or to organise and to protest, for example the CEF and anti-incinerator groups. The voice of those organising at a local level was strong, while a potential democratic way forward through partnership was exemplified by the work of the CEF, work which would appear to be supported, at least ideologically, by the DoE, and the everyday work of heritage officers.

An apparent contradiction existed within the regulatory discourse. While there was a distrust of regulators and scientific elites and a very strong sense that voices at a local level were not heard, there was also vigorous support for environmental regulation *per se*. The latter included widespread criticism of the lack of adequate implementation of existing regulations and praise among most groups for the plastic bag levy which impacted immediately on daily shopping behaviour. Thus, while regulators were criticised, regulation to protect the environment was sought, not only by the mobilised but also by the general public groups. Despite distrust, the regulatory route was the preferred option. No doubt the support for the ecomodernist policies of 'managing' the environment through regulation, while also supporting desired economic growth, contributed to this. Also contributing was a sense that regulation was needed to encourage and facilitate individuals to become more personally environmentally responsible, and to penalise them if they did not. Some of the more general cultural and social factors which may contribute to the strength of this regulatory discourse will be returned to in the next and concluding chapter.

7

Environmental Empowerment and Policymaking: Summary and Conclusion

Introduction

This research project was designed to explore the kinds of environmental discourses generated by different groups, and the social, organisational and cultural contexts that influence these discourses. To this end discussions were held with twenty-two focus groups, selected to include a wide range of different perspectives on the environment. Five sets of groups were selected: regulators and environmental scientists (three groups), business groups (two groups), farmers (two groups), mobilised and active environmental groups (four groups), and eleven groups drawn from the general public. The total number of participants was 168.

A review of both international and Irish literature led to the identification of five kinds of discourses in terms of which environmental attitudes and values might potentially be articulated – moral, radical political, romantic, scientific, and regulatory. Two-hour discussions were held with each of the twenty-two focus groups to explore how they talked about the environment with a group of their peers. In the first hour, the discussion was facilitated in a very open-ended manner, to ensure that other discourses could also be articulated. In the second hour, a set of discourse statements designed to explore further the five discourses was introduced to the participants. The focus groups were successful in eliciting wide-ranging discussions on the environment and environmental issues, enabling the researchers to explore how different groups elaborated, supported or contested the cultural themes identified as most salient.

Following the work of Fairclough (2003), discourses were defined as ways of representing aspects of the world from a particular perspective, as cultural lenses or frames shared by groups of people, drawn upon in communication with others, influenced by social and cultural history and thus relatively stable over time. However, discourses are also open to challenge and change, especially when, as social conditions change, previous patterns of trust are undermined and the discourses of those in power lose legitimacy. Embedded in discourses are constructions of identity, of a sense of self and of the other, as well as definitions of the social and natural worlds, not only of how these are but of how they ought to be. These discourses are not discrete cultural 'units'; rather, each tends to draw on overlapping, and indeed sometimes inconsistent, cultural themes, adding to their fluidity and potential to change and be challenged. They are not static but constantly being 'worked' – being narrated, supported, contested, argued over and changed. It was this dynamic aspect of discourses that the focus group research hoped to capture.

One of sociology's primary roles is to 'capture', describe and analyse such discourses, thereby opening up the possibility of a greater awareness and understanding of the range of different ways of looking at what might initially appear to be pre-defined issues. Sociology explores and describes this range, but also seeks to understand why various groups articulate different perspectives. It does this by analysing the social positions from within which these perspectives are enunciated. The aim of this description and analysis is to move towards a more informed civic culture or polity in which different perspectives are acknowledged and the existence of no one 'right' definition of nature recognised. This will increase opportunities for more informed democratic discussion in which different voices are heard and responded to, and more transparent policy decision-making facilitated. The significance of the research outlined in this book lies in the democratic centrality of the questions it raises regarding the relationship between self, society and nature, particularly in light of contemporary threats to the environment, the level of debate and rapidity of change in this area, and the importance of present policy decisions to the future trajectory of Irish society.

The focus group discussions about the environment were always embedded in broader discourses about the nature of Irish society and drew on central cultural themes. The two most frequently and spontaneously articulated discourses focused on moral and regulatory themes, such as waste, landfills and incineration; litter and dumping; pollution from farming and industry; and road building – the environmental issues on the public and media agenda during the first six months of 2003. The discourses in terms of which they were discussed drew on cultural themes that are deeply embedded in Irish society, both historically and in relation to current experiences of globally based economic growth and consumer wealth.

Moral Discourse Themes

Discussions of the relationship between human and non-human nature were found to be predominantly anthropocentric, with a strong emphasis on nature as a resource for human use and benefit. Moral discourses were no exception: human beings were seen as holding the centre ground as a right. There were, however, two sides to this anthropocentric moral theme. One had a social focus: the environment ought to be respected and protected in the interest of other people, and, likewise, care for others was strongly associated with care and respect for the environment. Thus it can be argued that a widespread, if sometimes rather weak, ethic of environmental care existed. Care for nature was seen as closely associated with, or similar to, care within the private sphere of the family and home, and particularly care of children.

The opposite was the greedy individualism of the public economic sphere and its environmental destructiveness. The latter were seen as driven by economic forces pushing for further growth in both production and consumption. There was broad awareness among all groups of these economic forces, of the consequences of greedy and irresponsible individualism and of the environmental destruction they entailed. However, while this recognition provoked some unease, it had not, for the majority, stimulated an incisive critique of these processes or a desire to jump the current economic ship.

Other, more critical, moral discourses were articulated, albeit in a fragmentary way. One hinted at a relational approach to nature, emphasising the autonomy of non-human nature, and the dependence of humans on it. The interconnectedness and interdependence of human and non-human nature were raised, leading to an ethic of partnership and co-operation rather than domination and exploitation, and a desire for the good of non-human nature for its own sake. This arose, for example, in the discourse of some teachers regarding the potential of a one-to-one relationship with domestic farm animals; as well as the discourse of nurses and the CEF regarding human and non-human nature going 'hand-in-hand', each needing and depending on the other. It is possible that if the term 'nature' rather the 'environment' had been used when the focus group participants were introduced to the research, further evidence of such an approach may have been elicited.

A relational approach appeared to be strongly underpinned by a romantic responsiveness to nature. Plumwood (1996: 159) notes of the relational approach that, in its emphasis on care, friendship and respect for nature, it is an approach that draws on both reason and emotion. It thus overcomes the dualistic characteristic of much contemporary culture, which sharply differentiates reason from emotion and undervalues the latter. She argues that this is a major source of current destructive attitudes to both human and non-human nature and the impoverished worldview that it entails. She argues that an emotional relationship with, and 'care for particular others is essential to a more generalised morality'. The capacity to care is 'as index of our moral being' and based on experiences and feelings for particular others, both human and non-human. She (Plumwood 1996: 159) believes that an ethic based only on a rational sense of ethical universalism is:

> ... seriously incomplete and fails to capture the most important elements of respect, which are not reducible to or based on duty or obligation any more than the most important elements of friendship are, but which are rather an expression of a certain kind of selfhood and a certain kind of relation between self and other.

In the focus group research, a relational approach, when articulated, was done so with feeling and high modality and as a source of environmental mobilisation and commitment. This, however, was not a prevalent perspective and was not expressed by regulators, scientists and engineers, among others. It is possible that regulators and scientists did not articulate a relational approach because of their self-distancing and sceptical approach to a romantic view of nature – or at least to the articulation of this approach among their occupational peers within a focus group setting.

The lack of a strong and articulate religious discourse underpinning an ethic of environmental care was notable. This was so for all groups except the returned missionaries, despite the possible opening given to a God-centred discourse by one of the moral discourse statements. Perhaps this is not so surprising given the lack of leadership by the Catholic Church in this matter – an issue vouched for by the returned missionaries themselves, much to their anger and frustration, given the centrality of their own God-centred and holistic environmental discourse, and their commitment to this both in Ireland and in the developing majority world.

Radical Political Discourse Themes

A moral discourse continued in the discussion of global environmental destruction, global inequalities and the economic dominance of the North over the developing South. Here a highly anthropocentric and socially conservative discourse legitimated what was acknowledged as an exploitative and environmentally destructive global economic system. A discourse of disempowerment regarding the possibility of radical economic change, as well as the theme of developing countries contributing to their own destruction, was articulated in particular by some environmental scientists, managers and engineers. Some in these groups noted over-population, inability to organise efficiently and effectively, as well as elite corruption in developing countries as contributing to continued environmental destruction.

These groups, along with the majority of the farmers and general public groups, noted how 'we Irish people' were dependent on this same globalised economic system, which has proven so destructive in the majority world. They reiterated that this economic system was based on greedy individualism, but this acknowledgement provoked little articulated sense of guilt or moral outrage. On the contrary, the collective conscience appeared to be absolved by statements about inability to effect change – '*we are only one small cog on the wheel'*, '*you can't not live as everyone else is living'*. No doubt this passivity and support for the status quo was considerably supported by the pleasures of an affluent lifestyle – '*my wallet says good luck to it'*.

To the extent that environmentally friendly action was promoted by an acknowledgement of global environmental damage, the emphasis was on individualised action. This, in particular, was noted by the heritage officers who stated that the inability to effect radical social change did not absolve society members from individual responsibility to act in an environmentally sensitive manner, even in such small actions as responsible behaviour regarding waste. However, because human-environment relationships were not seen in a holistic or relational way by most groups, the potential of small pro-environmental acts to contribute to changing broader social or environmental perspectives, which might subsequently feed into a more radical questioning of the existing economic system, was not envisaged or referred to by most.

Some of the participants in five of the twenty-two groups articulated more trenchant criticism of the global economic system and its consequences for the developing world. This criticism was most vocal among the returned missionaries whose moral outrage was fuelled by their own experiences in developing countries. They spoke of the '*robbery and rape'* of transnational corporations when, for example, these corporations patented the genes of plants essential to the livelihood of the poor. The CEF, walkers (especially teachers in this group) and nurses also acknowledged the exploitation of developing countries by the globalised economic system and its major and destructive environmental consequences, as well as raising the possibility of taking action to remedy this. These groups were well-embedded in their own local communities and voluntary associations, and drew on this sense of empowerment to seek to further inform themselves, to network and to act both in the political sphere *('we are the power', 'every voice is important', 'we change the government, we vote them in')* and private sphere (for example, buying Fairtrade products). Membership of the caring professions appeared to be a significant factor and will be examined later in the chapter.

A somewhat similar split among the focus groups was found regarding attitudes to radical environmental protest groups in Ireland. The mobilised groups, with the exception of the anti-incinerator group, as well as nurses, tended not to criticise these groups, while some of the consultant engineers articulated one of the most critical positions, with many of the general public and farmer groups taking a negotiated position that expressed ambivalence and unease. On the one hand their important democratic and political role in placing environmental issues on the public agenda was acknowledged by at least some in these groups, but on the other hand their mode of self-presentation and lifestyle were sharply criticised, and indeed seen as symbolic of their 'outsider' status, which drew attention away from the environmental message they hoped to publicise.

Romantic Discourse Themes

Romantic discourses about the natural world, often expressed in terms of an emotional and aesthetic identification with, and responsiveness to, a particular place or natural phenomena can be, and in the case of some of the focus groups were, a major cultural resource in mobilising and confirming a moral commitment to environmental care. Although a romantic discourse was not the most prevalent of the discourses in this research, it was nonetheless an important one to explore because of its role as motivator and mobiliser in relation to an ethic of environmental care, as well as its role in conferring or articulating a sense of personal identity and commitment. As the environmental anthropologist Kay Milton (2002: 109) notes:

> A recognition of the fundamentally emotional character of all personal commitments is essential if we are to understand any public discourse, including that on nature protection. Only if we start from the understanding that people are all and always emotional beings can we make sense of the debates that develop around matters of personal and public interest.

The spontaneous articulation of a romantic perspective was a characteristic of some of the mobilised groups, especially walkers and returned missionaries, as well as teachers, university students, young commuters and shop workers. Some among the latter were of particular interest because they drew on alternative medical and New Age discourses. Generally, however, romantic discourses were characterised by the remembered pleasures of the past, especially rural childhood experiences or leisure-time activities. This discourse, which was frequently associated with the home place or place of residence, was used to criticise destructive 'progress', such as the spread of concrete buildings and roads.

The same groups, along with the environmental managers, unemployed, and retired, tended to respond positively to the romantic discourse statement about Ireland and the beauty of its rural landscape. Again this discourse was articulated as an identification with particular places and natural phenomena, especially mountains, bogs, trees, or in terms of an embeddedness in one's local place of residence and its natural living world, as raised, for example, by dairy farmers and some shop workers. These identifications were of importance for group members' construction of a sense of self and the environment. It was a discourse carried and inculcated in particular by teachers, in this case rural primary teachers, but was only occasionally linked to a patriotic pride in being Irish. Only the retired articulated a strong discourse of romantic nationalism that idealised the rural. It was not a discourse readily articulated by West of Ireland small farmers, whose cryptic, *'you can't eat the scenery'*, summed up their sense of the crumbling economic basis of their world and their protest at depopulation.

Rural Ireland was not a romantic object for young Dublin-based and working-class groups of skilled workers or young mothers, for whom parks provided an alternative. Indeed young working-class mothers took great exception to the identification of Ireland with rurality. Traveller women were likewise dismissive.

While translocation, or seeing through the eyes of others, did occur, and with considerable facility, it was not discussed in detail. The privileging of the foreigner's viewpoint was questioned by the evocation of *'the gullible American'*, and the dismissal of Bord Fáilte advertising as offering a *'leprechaun image'* of Ireland. Some teachers, for example, queried this image, noting that it presented an outdated version of Ireland, which was now *'progressive, aware, affluent and educated'*.

The scepticism of the regulators, scientists and engineers regarding a romantic image of Ireland's landscape was notable. This lack of an articulated emotional sensitivity to nature may well reflect, as commented on by Milton (2002: 91), the underplaying of the '... emotional and constitutive role of nature and natural things ... in western environmental debates, which have been dominated by a rationalist scientific discourse in which emotion is suppressed and emotionalism denigrated'.

A possible consequence for regulators of ignoring the romantic or, worse, dismissing it as 'pure emotionalism', is the limiting of their capacity to recognise and work with the cultural resource of romanticism when attempting to understand the public's environmental concerns and promote pro-environmental practices.

Scientific Discourse Themes

In contemporary societies science holds a privileged place in decision-making about environmental issues, and it is often assumed, perhaps particularly by environmental regulators, that scientists are the most appropriate people to solve environmental problems. As a discourse, science is strongly anthropocentric, emphasising efficient resource use and prioritising humans over other species. Drawing on Enlightenment thinking that idealises human beings and their cognitive processes, it has been used to legitimate the domination and exploitation of non-human nature, especially during and following industrialisation. In its most idealised form it assumes that 'scientific facts' established in the laboratory are generalisable to other contexts and places and that these facts can be verified in an unbiased and disinterested way apart from political, economic or organisational interference. These assumptions have legitimated its predominant position in identifying environmental problems and offering solutions to them in the complex technological world of advanced industrial societies.

It was precisely these assumptions which were questioned by some of the focus groups, especially by environmental activists and also by many groups among the general public, a pattern not only characteristic of the Irish focus group discussions on science, but also of research undertaken elsewhere. The idealisation of science as generalisable from the laboratory to other contexts was questioned by the activists, the farmers, and some groups among the general public, drawing on their own local, sensory and common-sense knowledge to refute scientific claims. In doing this they also drew on deeply felt cultural themes which questioned the claims of 'outsiders', 'they', 'Dublin', to superior knowledge and their right to dominate and make decisions for their local area. Furthermore, they drew on a deeply held sense that this domination was maintained in the interest of an alliance of business and political elites, which used scientific knowledge in its own interest. Trust in this alliance was low, and science coming from this source was likewise seen as tainted. The independence of scientists was questioned, and there was a perception that science was being used as a smokescreen by the powerful to hide their particularistic economic and political interests.

Although they criticised the science that came from this elite, the activists, farmers, and general public did not rule out the possibility of establishing 'the scientific facts'. Indeed some in the activist groups were themselves scientists, and the inclusion of alternative scientists was frequently part of activists' game plan in refuting government or industry-based science. What was of particular importance was that when decisions about environmental issues in local areas were being made, contextual factors should be taken into account. Decisions taken only on the basis of scientific knowledge coming from the dominant centre were 'bad decisions', too rigid and too inflexible, uninformed by particularities of place and time, and by local knowledge of the past performance of particular industries or government agencies and local experiences of them. The focus groups of environmental scientists, managers and engineers were aware of these claims and not entirely insensitive to them. While stating that environmental groups on occasions misrepresented the facts of a case or changed the issue being complained about in their own interest, they recognised the preferred practice of local consultation if environmental decisions were to hold and gain acceptance and compliance in the local area. The consultant engineers felt that the large infrastructural companies that hired them should show a greater interest in early consultation with local groups and a willingness to pay for this process.

Many environmental decisions are ultimately decisions about local areas. However, the particularities of the local are frequently anathema to the centralising tendencies of the state and to the standardising and translocal practices of contemporary production. Science has come to be associated with this power centre of 'money', and has thus become tainted with the themes of greed and vested interests. For the locally based focus groups, these vested interests were contrasted with the 'I' of one's own senses and experiences, of *'seeing things as they really are'*, and the 'we' of the local community with knowledge of the local area. What was sought was a situation in which scientific knowledge was balanced with appropriate local inputs of knowledge, context and values. This ideal suggested a potentially strong role for science once current patterns of misuse were addressed. For the present, however, discussions regarding science among the activists and some of the public groups tended to become discourses based on the issues of overly centralised power, a lack of trust and a democratic deficit.

Regulatory Discourse Themes

The continuing widespread political and popular support for, and indeed prioritisation of, the project of economic growth, 'progress' and affluence were evident in the regulatory discourse. Given that any attempt to limit economic growth in the interests of the environment was seen as undesirable by the great majority of groups, the ecomodernist or sustainable development goals of aligning growth and environmental protection through good environmental management and appropriate regulation gave environmental regulators a focus and an agenda. However, regulators complained that under-resourcing at both national and local levels of their department and of local government, as well as a lack of co-ordination of environmental policy across departments, were weakening this effort. They also spoke of the public's unwillingness to take ownership of public spaces, explaining this in terms of Irish political culture, 'the national psyche', and indeed post-colonial mentality. The general public themselves, at least as indicated by the focus group discussions with them, reflected perhaps a greater concern to care for the environment than regulators perceived. However, the public frequently recognised that this stated concern was not always translated into practice, often due to lack of facilities or support. Regulators also felt that the general public had an antipathy to 'the voice of authority', to environmental taxes and policies, seeing them as 'another scam by the government'. The focus group research would appear to support this analysis, and to take it further in terms of indicating that this lack of trust grew from, and was supported by, a perception that cliques of powerful economic and political interests were making decisions about the lives of local people without consultation.

As might be expected, business groups were also strongly pro-growth. Environmental managers from large industrial firms felt that some industries, under EPA licences, had achieved a level of maturity in their environmental protection strategies. Echoing British research (see Schaefer et al. 2003), they noted the limiting factors of profitability, competitiveness and different production and trading conditions as constraints in pushing out the frontiers. The consultant engineers working on major infrastructural projects were particularly pro-growth, but also realised that their work projects were the focus of much environmental criticism. They felt limited in the extent to which they could propose environmental protections, given that the construction firms for which they worked were their paymasters.

There were also some differences between the two groups of farmers regarding their regulatory discourse and its tenor. Small farmers strongly favoured the ideology of economic growth. This, however, was not necessarily to save the economy of small farms, which they felt was already economically compromised because of its over-dependence on subsidies, while, furthermore, the next generation had little interest in becoming farmers. Small farmers wanted continued growth so that their local communities could be saved from depopulation and to prevent the land from turning into, as they saw it, a wilderness. Their current economic weakness, however, appeared to have led to a considerable level of disempowerment and despondency. This contrasted sharply with the large dairy farmers who, while severely critical of environmental regulations, which they felt were imposed by bureaucrats from outside who knew little about the actual daily process of farming in local conditions, felt enabled to challenge these on the basis of their own alternative knowledge and to act autonomously in their own interest. This interest included, in their view, protecting the environment of their farms, of which they themselves had the most detailed knowledge and to which they had commitment and emotional attachment, underpinned by their daily work, long-term experience and economic and livelihood interests.

The regulators, activists and the general public all complained about the lack of rigorous implementation of environmental policies and a lack of facilities which would enable the public to comply more easily. Being facilitated to be environmentally active brought the added rewards (as with the plastic bag levy) of increased environmental awareness and, perhaps even more importantly, empowerment, the capacity to do something about it and to feel that it was possible to act constructively.

In the remainder of the chapter three interrelated themes will be addressed. These themes cross-cut the five discourses reviewed above. One is the theme of empowerment and its basis in a sense of local identity; the second is the perceived lack of local democratic consultation; and the third examines the contradictory stance of distrust in regulators and yet the desire for regulation. Some of the findings from the survey undertaken as part of the 'Research Programme on Environmental Attitudes, Values and Behaviour in Ireland' will also be briefly drawn upon in this discussion. The final section of the chapter will highlight some of the challenges the findings of this research pose for policymakers.

Empowerment and the Local

Investigating environmental empowerment requires an exploration of the factors that contribute to a sense that one's pro-environmental actions make a difference and that they are important both for one's own sense of identity and well-being as well as that of others.

Among the focus groups, the most empowered were those who were most strongly committed to a moral ethic of environmental care, most emotionally or aesthetically attached to nature, and actively involved with others in promoting environmental issues at a local level. It was also the same participants who felt that, despite the dominance of the global economic system, it was possible for individuals and groups to contribute to social and economic change. These participants were among the most critical of the lack of local consultation and democracy.

It is of interest to note some similarities in the findings of the survey research completed within the broader 'Research Programme on Environmental Attitudes, Values and Behaviour in Ireland'. Here those who strongly agreed with a number of attitudinal variables that together constituted the 'New Environmental Paradigm' (in which nature is seen as fragile, limited and in need of the care and attention of humans to protect it) were found to be more likely to act in an environmentally friendly manner, to be willing to pay more to protect the environment, to have signed an environmental petition, to have protested and to have given money to support an environmental group (see Kelly et al. 2003: 35 seq.). It was also found that a questioning attitude to authority and a strong sense of personal and political efficacy contributed to pro-environmental mobilisation. For example, these values were related to an increased willingness to pay for protecting the environment, to a heightened tendency to recycle and cut back on driving, as well as to increased support for environmental activism (Kelly et al. 2003: 84).

What further information did the focus group research offer regarding the social and cultural context in which these questioning attitudes to authority and a sense of empowerment develop? One contextual fact was the importance of the local area and activism within it. A second was level of education and membership of the caring professions.

The importance attached by many focus group members to one's local area of residence was a theme that arose across a number of discourses. It was one of a number of dichotomous and interrelated cultural themes which included:

Local area	vs. Metropolitan centres of power
Care for nature	vs. Greedy individualism destroying nature
Home, private world	vs. Global economy, public world
Care for children and others	vs. Carelessness and lack of respect for others
'Little people', unless mobilised	vs. Economic and political elites
Mobilised environmental activism at the local level	vs. Authoritarian and arrogant centralised decision-making
Local knowledge	vs. Scientists and experts legitimating the power of economic and political elites

| Local sensory and common-sense knowledge | vs. | 'Superior' scientific claims from the centre |

The local area was the environment of the home, and the protection of the environment in the interests of the home and children was a frequent moral theme. It was local environmental issues that the general public groups spontaneously discussed – domestic and local waste management, the proposed local siting of incinerators, impinging roads or invading smells – rather than, for example, climate change. The local area was also for many the site of leisure-time activities, and here the frequency with which general public groups mentioned membership of the GAA and other sports clubs is worth noting. When discussing identification with particular natural phenomena it was often those in the local area, for example trees, which were important and which contributed to a sense of place; while again, if local experts were available, these were preferred to those from outside, particularly those identified with economic and political elites, situated elsewhere, and attempting to impose undesirable changes on the locality without consultation.

Environmental protest activism in Ireland tends to be strongly locally based, and indeed conflict between local and national (often perceived as 'Dublin-based') environmental groups is not unusual (see Tovey 1993 and currently regarding one-off-housing). As Ireland moved to industrialise from the 1970s onwards, local environmental protests regarding the siting of, for example, potentially dirty industries was a frequent point of local contention and mobilisation. In this regard some local groups perceived the incursions into the locality by powerful interests from the centre as illegitimate and refused to cede privilege to them. The use of the appeals process allowed by planning legislation provided a ready 'access point' to acquire experience of how decisions came to be taken and, in particular, the role of scientists and experts in legitimating these decisions and marginalising the voice of the local community (see also Peace 1993, Keohane 1998). This is how experiences of trust and distrust were learned and the need for alternative sources of knowledge and expertise recognised.

The local was not at all a closed world. Its porous boundaries allowed for outward and inward migration, extensive commuting and tourism, all of which facilitated widespread translocal perceptions, including that of the returned migrant and traveller. However, regarding behaviour in one's local community, a certain level of conformity was required, a conformity not shown by eco-warriors, and hence the very frequent labelling and denigration of their self-presentation, which was seen as confirming their 'outsider' status.

Identification with one's home area was least frequently mentioned by environmental scientists and engineers whose focus was at the more general and occupationally defined levels of science and regulatory endeavours, and the interests and demands of economic growth at the level of the nation-state. This perhaps bears out Appadurai's (2003: 338) analysis that localities, and all the differential personal and social identifications that they entail, challenge the order and orderliness of the nation-state in its promotion of economic growth and environmental regulation. He continues:

> The work of producing localities, in the sense that localities are the life-worlds constituted by relatively stable associations, relatively known and shared histories, and collectively traversed and legible spaces and places, is often at odds with the projects of the nation-state. This is partially because the commitments and attachments that characterize local subjectivities ... are more pressing, more continuous, and sometimes more distracting than the nation-state can afford ... [and] are often at odds with the needs of the nation-state for regulated public life.

Thus, in conflict situations between the interests of the state and their legitimating experts on the one hand, and the local community on the other, each may be talking past the other. The latter will tend to emphasise local knowledge and perspectives, underpinned by a moral sense of the right to be heard and an identification with the local area, while accredited 'experts' from the centre emphasise the general, the abstract and the national interest.

Apart from an identification with the local, a second social factor associated with pro-environmental sentiments, empowerment and activism was level of education and membership of the caring professions. Again the quantitative survey research gave support to these patterns. Having a third-level education was found to be related to both increased environmental concerns and commitments (Motherway et al. 2003: 49 seq.) and to stronger New Environmental Paradigm values (Kelly et al. 2003: 49). It was also found that a willingness to challenge authority – whether this was derived from expert knowledge, experience or religion, and a sense of one's own efficacy in both the private and public spheres – was related to having a higher level of education (Kelly et al. 2003: 59).

Within the focus groups, an ethic of environmental care appeared to be particularly frequently articulated by those in the caring professions rather than among environmental managers and consulting engineers. Some support for this is present in the survey data, which show lower levels of environmental concern and commitment among senior officials and managers than among professionals (Motherway et al. 2003: 53). The different educational and occupational interests, constraints and opportunities of various groups within the middle class and their impact on environmental values and discourses have also been noted in other societies (see Cotgrove and Duff 1980).

However, although level of education was an important factor related to both environmental concern and commitment, it should not be forgotten that an ethic of environmental care was articulated by all groups. It was the strength of this articulation that varied (see also Kelly et al. 2003: 35). Some individual participants within almost all focus groups articulated a strong ethic of care even against the grain of the discussion among others in the group (for example, in the young mothers' group), thus indicating its broad diffusion within all sectors of Irish society. However, its mobilisation into activism may be related not only to having the resources of time and money, but to the confidence consequent to receiving third-level education and the related willingness to question authority, reinforced by working in a caring people-oriented profession. This also appears to encourage an anthropocentric attitude to nature, which is socially oriented and which sees care of non-human nature as part of, and essential to, the care of humans. It also seems to activate pro-environmental behaviour and activities and on occasions may go further, encouraging a relational approach to nature.

Participatory Democracy

Decisions with environmental consequences for the local community taken by outside interests, by business and political elites, by bureaucrats and 'suits' without adequate local consultation were major themes among the activists, farmers and many of the general public groups. This led to criticism not only of what was seen as an arrogant form of decision-making, but of the scientific and technocratic discourse themes on which it was frequently based. It also led to a significant weakening of trust and a questioning of the legitimacy of these decisions and of the groups making them. As economic development pushes further environmental change, similar instances of what are seen as arrogant decision-making are likely to continue and indeed increase, offering significant 'access points' at which local groups confront these undesirable decisions, question their legitimating discourses, and mobilise against them. A discourse of the local right to be consulted and to stop what are perceived to be environmentally harmful developments already exists as a significant mobilising tool, as do identification with, and desire to protect, one's local area.

Because of a perceived lack of local consultation, the level of trust in business, industry and government departments was palpably low among general public, activist and farmer groups. This was also found to be the case in the survey research. Here only 7 per cent of the respondents stated that they had a great deal of trust or quite a lot of trust in the information they received about the causes of pollution from business and industry, with 25 per cent making similar judgements regarding government departments. In contrast, 61 per cent said they trusted the information they received from environmental groups, and 70 per cent said they trusted the information received form university research centres (Motherway et al. 2003: 42). Trust in environmental groups was particularly high among those committed to the New Environmental Paradigm, which was itself related to level of education (Kelly et al. 2003: 34 and 73). Trust in environmental groups was also higher among those respondents who were less willing to accept external direction, and who had a sense of their own efficacy in both the public and private spheres.

While local authorities might be expected to be seen as the representative voice of local areas and as offering a public space for articulating local concerns, their weakness in terms of legislative, administrative and financial remits undermines this expectation. Government-appointed quangos were often seen by local groups as representing the interests of the already dominant centre. Increasing the democratic remit of local authorities has been stated government policy for the last decade, and partnership arrangements between local governments and organised interest groups regarding local development plans have been put in place. It remains to be seen if these increase the local population's sense of ownership over local areas or simply become another arm of existing powers, a way for the centre to further encroach into local areas, while not engaging in effective participatory and deliberative decision-making practices.

A focus on greater democracy at the local level should not hide the equally important role of central state institutions, and of partnership at this level. It is the role of the state to formulate the overall direction of environmental policy and in particular its relationship to economic interests and the direction of the economy as a whole, to establish departmental and cross-departmental structures that facilitate the formulation and implementation of environmental policies, to ensure that local authorities are adequately resourced to fulfil their environmental obligations, as well as to establish the legal and organisational framework which facilitates participatory, deliberative and inclusive decision-making.

The importance of democratic practices in increasing the relative success of ecomodernist or sustainable development environmental management processes has been attested to in comparative studies of European polities (see Jänicke 1996 and also Lafferty 2001). However, there is widespread recognition that ecomodernist policies have tended to emphasise the managerial and regulatory aspects in relation to limiting environmental damage rather than its potential democratic aspects. A review (Berkhout et al. 2003: 6) of a decade of social scientific research into environmental policies in Britain in the 1990s, characterised in particular by the sustainable development project, has concluded that:

> During the decade following the 1992 Rio conference highpoint, the weaknesses of the analytical and policy 'programme' that it expressed have become increasingly apparent. Even if much has changed for the better, the formula that science reveals, states coordinate and incentives push private actors to enact solutions to environmental problems has proven incapable of achieving its goals.

They note that research has indicated that science cannot provide 'certain' environmental knowledge to policymakers and is also being questioned by lay actors; there is decreasing trust in the state and an increasing divergence between policy and lay opinion; citizen perspectives are deployed to register protest and boycott, both locally and globally; and incentives appear to be appropriate and effective only in rather specific circumstances (Berkhout et al. 2003: 24 seq.). Echoes from the current research findings regarding Ireland are evident.

From these conclusions, the British researchers argue that the way forward is 'a knowledge partnership', drawing on reflexive and critical citizenship, and multilevel government which is capable of local adaptability and flexibility. The emphasis is on establishing democratic practices that will not impose, but negotiate. Explaining the title of the book, *Negotiating Environmental Change*, the editors (Berkhout et al. 2003: xi) note:

> By 'negotiating' we want to capture three meanings: in the sense of the dialogue and deliberation now viewed as central to the framing and handling of environmental problems; in the sense of travelling through an uncertain landscape towards the objective of greater sustainability; and in the sense of formal processes of governance that lead to new norms, expectations, agreements and commitments.

The uncertainties and ambiguities of contemporary society are not something new, although their level, as Beck and Beck-Gernsheim (2002) and Bauman (2001) would argue, has been considerably heightened. Every society faces contradictions. The contradiction between the drive for economic growth and environmental protection is central in the current world, and how this contradiction is negotiated or hidden is one of the most important questions facing society. Democratic negotiation of the issue at least lays the contradiction on the table. It does not offer clear solutions.

However, deliberative democracy and the form of partnership arrangements it may adopt in Ireland should not be seen as a panacea. Powell and Geoghegan (2004), having examined in some detail how partnership arrangements have been operating in the community development sector in Ireland, noted how they may serve to further legitimate the incursion of the administrative centre into the local, and contribute to the weakening of local groups. Munton (2003) reviews the existing research on how DIPs (deliberative and inclusionary practices) in relation to the environment have been operating in Britain. He recognises their capacity to mobilise active citizen engagement, but also notes (Munton 2003: 130) that 'significant, transformative changes will not be realised from DIPs until their findings are accepted by powerful stakeholders as making legitimate and necessary contributions to environmental decision-making in democratic societies'. Considerably more research needs to be done to explore best practice in this area, as well as the capacity of different forms of deliberative practices to re-establish trust, to empower and to deliver on greater environmental care and protection. Research into the discourses on which empowerment draws, and how these discourses operate at the local and national levels, offers insights into the socio-cultural dynamics which underpin or undermine these democratic processes. It may also offer insights into how best to mobilise or attempt to reconcile different discourses in the interests of the environment, and of local and national communities.

Contradictions between Loss of Trust and Commitment to Regulation

Despite a lack of trust in regulatory, scientific and business elites, the desire for regulation was strong among the focus groups, and indeed a major criticism of the groups was the lack of adequate implementation of existing environmental laws. Again the survey research confirmed this. When respondents were asked whether governments should allow individuals to decide for themselves how to protect the environment, even if this meant individuals didn't always do the right thing, or whether governments should pass laws to make ordinary people protect the environment, even if this interfered with people's right to make their own decisions, 72 per cent favoured the government option of passing laws. When the same question was asked regarding business, an even higher percentage (84 per cent) favoured the government passing laws rather than trusting business; only 7 per cent chose the business option (Motherway et al. 2003: 39–40). There was thus very considerable consent to being forced to be environmentally responsible.

Some participants in the focus groups articulated these sentiments further, noting that irresponsible environmental behaviour was due to carelessness and the lack of habituation; they believed that strong government implementation would counter this. The focus groups' moral and regulatory discourses were replete with moral phrases indicating how individuals ought to behave and criticising careless, selfish and greedy behaviour. However, there was little sense of strongly internalised guilt or shame about careless behaviour among most groups. Likewise, while an ethic of environmental care was articulated, it could not be said to be very strong, and stronger pro-environmental themes including a relational approach to nature were fragmentary. This appears to confirm the focus groups' assessment of 'we Irish people' as a rather irresponsible and selfish lot, delighted to make hay while the Celtic sun shines, and somewhat unwilling to be individually responsible or to take hold of our own destiny.

A number of political, social and cultural factors may contribute to citizen support for environmental regulations. Despite stated distrust, in particular regarding unwelcome decisions that impact at a local level, participants still adhered to a collective discourse of commitment to the Irish state, which they saw as responsible for 'managing' the relationship between economic growth and environmental destruction. The civic bond between state and citizens may in fact have been reaffirmed through continued economic growth. However, questions regarding how this wealth is spent are more frequently being raised, with concerns regarding ineffectual health policies heading the list of public policy issues for many of the focus groups. The civic bond in Ireland is also characterised by a belief in democracy and a certain level of egalitarianism. In this context another of the findings of the survey research should be mentioned: heightened environmental concerns were found to be related to a strong sense of egalitarianism and an approval of collective political action to redistribute income more equitably (Kelly et al. 2003: 84). This is not just a feature of Irish society but has been noted elsewhere, and the argument is made that environmentalism can be a political weapon used to criticise what is seen as an inequitable and unjust society, as well as an environmentally destructive one.

The focus group research indicated that romantic nationalism based on an idealisation of the rural has all but disappeared except among the retired, as has the centrality of the Catholic Church. The articulation of a strong religious or God-centred discourse on the environment was notable for its absence among all groups except the returned missionaries. However, the authoritarian legacy of the Catholic Church may continue to contribute to a desire to be regulated. The survey research indicated that those who attended religious services once a week were more willing to accept external direction uncritically than those who attended less frequently or not at all. Committed religious attendees were also somewhat less likely to support the New Environmental Paradigm (Kelly et al. 2003: 34 and 58) but were more likely to recycle their waste.

As nationalist and Catholic sentiment and beliefs continue to weaken, so may a sense of collective identity and responsibility. If neither nation nor God provides a secure ground or sense of direction, undoubtedly more responsibility will fall on the family and on education. There was perhaps some sense of this already within the focus groups who spoke of these institutions as the sites where the teaching of 'care' and individual, social and environmental responsibility were located. In what may increasingly become an economically rich but morally barren and highly individualised society (see Beck and Beck-Gernsheim 2002, Bauman 2001), the importance of encouraging a recognition of the centrality of the natural world and human interdependence with it, and an integration of this perspective into one's personal sense of space and place, may be key to taking responsibility for the kind of society created both nationally and globally. The state, working to support both families and education in these tasks, as well as working in partnership with local groups, would do well to reaffirm the link between the private and the public and, through horizontal rather than vertical and hierarchical relationships, re-establish trust. Thus, the consumer might be encouraged to become a citizen with the ability to make choices responsibly in the context of the broader public and environmental interest and to identify with 'our world', a world in which both human and non-human beings are fundamentally interconnected and interdependent.

Challenges for Policymakers

For policymakers, each of these three cross-cutting themes – empowerment and involvement at the local level, the demand for consultation rather than imposed decisions regarding the local area, and the contradiction between lack of trust on the one hand and a desire for regulation on the other – has relevance.

People are exercised by local, immediate issues, and evaluate their environmental concerns and priorities in socially and politically embedded terms. For the most part, they do not isolate environmental issues from other broader social issues, and indeed strong, explicit 'environmental' concern is thin on the ground. They do, however, tend to have quite sophisticated and knowledgeable views on issues that concern them, without always using the 'environmental' labels that regulators and scientists may use for them. This sets an agenda for integrated thinking on the part of policymakers and regulators, something that is already at the heart of the sustainability project. Local priorities are just that, local, and they cut across traditional departmental and sectoral structures. They are best addressed in the same manner.

People include the social and political in their thinking on the environment. The views expressed in this data set point strongly to a need to accept the political nature of environmental issues, rather than trying to treat them as apolitical. In this regard, the degree of perceived disempowerment is striking. Many expert-led issues are seen as nothing more than attempts to dominate and manipulate. Before any real progress can be made on changing environmental practices, trust must be regained.

The means of building up such trust is the subject of the second strong theme emerging from the data, that of participation in planning and decision-making processes. This is a very controversial issue at the moment, and in many ways public involvement in planning is in crisis. However, the remedy is not less democracy, but more. Criticisms of participation processes are invariably criticisms of such processes done badly. There are virtually no published case studies of participatory processes in Ireland in relation to the environment, where genuine creative deliberation is fostered, and the link to policy outcomes is strong and transparent.

Two things are clear from the range of discussions across all the focus groups set out here: first, people have much to contribute to debates about how to address environmental imperatives, and second, they will not confer legitimacy on any system or decision that refuses to allow them to make their contributions and that makes decisions opaquely or on narrow grounds. Such legitimacy is essential if environmental politics is to bring people and their behaviour along as part of the project. It will always be counter-productive to address issues that require public support and behavioural responses in ways that the general public do not see as valid or acceptable. Furthermore, the weakening by government of the possibility of local consultation will also weaken precisely that which policymakers are attempting to foster – commitment to pro-environmental action. In other words, if regulators wish to enhance ecological sensitivity, they need to take care not to destroy or undermine one of the most important grounds of this sensitivity – identification with the local.

Views expressed by the focus groups on the role of regulation and how to change people's behaviour are insightful, if apparently contradictory. At the same time as expressing strong distrust of experts and regulators in trying to manipulate their lives, many expressed support for stronger legal regulation on environmental issues. This is evident both in the quantitative survey and qualitative focus group data. However, the public would need to be confident that the same rules are applied to everyone, and suspicions that others are getting away with ignoring the law (including, in particular, those with power and money) need be allayed.

The role of environmental policy as enabler of social and environmental action rather than policy as control takes seriously on board citizens' demands for fair and robust environmental regulation and implementation as well as for participation in decision-making. Participation does not lessen the role of either central or local state institutions, which are the representative institutions responsible for creating both the policy and the legal and organisational frameworks that facilitate participation and the implementation of policy outcomes. In this process, the range of environmental discourses that citizens will bring to the table needs to be acknowledged and worked with, however contentious. This research has identified and discussed a number of these discourses as articulated by different groups. They included an ethic of environmental and social care; an identification with the local and a strong sense of place; a minority radical perspective severely critical of the socio-economic and environmental characteristics of the society in which we live; scientific perspectives deconstructed in terms of the political and social interests they are seen to represent; as well as a sustainable development discourse (although infrequently labelled as such) arguing for both economic growth and environmental protection through regulation. It is a fundamental task for Irish society to find just and equitable ways of dealing with such plurality, in the interests of citizens, society and the environment.

Appendix

Undertaking Focus Group Research

1 Focus Groups as a Research Method

Focus groups, or 'group discussions exploring a specific set of issues' (Barbour and Kitzinger 1999: 4), are a recognised social scientific method used to examine in depth how groups talk about and discuss issues related to the research questions in hand. This gives the researcher access to the kinds of discourses the group articulates. In focus groups, participants are facilitated by the moderator of the group to discuss their own interpretation of topics and to compare their own experiences, feelings and knowledge with that of others in the group. For some this may mean becoming aware of what has been implicit in their perspectives. Talking and discussing these gives the researcher access to information that would be difficult to get using other methods (Morgan 1997: 46).

A focus group methodology emphasises the interactive and constructed nature of discourses. It recognises that attitudes and worldviews are formed and changed in interaction with others within a number of different social contexts. Focus groups allow researchers to examine this process of interaction and discussion, or discourse formulation and articulation, in action.

In their discussion, focus group participants will highlight other social contexts and sources of knowledge of importance to them in formulating their particular attitudes and worldviews. For example, in focus group research on environmental risks (from chemical and nuclear industries sited in their neighbourhood), it has been found that participants talked and reasoned about risk in complex ways – albeit differently from risk experts. They drew on their own experiences of risk and regulation (or lack of it) in their work places or in other industries they knew; on their historical knowledge of previous accidents; on their knowledge of regulatory institutions and their trust – or otherwise – in them; and on their sense of agency or power to do something about the risk or, on the contrary, their perceived economic dependency and political weakness (see Walker et al. 1998, Waterton

217

and Wynne 1999: 130). Thus, risks were socially constructed and the discourse on risks formulated and articulated in the context of social, economic, political and cultural relationships. Group discussions enabled researchers to identify how risks were constructed in particular ways and the social and cultural discourses drawn upon.

Focus groups also allow for the detailed examination of how groups discuss the research issues, 'how accounts are articulated, censured, opposed and changed' through the interaction of group members (Barbour and Kitzinger 1999: 5). It is a method that allows 'participants to generate their own questions, frames and concepts and pursue their own priorities on their own terms and in their own vocabulary' (1999: 5). It enables the researcher to examine not only what people think but also how and why they think as they do. It is thus possible to explore the evidence that participants bring to bear on an issue, what sources they cite and what arguments they use (Kitzinger 1994). It is a method that sees attitudes as arguments. It examines how individuals mobilise evidence, tell stories and use humour; how conflict – or consensus – is generated; and how participants draw on pre-existing knowledge and cultural resources to make their case (Marris et al. 2001: 20–21).

Because of the interaction among group members, the co-participants may act as co-researchers. As Kitzinger (1994: 107) notes:

When group dynamics worked well the co-participants acted as co-researchers taking the research into new and often unexpected directions and engaging in interactions which were both complementary (such as sharing common experiences) and argumentative (questioning, challenging, and disagreeing with each other).

Focus groups are thought to be particularly useful when the participants have not fully thought through their ideas (see Morgan 1997) or when they are ambivalent, or hold contradictory positions. Environmental discourses are replete with such ambivalence. We express support for sustainability yet find the pleasures of consumption hard to resist; we love our pets, yet eat animals as food. While it may be difficult in a face-to-face interview for the interviewer to challenge such contradictions, in focus groups participants may well challenge one another (Marris et al. 2001: 18).

A considerable amount of research outside Ireland, which was undertaken to examine environmental discourses using focus groups, indicates that it is an eminently suitable method in this regard. The range of environmental topics that have been investigated include sustainability, environmentally friendly consumption, perceptions of environmental risks, genetic modification of both plants and animals, and climate change.

2 Selecting Groups

In choosing focus groups statistical representativeness is not the aim. Rather, groups are selected on the basis of theoretically motivated sampling, that is, on the basis of the research questions to which answers are being sought. In the research in hand, which sought to explore environmental discourses, it was appropriate to include groups that might be expected to explicitly articulate these discourses as well as other groups whose discourse allegiance was not known but was being explored. In selecting other groups it was important to ask, what kinds of occupations, interests or other activities might contribute to participants drawing on different environmental discourses? It was also considered important to include demographic diversity and to make particular efforts to consider the voices that might be excluded (Barbour and Kitzinger 1999: 7).

In order to facilitate group interaction it is important to structure groups in terms of similarity within groups and differences between groups. There should be sufficient similarity within groups to make participants feel comfortable discussing the topic. Similarity in level of education is considered important in this regard (Morgan 1997: 360).

While between eight and twelve participants is advised in some of the focus group literature, some of the more recent writing in this area has questioned this orthodoxy and the adequacy of smaller numbers has been raised. Here again the possibility – or indeed the necessity – of flexibility is recommended (Barbour and Kitzinger 1999: 8) It is also appropriate to recognise that the number who actually turn up for a focus group discussion is often outside the control of the researcher, and is 'a product of circumstance rather than planning' (Barbour and Kitzinger 1999: 8). Also, although the research team may seek to recruit particular types of groups, this cannot always be guaranteed, as participation is normally voluntary.

In the research project in hand recruitment of the participants in the general public groups (with the exception of the student groups), as well as the recruitment of the two groups of farmers, the anti-incinerator group and the walkers, was by experienced focus group recruiters based in the local area, who recruited according to strict selection criteria established by the research team, noting that the discussion would be about the environment. Recruitment to the focus groups, which consisted of regulators and environmental scientists, the business groups, the Cork Environmental Forum (CEF) and the returned missionary group, was initiated by the members of the research team rather than local recruiters.

3 Facilitating Groups

The great majority of the focus group discussions were completed between January and July 2003. The two-hour discussion was usually completed in a convenient pre-booked hotel room, with refreshments served mid-way. The discussion was audio-taped. Facilitation was by two members of the research team, one facilitating the discussion, the second taking notes (particularly of who said what). Thus it was possible to edit the transcribed audiotape by adding which participant was speaking, when identifiable.

A discussion guide was prepared for the general public groups, and the same guide was used for the farmers and the environmentally mobilised groups, with the exception of the CEF. For the regulators, environmental scientists, business groups and the CEF, the discussion guide was adapted to the requirements of each of these groups to ensure relevant focused discussion.

The research was introduced to the groups as follows:

This research is part of a research study on environmental attitudes, values and behaviour in Ireland. It is an academic study and is the first of its kind in Ireland. The research will involve a series of group discussions among various groups of people throughout Ireland. For this reason, the attitudes and opinions expressed in this group will form an important part of the overall findings.

The role of the moderator is to introduce the discussion theme(s) and facilitate group discussion, 'allowing interaction between participants to develop unencumbered by heavy-handed interventions' (Barbour and Kitzinger 1999: 13). Encouraging interaction between participants is an essential skill for the group facilitator. To ensure this, he/she needs to be culturally sensitive and non-judgmental, and to be sufficiently knowledgeable about the issues in hand so as not to lose credibility with the group or close off potentially interesting exploratory discussions that may appear off the point. He/she also needs to be aware of group dynamics in order to know when and how to seek clarification or elaboration of topics, to ask appropriate questions or to move the discussion forward, as well as how to begin and end the discussion appropriately.

In this research, the first hour of the discussion was kept as open as possible to allow participants to articulate their own environmental interests, concerns and priorities and to allow them to bring their own modes of representing these, i.e. their own voices and discourses, to the discussion. As particular environmental issues were raised by the participants, these were noted on cards, which might then be used subsequently to move the discussion to another topic, as appropriate. The process was generally highly successful, and facilitator intervention was most frequently used to encourage further exploration of a topic or to refocus the discussion if necessary. Hence the discussion guide was used in a manner highly sensitive to each group's discussion and dynamics. A major use of the guide was, in many instances, to help the facilitator, before the discussion started, to focus on the central research issues in order to facilitate the meeting.

The second hour of the discussion was used to present each group with three or four (depending on time) 'discourse statements'. These were prepared by the research team in order to stimulate discussion around some of the discourses in which the research was particularly interested. These discourse statements are given in Table A1, pp. 224–5 below, along with the groups to whom they were presented.

The research team selected four of these statements before each focus group took place. One criterion for selection was to raise issues and possible discourse themes that might not have been raised spontaneously, thereby opening up further discussion. For example, because it was anticipated that the focus groups that included environmental scientists, engineers and environmental managers might articulate a scientific or expert technical discourse spontaneously in the first hour, these groups were not presented with the scientific discourse statements. In order to ensure that all participants took part in the subsequent discussion around these statements, each participant was given pen and paper on which they briefly entered their responses to the statement. These responses then formed the initial basis for the subsequent discussion. This process was found to work very well.

Further demographic and attitudinal information, which was regarded as relevant to the type of environmental discourses being articulated, was also gathered by means of brief recruitment and exit questionnaires, which each participant in the general public groups, the farmers, and most of the environmentally mobilised groups completed. Thus, the research team had available to it demographic data on almost all participants, including information on age, education, occupation and present residence, household composition, area in which the participant grew up, community and voluntary associations of which each was a member, extent of environmental mobilisation through support for environmental groups over the previous five years, and priority given to a range of public policy issues.

4 Analysis of the Focus Group Data

A limitation in the use of focus groups which should be recognised is that the particular groups chosen are not a representative sample and the perspectives and discourses they articulate will reflect the particular constitution of the group and the context of discussion. These social and contextual influences also exist in face-to-face interviews in both qualitative and quantitative research. The obligation on researchers is to be aware of and to acknowledge these factors in analysing the data. It also might be noted regarding the general public groups that participants may have held more pro-environment sentiments than others in a similar educational or occupational position, given that they had willingly agreed to give up two hours of their own time to participate in a focus group discussion on the environment. This may have been countered somewhat by the payment of a small honorarium to participants.

A range of methods can be used in analysing the discourses made available through focus group discussions. These may be plotted along a continuum from content analysis of meaningful units to detailed linguistic and interactional analysis. In the main in this research, the textual analysis undertaken was closer to the content analysis side of this continuum (see Macnaghten and Myers 2004). This included the identification within the data of each of the five environmental discourses in which the research was particularly interested and the central themes within them, in particular what themes were given greater salience, and what themes were included and excluded by which groups. The research team was also interested in an analysis of the particular perspective or point of view from which these themes were represented (see also Fairclough 2003: 129 and 154; Myers and Macnaghten 1999a; Kelly 1997).

This analysis does not exhaust the rich potential of the very extensive focus group data collected. Many more ways of analysing the data set – for example, in terms of the specific environmental issues discussed, or in terms of other discourses such as that regarding education and the environment – would be possible. However, this book would argue that the five discourses identified were not only centrally important in themselves, but allowed many other sub-themes and issues to be explored in a rigorous and fruitful manner.

A detailed linguistic analysis of the data was not carried out, although certain linguistic features such as the use of metaphors were referred to. Nor was there a detailed analysis of interaction within the groups, although, again, on occasions this was referred to if deemed relevant. The focus was on identifying the major discourses and themes, their salience and the perspective from which they were discussed, elaborated or argued about.

Environmental discourses define not only perspectives on the environment *per se*, but also the appropriate relationship between self, other and the environment. Many of the discourses, having been analysed in terms of the themes that constituted them, were further explored in relation to how the latter contributed to the articulation of a sense of self; to the definition of others, in terms of 'we' or 'they'; as well as how they defined the environment in particular ways. Thus the responsibilities of 'I', 'we' and 'they' in relation to 'it', the environment, were explored.

To enable this analysis to be undertaken, discussions were audio-taped and transcribed. A detailed coding frame identifying major themes and discourses was drawn up based on a careful reading of the transcripts as well as focusing on the original research questions asked. Given the large number of groups involved, the discussions were coded and analysed using the computer package 'Nud*ist'.

Table A1: Discourse Statements and Focus Groups given each Statement

Discourse Statements	Focus Groups given this statement				
	Regulators & Scientists	Business	Farmers	Mobilised	General Public
1 Moral discourse statements:					
– Trees are not commodities. Trees are nature. They are nature's gift to us and we should protect them.	Environmental Scientists, Heritage Officers	Environmental Managers, Consultant Engineers	Dairy Farmers Small Farmers	Walkers	Teachers, Nurses, Students 1, Skilled Workers, Young Mothers
– Trees are not commodities. Trees are nature. They are God's gift to us and we should protect them.				CEF, Anti-Incinerator	Students 2, Shop Workers, Unemployed, Retired, Travellers
2 Radical political discourse statement:					
– It is the worldwide economic system today that is not only destroying the environment but destroying many Third World countries. We need to do something about that.	DoE, Environmental Scientists, Heritage Officers	Environmental Managers, Consultant Engineers	Dairy Farmers, Small Farmers	Returned Missionaries, Walkers	Nurses, Skilled Workers
3 Romantic discourse statement:					
– The central plain of Ireland is surrounded by a ring of mountains. Hues vary from the deep purple of heather to the black of the turf bogs and vistas range from the gentle Slieve Bloom mountains to the steep wooded valleys and the awe-inspiring Cliffs of Moher.	DoE, Environmental Scientists	Environmental Managers, Consultant Engineers		CEF, Walkers	Teachers, Students 1 & 2, Shop Workers, Unemployed, Retired, Young Mothers, Travellers

4 Scientific discourse statements:

Statement					
– Sometimes you just have to accept what scientific experts say about an environmental problem. But sometimes, for example, if it is a local environmental issue, local people may know as much or more about it than the experts do.				Anti-Incinerator	Teachers, Commuters, Shop Workers
– Before doing anything we should be sure we know everything about the problem. We need more facts and figures.	DoE		Dairy Farmers	CEF, Returned Missionaries	Unemployed, Retired, Young Mothers

5 Regulatory discourse statements:

(a) Ecological modernisation

Statement					
– Is it possible to have economic progress and protect the environment?	Heritage Officers		Small Farmers	CEF, Returned Missionaries	Nurses, Skilled Workers
– Economic progress in Ireland will slow down unless we look after the environment		Consultant Engineers		Anti-Incinerator	Commuters, Unemployed
– Business is about making profits but not about protecting the environment	DoE, Heritage Officers	Environmental Managers		CEF	Skilled Workers, Travellers

(b) Environmental regulations

Statement					
– We need environmental regulations to protect the environment, for example waste disposal, but we are also turning a blind eye to these same regulations when it suits us.			Dairy Farmers, Small Farmers	Returned Missionaries, Anti-Incinerator	Returned Missionaries, Nurses, Retired, Young Mothers, Travellers
– We need environmental regulations. However, it's all very well saying that we should all recycle more or whatever but at the end of the day the authorities aren't putting their money where their mouth is. If they don't set the example or provide the facilities, why should we make the effort?					Commuters, Shop Workers

References

Agyeman, Julian, Robert Bullard and Bob Evan (2003), *Just Sustainabilities*, London: Earthscan

Appadurai, A. (2003), 'Sovereignity without Territoriality: Notes for a Postnational Geography', in S. Low and D. Lawrence-Zúniga (eds) *The Anthropology of Space and Place: Locating Culture*, Oxford: Blackwell

Baker, Susan (1990), 'The Evolution of the Irish Ecology Movement', in W. Rüdig (ed.) *Green Politics One*, Carbondale, Ill.: Southern Illinois University Press

Barbour, Rosaline and Jenny Kitzinger (eds) (1999), *Developing Focus Group Research*, London: Sage Publications

Bauman, Zygmunt (2001), *The Individualised Society*, Cambridge: Polity Press

Beck, Ulrich (1992), *Risk Society: Towards a New Modernity*, London: Sage Publications

Beck, Ulrich and Elizabeth Beck-Gernsheim (2002), *Individualization*, London: Sage Publications

Berkhout, Frans, Melissa Leach and Ian Scoones (2003), 'Shifting Perspectives in Environmental Social Science', in Frans Berkhout, Melissa Leach and Ian Scoones (eds) *Negotiating Environmental Change, New Perspectives from Social Science*, Cheltenham, UK: Edward Elgar

Berry, Thomas (1999), *The Great Work*, New York: Bell Tower

Bonanno, Alessandro and Douglas Constance (1996), *Caught in the Net: The Global Tuna Industry, Environmentalism and the State*, Kansas: University of Kansas Press

Boyle, Mark (2002), 'Cleaning up after the Celtic Tiger: Scalar "Fixes" in the Political Ecology of Tiger Economies', *Transactions of the Institute of British Geographers*, 27, 172–94

Broderick, Sheelagh (1999), 'The State versus Civil Society: Democracy and Sustainability in Ireland', *Democracy and Nature*, 5 (2) 343–56

Bryant, Raymond L. and Sinead Baily (1997), *Third World Political Ecology*, London: Routledge

Burgess J., J. Clark and C. M. Harrison (2000), 'Knowledge in Action: An Actor Network Analysis of a Wetland Agri-Environmental Scheme', *Ecological Economics*, 35 (1), 119–32

Casey, Ruth (2000), 'Virtual Locality', in Eamonn Slater and Michael Peillon (eds) *Memories of the Present: A Sociological Chronicle of Ireland, 1997–1998*, Dublin: Institute of Public Administration

Castells, M. (1997), *The Power of Identity*, Oxford: Blackwell

Clarke, J. and J. Murdoch (1997), 'Local Knowledge and the Precarious Extension of Scientific Networks: A Reflection on Three Case Studies', *Sociologia Ruralis*, 37 (1), 38–60

Coakley, John (1999), 'Society and Political Culture', in John Coakley and Michael Gallagher (eds) *Politics in the Republic of Ireland*, 3rd edn., London: Routledge

Cotgrove, Stephen and A. Duff (1980), 'Environmentalism, Middle-Class Radicalism and Politics', *Sociological Review*, 28, 333–51

Curtin, Chris and Dan Shields (1988), 'The Legal Process and the Control of Mining Development in the West of Ireland', in Mike Tomlinson et al. (eds) *Whose Law and Order?* Galway: Galway University Press

Darier, Eric, Simon Shackley and Brian Wynne (1999), 'Towards a Folk Integrated Assessment of Climate Change?' *International Journal of Environment and Pollution*, 11 (3), 351–72

De Paiva Duarte, Fernanda (2001), '"Save the Earth" or "Manage the Earth?" The Politics of Environmental Globality in High Modernity', *Current Sociology*, 49 (1), 91–111

Department of the Environment (DoE) (1997), *Sustainable Development – A Strategy for Ireland*, Dublin: Government of Ireland

Department of the Environment (DoE) (1999), *Green Paper on Sustainable Energy*, Dublin: Government of Ireland

Department of the Environment (DoE) (2000), *National Climate Change Strategy*, Dublin: Government of Ireland

Department of the Environment (DoE) (2000), *The Planning and Development Act*, Dublin: Government of Ireland

Douthwaite, Richard (1996), *Short Circuit*, Totnes: Green Books

Douthwaite, Richard (2002), *The Growth Illusion*, (rev. edn.) Dublin: Lilliput Press

Dryzek, John, David Downes, Christian Harrold and David Schlosburg (2003), *Green States and Social Movements*, Oxford: Oxford University Press

Earth Summit Ireland (2002), *Telling it Like it is*, Dublin: Earth Summit Ireland

Eckberg, D. L. and T. J. Blocker (1989), 'Varieties of Religious Involvement and Environmental Concerns: Testing the Lynn White

Thesis', *Journal for the Scientific Study of Religion*, 28, 507–517

Eckberg, D. L. and T. J. Blocker (1996), 'Christianity, Environmentalism and the Theoretical Problem of Fundamentalism', *Journal for the Scientific Study of Religion*, 35, 343–355

Eipper, Chris (1989), *Hostage to Fortune: Bantry Bay and the Encounter with Gulf Oil*, St John's, Newfoundland: ISER

Environmental Protection Agency (EPA) (2004), *Ireland's Environment 2004*, Wexford: EPA

Fairclough, Norman (2003), *Analysing Discourse: Textual Analysis for Social Research*, London: Routledge

Fairclough, Norman, Simon Pardoe and Bronislaw Szerszynski (2003), 'Critical Discourse Analysis and Citizenship', in A. Bora and H. Hasendorf (eds) *Constructing Citizenship*, Amsterdam: John Benjamins

Flynn, Brendan (2003), 'Much talk but Little Action? "New" Environmental Policy Instruments in Ireland', *Environmental Politics*, 12 (1) 137–56

Foster, John Wilson (1997), *Nature in Ireland: A Scientific and Cultural History*, Dublin: Lilliput Press

Franklin, A. (2002), *Nature and Social Theory*, London: Sage Publications

Gadgil, Madhav and Ramachandra Guha (1995), *Ecology and Equity*, London: Routledge

Gibbons, Luke (1987), 'Romanticism in Ruins: Developments in Recent Irish Cinema', *The Irish Review*, 2, 59–63

Giddens, A. (1990), *The Consequences of Modernity*, Cambridge: Polity Press in association with Blackwell

Gilligan, Carol (1982), *In a Different Voice: Psychological Theory and Women's Development*, Cambridge, Mass.; London: Harvard University Press

Government of Ireland (2000), *Programme for Prosperity and Fairness*, Dublin: Stationary Office

Graham, Colin (2001), *Deconstructing Ireland: Identity, Theory and Culture*, Edinburgh: Edinburgh University Press

Greeley, Andrew (1993), 'Religion and Attitudes Toward the Environment', *Journal for the Scientific Study of Religion*, 32, 19–28

Grove-White, Robin, Phil Macnaghten and Brian Wynne (2000), *Wising Up: The Public and New Technologies*, Lancaster: Lancaster University IEPPP

Guth, J. L., J. C. Green, L. A. Kellstedt and C. E. Smidt (1995), 'Faith and the Environment: Religions, Beliefs and Attitudes on Environmental Policy', *American Journal of Political Science*, 39 (2), 364–82

Hajer, Maarten A. (1995), *The Politics of Environmental Discourse: Ecological Modernization and the Policy Process*, Oxford: Clarendon Press

Hajer, Maarten A. (1996), 'Ecological Modernization as Cultural Politics', in Scott Lash, Bronislaw Szerszynski and Brian Wynne (eds) *Risk, Environment, Modernity: Towards a New Ecology*, London: Sage Publications

Halkier, Bente (2001), 'Risk and Food: Environmental Concerns and Consumer Practices', *International Journal of Food Science and Technology*, 36, 801–12

Harvey, David (1996), *Justice, Nature and the Geography of Difference*, Oxford: Blackwell

Hepburn, Ronald W. (1984), *Wonder and Other Essays*, Edinburgh: Edinburgh University Press

International Forum on Globalisation (2002), *Alternatives to Economic Globalization*, San Francisco: Berrett-Koehler

Irwin, Alan and Brian Wynne (1996), *Misunderstanding Science: The Public Reconstruction of Science and Technology*, Cambridge: Cambridge University Press

Irwin, Alan and Mike Michael (2003), *Science, Social Theory and Public Knowledge*, Maidenhead: Open University Press

Jamison, Andrew (2001), *The Making of Green Knowledge: Environmental Politics and Cultural Transformation*, Cambridge: Cambridge University Press

Jänicke, M. (1996), 'Democracy as a Condition for Environmental Policy Success: The Importance of Non-Institutional Factors', in W. Lafferty and J. Meadowcroft (eds) *Democracy and the Environment: Problems and Prospects*, Cheltenham: Edward Elgar

Kelly, Mary J. (1997), 'Particpatory Media and Audience Response', in Mary J. Kelly and Barbara O'Connor (eds) *Media Audience in Ireland*, Dublin: UCD Press.

Kelly, Mary, Brian Motherway, Pauline Faughnan and Hilary Tovey (2003), *Cultural Sources of Support on which Environmental Attitudes and Behaviours Draw*, Dublin: Department of Sociology, University College Dublin

Kelly, Mary, Fiachra Kennedy, Pauline Faughnan and Hilary Tovey (2004), *Environmental Attitudes and Behaviours: Ireland in Comparative European Perspective*, Dublin: Social Science Research Centre, University College Dublin; also www.ucd.ie/environ/home.htm

Kempton, Willett, James S. Boster and Jennifer Hartley (1995), *Environmental Values in American Culture*, Cambridge, Mass.; London: MIT Press

Keohane, K. (1998), 'Reflexive Modernisation and Systematically Distorted Communications: An Analysis of an Environmental Protection Agency Hearing', *Irish Journal of Sociology*, 8, 71–92

Khor, Martin (1999), 'Introduction', in Caoimhin Woods and Philip Davie (eds), op. cit.

Kitzinger, Jenny (1994), 'The Methodology of Focus Groups: The Importance of Interaction between Research Participants', *Sociology of Health and Illness*, 16 (1), 103–121

Knorr-Cetina, K. (1981), *The Manufacture of Knowledge: An essay on the constructivist and contextual nature of science*, Oxford: Pergamon Press

Knorr-Cetina, K. and M. Mulkay (eds) (1983), *Science Observed*, London: Sage Publications

Korten, David (2001) 'Life after Capitalism', *Feasta Review*, 1, 64–76

Laffan, Bridget and Jane O'Mahony (2004), 'A Cocktail of Mis-fit and Politicisation: The Tortuous Implementation of the Habitats Directive in Ireland', Paper presented to Department of Politics Seminar, UCD, March 2004

Lafferty, William (ed.) (2001), *Sustainable Communities in Europe*, London: Earthscan

Lash, Scott (2000), 'Risk Culture' in Barbara Adam, Ulrich Beck and Joost Van Loon (eds) *The Risk Society and Beyond*, London: Sage Publications

Latour, B. (1987), *Science in Action*, Cambridge, Mass.: Harvard University Press

Leopold, Aldo (2001), *A Sand County Almanac: With Essays on Conservation*, illustrated ed., New York; Oxford: Oxford University Press

Lukács, Georg (1971), *History and Class Consciousness*, London: Marlin Press

Lysaght, Sean (1998), *Robert Lloyd Praeger: The Life of a Naturalist*, Dublin: Four Courts Press

Macnaghten, Phil and Greg Myers (2004), 'Focus Groups', in Clive Seale et al. (eds) *Qualitative Research Practice*, London: Sage Publications

Macnaghten, Phil and John Urry (1998), *Contested Natures*, London: Sage Publications

Marris, Claire, Brian Wynne, Peter Simmons and Peter Waldon (2001), *Public Perceptions of Agricultural Biotechnologies in Europe: Final Reports of the PABE Research Project*, Lancaster: Lancaster University IEPPP

McDonagh, Seán (2001), *Why Are We Deaf to the Cry of the Earth?* Dublin: Veritas

McMichael, Philip (2000), *Development and Social Change: A Global Perspective*, Thousand Oaks, California: Pine Forge Press

Meadowcroft, James (2004), 'Participation and Sustainable Development', in William Lafferty (ed.) *Governance For Sustainable Development*, Cheltenham, UK: Edward Elgar

Merchant, Carolyn (1992), *Death of Nature: Women, Ecology and the Scientific Revolution*, San Francisco: Harper Row

Merchant, Carolyn (1996), *Earthcare, Women and the Environment*, New York: Routledge

Merchant, Carolyn (2003), *Reinventing Eden: The Fate of Nature in Western Culture*, New York: Routledge

Milton, Kay (2002), *Loving Nature, Towards an Ecology of Emotion*, London: Routledge

Morgan, David (1997), *Focus Groups as Qualitative Research*, London: Sage Publications

Morley, David (1980), *The Nationwide Audience*, London: British Film Institute

Motherway, Brian (2002), 'The Changing Face of Community Planning in Ireland, Lessons from Cross Border Research on Local Agenda 21', Paper presented to Sempa conference, 'Encouraging Public Participation in Planning for Suburban and Urban Environment Management', 6 September 2002

Motherway, Brian, Mary Kelly, Pauline Faughnan and Hilary Tovey (2003), *Trends in Irish Environmental Attitudes between 1993 and 2002*, Dublin: Department of Sociology, University College Dublin

Mullally, Gerard (2001), 'Starting Late: Building Institutional Capacity on the Reform of Sub-National Governance?', in William Lafferty (ed.) op. cit.

Munton, Richard (2003), 'Deliberative Democracy and Environmental Decision-Making', in Frans Berkhout, Melissa Leach and Ian Scoones (eds) *Negotiating Environmental Change, New Perspectives from Social Science*, Cheltenham, UK: Edward Elgar

Myers, Greg and Phil Macnaghten (1999a), 'Can Focus Groups be Analysed as Talk?', in Rosaline Barbour and Jenny Kitzinger (eds) op. cit.

Myers, Greg, Bronislaw Szerszynski and John Urry (1999), *Global Citizenship and the Environment*, End of Award Report, Swindon: ESRC

Naess, Arne (1989), *Ecology, Community and Lifestyle, Outline of an Ecosophy*, Cambridge: Cambridge University Press

Nash, Roderick (1989), *The Rights of Nature, A History of Environmental Ethics*, Wisconsin: University of Wisconsin Press

O'Cinnéide, Seamus (1998–99), 'Democracy and the Constitution', *Administration*, 46 (4), 41–58

O'Connor, Barbara (1987), 'Women and the Media: Social and Cultural Influences on Women's Use of a Response to Television', Doctoral Dissertation, Department of Sociology, University College Dublin

O'Connor, Barbara (1993), 'Myths and Mirrors: Tourist Images and National Identity', in Barbara O'Connor and Michael Cronin (eds) *Tourism in Ireland: A Critical Analysis*, Cork: Cork University Press

O'Tuama, Sean (1985), 'Stability and Ambivalence: Aspects of a Sense of Place and Religion in Irish Literature', in J. Lee (ed.) *Ireland, Towards a Sense of Place*, Cork: Cork University Press

Owens, Susan (2000), '"Engaging the Public": Information and Deliberation in Environmental Policy', *Environment and Planning A*, 32, 1141–8

Palmer J. A. (1998), 'Spiritual Ideas, Environmental Concerns and Educational Practice', in D. E. Cooper and J. A. Palmer (eds) *Spirit of the Law: Religion, Value and Environmental Concern*, London: Routledge

Payne, Diane and Peter Stafford (2004), 'The Politics of Urban Regeneration in Dublin', Paper presented to Department of Sociology Seminar, UCD, April 2004

Peace, Adrian (1993), 'Environmental Protest, Bureaucratic Closure: The Politics of Discourse in Rural Ireland', in Kay Milton (ed.) *Environmentalism: The View from Anthropology*, London: Routledge

Peace, Adrian (1997), *A Time of Reckoning: the Politics of Discourse in Rural Ireland*, St John's, New Foundland: ISER, Memorial University

Peet, Richard and Michael Watts (2004) *Liberation Ecologies, Environment, Development, Social Movements*, 2nd edn., London: Routledge

Peillon, Michael (2002), 'Culture and the State in Ireland's New Economy', in Peadar Kirby, Luke Gibbons and Michael Cronin (eds) *Reinventing Ireland, Culture, Society and the Global Economy*, London: Pluto Press

Pepper, David (1996), *Modern Environmentalism*, London: Routledge

Plumwood, Val (1993), *Feminism and the Mastery of Nature*, New York: Routledge

Plumwood, Val (1996), 'Nature, Self and Gender: Feminism, Environmental Philosophy and the Critique of Rationalism', in Karen J. Warren (ed.) *Ecological Feminist Philosophies*, Bloomington: Indiana University Press

Plumwood, Val (2002), *Environmental Culture, the Ecological Crisis of Reason*, London: Routledge

Portes, Alejandro (1997), 'Neoliberalism and the Sociology of Development: Emerging Trends and Unanticipated Facts', *Population and Development Review*, 23, 229–60

Powell, Fred and Martin Geoghegan (2004), *The Politics of Community Development*, Dublin: A & A Farmar

Praeger, Robert Lloyd (1901), *Irish Topographical Botany: Compiled Largely From Original Material*, Dublin: The Academy

Praeger, Robert Lloyd (1937), *The Way That I Went: An Irishman in Ireland*, 3rd edn., Dublin: Hodges Figgis

Regan, Tom (1984), *The Case for Animal Rights*, London: Routledge

Reilly, Jacquie (1999), 'Just Another Food Scare? Public Understanding of the BSE Crisis', in Greg Philo (ed.), *Message Received*, Essex: Longman

Rodman, M. (2003), 'Empowering Place: Multilocality and Multivocality' in S. Low and D. Lawrence-Zúniga (eds) *The Anthropology of Space and Place, Locating Culture*, Oxford: Blackwell

Schaefer, Anja, Andrea Coulson, Ken Green, Steve New and Jim Skea (2003), 'Sustainable Business Organisations? in Frans Berkhout, Melissa Leach and Ian Scoones (eds) *Negotiating Environmental Change, New Perspectives from Social Science*, Cheltenham, UK: Edward Elgar

Schifferstein, Henrik N. J., Oude Ophuis, Peter A. M. (1998), 'Health-related Determinants of Organic Food Consumption in the Netherlands', *Food Quality and Preference*, 9 (3), 119–33

Skillington, Tracey (1997), 'Politics and the Struggle to Define: A Discourse Analysis of the Framing Strategies of Competing Actors in a "New" Participatory Forum', *British Journal of Sociology*, 48 (3), 493–513

Skillington, Tracey (1998), 'The City as Text: Constructing Dublin's Identity through Discourse on Transportation and Urban Re-development in the Press', *British Journal of Sociology*, 49 (3), 456–73

Sklair, Leslie (2002), *Globalization, Capitalism and its Alternatives*, 3rd edn., Oxford: Oxford University Press

Slater, Eamonn (1993), 'Contested Terrain: Differing Interpretations of Co. Wicklow Landscape', *Irish Journal of Sociology*, 3, 23–55

Smith, Mick (2001), *An Ethics of Place*, New York: State University of New York Press

Smyth, William (1985), 'Explorations of Place', in J. Lee (ed.) *Ireland, Towards a Sense of Place*, Cork: Cork University Press

Spaargaren, Gert, Arthur P. J. Moll and Fredrick H. Butler (eds) (2002) *Environment and Global Modernity*, London: Sage Publications

Strydom, Piet (2002), *Risk, Environment and Society*, Buckingham: Open University Press

Szerszynski, Bronislaw (1997), 'Voluntary Associations and the Sustainable Society', in Michael Jacobs (ed.) *Greening the Millennium, The New Politics of the Environment*, Oxford: Blackwell

Taylor, George (1999) 'Environmental Democracy, Oral Hearings and the Public Register in Ireland', *Irish Planning and Environmental Law Journal*, 3 (4), 143–151

Taylor, George (2001), *Conserving the Celtic Tiger: the Politics of Environmental Regulation in Ireland*, Galway: Arlen House

Taylor, George and Avril Horan (2001), 'From Cats, Dogs, Parks and Playgrounds to IPC Licensing: Policy Learning and the Evolution of Environmental Policy in Ireland', *British Journal of Politics and International Relations*, 3 (3), 369–92

Taylor, George and Brendan Flynn (2003), 'It's Green, but is it of a Light Enough Hue? Past Performance, Present Success and the Future of the Irish Greens', *Environmental Politics*, 12 (1), 225–32

Taylor, Paul (1986), *Respect for Nature, A Theory of Environmental Ethics*, Princeton, New Jersey: Princeton University Press

Torgenson, Douglas (1999), 'Images of Place in Green Politics: The Cultural Mirror of Indigenous Traditions', in Frank Fischer and Maarten Hajer (eds) *Living with Nature: Environmental Politics as Cultural Discourse*, Oxford: Oxford University Press

Torode, Brian (1984), 'Ireland the Terrible', in Chris Curtain, Mary Kelly and Liam O'Dowd (eds) *Culture and Ideology in Ireland*, Galway: Galway University Press

Tovey, Hilary (1990), 'Of Cabbages and Kings: Restructuring in the Irish Food Industry', *Economic and Social Review*, 22, 333–52

Tovey, Hilary (1993), 'Environmentalism in Ireland: Two Versions of Development and Modernity', *International Sociology*, 8 (4), 413–30

Tovey, Hilary (1996), 'Natural Resource Development and Rural Poverty in Ireland', in Chris Curtin, Trutz Haase and Hilary Tovey (eds) *Poverty in Rural Ireland*, Dublin: Oaktree Press

Tovey, Hilary (1997), 'Food, Environmentalism and Rural Sociology: On the Organic Farming Movement in Ireland', *Sociologia Ruralis* 37 (1), 21–37

Tovey, Hilary (1998), 'Agricultural Development and Environmental Regulation in Ireland', in Henry Buller and Keith Hoggart (eds) *Agricultural Transformation, Food and the Environment – Perspectives on European Rural Policy and Planning*, Vol. 1, 2001, Aldershot: Ashgate, 109–130

Tovey, Hilary (1999), 'Messers, Visionaries and Organobureaucrats: Dilemmas of Institutionalisation in the Irish Organic Farming Movement', *Irish Journal of Sociology*, 9, 31–59

Tovey, Hilary (2002), 'Risk, Morality and the Sociology of Animals – Reflections on the Foot and Mouth Outbreak in Ireland', *Irish Journal of Sociology*, 11 (1), 23–42

Tovey, Hilary (2002a), 'Alternative Agriculture Movements and Rural Development Cosmologies', *International Journal of Sociology of Agriculture and Food*, 10 (1), www.cface.org.nz/ijsaf/

UNDP (2005), *Millennium Ecosystem Assessment Synthesis Report*, www.millenniumassessment.org

Viney, Michael (2003), *A Living Island. Ireland's Responsibility to Nature*, Dublin: Comhar (The National Sustainable Development Partnership)

Walker, Gordon, Peter Simmons, Brian Wynne and Alan Irwin (1998), *Public Perception of Risks Associated with Major Accident Hazards*, London: HSE Books

Waterton, Claire and Brian Wynne (1999), 'Can Focus Groups Access Community Views?' in Rosaline Barbour and Jenny Kitzinger (eds) op. cit.

White, Lynn (1967/1996), 'The Historical Roots of Our Ecological Crisis', reproduced in Roger Gottlieb (ed.) *This Sacred Earth: Religion, Nature, Environment*, New York: Routledge

Wilson, Edward O. (1993), *The Diversity of Life*, London: Penguin Press

Woods, Caoimhin and Philip Davie (eds) (1999), *Sustainable Ireland Source Book 2000: A Guide for Living in the 21st Century*, Dublin: United Spirits Publications

World Bank (2001), *World Development Indicators*, New York: World Bank

Worster, Donald (1985) *Nature's Economy: A History of Ecological Ideas*, Cambridge: Cambridge University Press

Wynne, B., R. Grove-White, T. Mansfield and C. Waterton (2000), *Scientists Reflect on Science: How Scientists Encounter the Environment-Risk Policy Domain*, End of Award Report, Swindon: Economic and Social Research Council

Wynne, Brian (1996), 'Misunderstood Misunderstandings: Social Identities and Public Uptake of Science', in Alan Irwin and Brian Wynne, *Misunderstanding Science: The Public Reconstruction of Science and Technology*, Cambridge: Cambridge University Press

Wynne, Brian (1996a), 'May the Sheep Safely Graze? A Reflexive View of the Expert–Lay Knowledge Divide', in Scott Lash, Bronislaw Szerszynski and Brian Wynne (eds) *Risk, Environment, Modernity: Towards a New Ecology*, London: Sage Publications

Index

The suffix 't' following a page number indicates a table.